SUE KREITZMAN'S
SUNDAY BEST

SUE KREITZMAN'S SUNDAY BEST

Designer: Becky Hollingsworth
Cover illustration: Arless Day
Text illustration: Sandi Glass

ISBN 0-939114-33-x

Copies of Sue Kreitzman's Sunday Best may be obtained from:
Sue Kreitzman's Sunday Best
P.O. Box 15464
Atlanta, Georgia 30333-0464

For Steve and Shawm, who illuminate my life.

Acknowledgements

Without the support and help of many friends and colleagues this book would be just a fond dream. I particularly wish to thank the following: Dr. Brown Whittington, Dean George "Chip" Parks, Martha Gooch, Jerry Thompson and Elmer Schneid Jr. Also Kay Lumsden and Dr. Peter Day at the Emory Computer Center; Marie Nitschke at the Emory Library; Patty Nuzzo and her flying fingers; Dilys Winn who deduced that Nero Wolfe's sausage would make a dandy pate; and Fred DuBose, Doug Allila, Marianne McGeorge and Allida Black who were generous with much needed advice.

Special thanks go to those friends with whom I have traded recipes, discussed food endlessly, and cooked incessantly: Frank and Amy Ma, Paul and Ann Masselli, Nick and Anna Letsos, Jep and Linda Morgan, Jeanne Schwartz, Susan Steel, Ann Abbott, Connie Richardson and Ron Cohn.

And finally, much love and many thanks to my family: my husband Steve whose support, love and editing skills have meant more to me than I can ever say; my son Shawm whose good humour and loving nature enrich our household; and my beagle Shallot, who is always enthusiastically ready to taste absolutely anything at any time of the day or night.

Introduction

Many years ago, when I was a high school creative writing student, I knew that I would grow up to be a major poet. Here I am in what I am sure is the prime of my life. A poet? No. A food writer. In the cold light of adulthood, poetry ambitions were abandoned, but my chosen field is one that has been glorified by the likes of M. F. K. Fisher and Calvin Trillin so I am shedding no tears. When I sit down to write about a sauce or a bean, words flow, (salivary juices also), and I almost feel like the poet I had hoped to be.

This book is a compendium of my culinary and literary ramblings for the food pages of *Atlanta Weekly*—The Atlanta Journal and The Atlanta Constitution's Sunday Magazine—plus a good deal of new material. My special interest is old fashioned ethnic food, the home cooking of many cultures that is vanishing under our national onslaught of fast foods and convenience foods. You will find recipes for such old fashioned, soul satisfying food in these pages along with recipes featuring seasonal produce, elegant recipes for entertaining, and in depth advice on such matters as souffles, bread baking, crepes, omelets and so on. Please note that most of the longer recipes can be made ahead of time, at leisure, and then quickly reheated and enjoyed on busy days.

Cooking for oneself and for one's friends and family is one of the great joys of life. As you use this book, I hope that some of that joy will be yours.

Table of Contents

Chapter 1

Kitchen Wisdom

The Well Equipped Kitchen

Nothing makes cooking more of a chore than a dull knife, a thin walled pot or an absence of wooden spoons. Good tools are as important to a cook as to a carpenter or a plumber. Despite the overwhelming array of space age equipment currently being offered in kitchenware shops, a competent cook needs only a very simple selection of carefully chosen equipment to make cooking a pleasure. The basic necessities are a source of heat, a few good knives and a board to cut on, some cooking pots, a bowl or two, and a few stirring utensils.

Knives

Most important of all are knives; they should be chosen carefully, stored safely and sharpened often. Many cooks love old fashioned carbon steel knives, although they have become increasingly hard to find. Carbon steel knives are easy to sharpen and keep their edge well, but they must be rinsed and wiped meticulously after each use, or they will rust. The disadvantage of carbon steel cutlery is that it reacts with acidic foods—the metal stains, and the food itself darkens and takes on a metallic flavor if left in contact with the knife blade. Even so, carbon steel knives are excellent to work with and worth the extra time and effort involved in caring for them and using them properly.

Stainless steel knives are non-reactive, therefore they will not darken, rust or impart an off flavor to foods, but they do not keep an edge very long. Many firms make excellent quality high carbon stainless steel knives that combine the best of both worlds; they retain their edge, yet are non-reactive and do not rust or stain. They are expensive, as are all good knives, but an important and worthwhile investment for a serious cook—if cared for properly they should last several lifetimes.

A well equipped kitchen needs four basic knives: a chef's knife, a paring knife, a slicer—sometimes called a ham slicer—for slicing meat, and a serrated knife for bread and tomatoes. When buying knives, shop carefully. Heft each knife in your hand—it must feel well balanced and comfortable. A good, well loved knife will eventually seem like an extension of your hand and arm; if you buy one that feels uncomfortable in your grip, it will never be anything but a clumsy and wickedly dangerous stranger.

To insure a properly long life for your chosen set of knives, invest in a good sharpening steel and train yourself to use it before putting each knife away. This is especially important if you buy stainless steel knives. Even with a sharpening steel, however, your knives should be sharpened professionally once a year. It is also important to have a strong knife rack. Hang it on a safe place on your wall, away from the curious hands of children. Always rack your knives immediately after use, with their sharp edges facing the wall. Nothing is more dangerous to fingers or destructive to knife blades than a haphazard tangle of knives in a drawer.

A good cutting board is vital to the survival of your knives. If you were to chop or slice on a Formica or tile surface, the blades would soon be dull and nicked. When buying wooden cutting boards, there are three basic choices: a slice right out of a tree trunk—usually available in Asian food markets; a thick, heavy, conventional butcher's block; or a professional pizza peel. The pizza peel is a flattish length of finished wood used to slide pizzas into deep ovens; it is remarkably inexpensive, and perfectly suitable for home use as a cutting board. Pizza peels are available in restaurant supply stores; most establishments will sell a pizza peel, or anything else for that matter, to a non-professional customer. All chopping blocks and cutting boards must be periodically scrubbed and kept meticulously clean and dry to avoid bacteria buildup and warping, and oiled occasionally with mineral oil or a tasteless salad oil.

Pots and Pans

Good cookware, both stove top and oven, should be heavy and thick for slow, even cooking. Aluminum and cast iron are excellent heat conductors, and do very well for sauteing and frying, but they will react with high acid foods and egg yolks, producing discolored sauces, off flavored spinach, and so on. The best cookware there is, as far as I am concerned, is heavy, enameled, cast iron. These pots are handsome, colorful, and extremely functional. Like good knives, they are an investment; properly cared for, they last for generations. Once or twice a year, such pots are offered at reduced prices; it pays to wait for a sale to stock up. A well rounded, workable collection of enameled cast iron should include a deep 12 inch skillet with lid (sometimes called a chicken fryer), a regular 12 inch skillet, a saucepan, a dutch oven, and a gratin pan.

Commercial Aluminum Company manufactures an impressive line of cookware; if you are not immediately seduced by the handsome lines, brilliant color, and functionality of enameled cast iron, you might wish to invest in Commercial's good looking pots and pans instead. These heavy, beautifully balanced pots are electro-chemically treated with a smooth, black, inert surface called Calphalon. Because it is inert, it will not react with food, therefore, the pots provide the advantages of aluminum with none of its drawbacks.

If you are not ready to invest large sums of money in pots and pans, yet need a few things for those times when a basic black cast iron skillet won't do, try Corning Ware. Corning's glass-ceramic pots are non-reactive, and go from freezer, to oven or stove, to table with the greatest of ease. Corning Ware (except for their excellent "range-toppers," which have heavy, aluminum bottoms) is thinner than ideal cookware should be, therefore an asbestos pad should be placed on the burner under the pot in order to add an extra layer of thickness to the underside of the pot and spread the heat evenly. The most versatile Corning Ware vessel is the roaster; even if you own an expensive set of fine cookware, it pays to buy the glass ceramic roaster as well. It serves as a roaster, of course, but also as a gratin or lasagna pan, a top of the stove skillet or saute pan, and a cake pan. If you buy only one pot, and your budget is limited, this is the one.

To round things out nicely, add an omelet pan to your collection; an 8 inch one with a fool-proof non-stick lining. It will turn out perfect, fluffy 3-egg omelets, and double as a crepe pan. A big stock pot is needed also; look for one that comes with a perforated steamer-bucket insert that will enable you to steam fresh vegetables when not turning out quarts of basic stock or boiling water for pasta. Bake ware is important, too; a sheet for cookies, roulades and jelly rolls; loaf pans for breads and pound cakes; and cake tins of various sizes. And finally, don't forget a colander for draining, and a sieve for straining and pureeing.

Utensils

Wooden spoons and spatulas are essential kitchen tools. They stir, whip, scrape, and beat without ever scratching the surface of a pot or burning a finger. Chopsticks are handy, too, for stirring

9

or for fishing test pieces of spaghetti or vegetables out of seething liquid. Good wooden utensils keep for years and soon take on a comfortable, familiar feeling in the hand. Many cooks keep them standing in a crock or canister right next to the stove for easy accessibility. The crock should also contain several sizes of rubber bladed spatulas for folding egg whites into souffle bases, grated cheeses into hot sauces, and for scraping thick mixtures out of pots; a slotted spoon or two; and a nylon spatula for flipping crepes in a non-stick pan without marring its finish.

A fat bouquet of wire whisks should be standing in its own crock near your stove; these fanciful looking implements are invaluable for all beating jobs. Use balloon whisks of flexible wire for jobs that involve incorporating air into the beaten mixture—egg whites or heavy cream, for instance—and narrower whisks of rigid wire for beating thick sauces and batters. The best and sturdiest whisks are available in restaurant supply shops; they are designed for heavy usage and long life.

And So On

Every kitchen should have several sets of measuring spoons and several kinds of measuring cups—the plastic stacking kind that can be lightly filled with flour and leveled off, the glass pitchers for liquid, and the two quart and four quart graduated bowls that double as mixing bowls. Two or three timers with long, loud bells are vital as well, and of course, pot holders and trivets for hot pots and serving dishes.

There are other gadgets, large and small, that help make a cook's life easier; they should all have a place in your kitchen. A potato ricer for perfect purees of cooked potatoes and other vegetables; a square sided grater—an old fashioned and invaluable gadget for grating fine or coarse, and slicing; a food mill for pureeing soups and sauces to a perfect, not-too-smooth consistency; a swivel bladed vegetable peeler for peeling vegetables and zesting citrus fruits; an ordinary wooden 12 inch ruler for measuring the thickness and width of dough, vegetable slices, etc.; a large and a small wooden chopping bowl with appropriately sized choppers for chopping garlic and herbs, old fashioned liver pates, egg salad and a myriad of other things; an oven thermometer to keep your oven honest; and two Bi-therm instant thermometers, one for liquids, one for roasts. The Bi-therms take the temperature of meat or of liquids instantly—no need to keep a thick, unwieldy thermometer stabbed into a roast during its entire cooking time.

You will also need a rolling pin for rolling out pie crusts, pasta dough, and so on; racks for cooling cakes and pies, and drying breaded foods; a Swing-a-Way can opener which is the simplest and best of its kind; kitchen scales; a cake tester—a thin, flexible skewer for testing roasts, daubes and vegetables as well as cakes (keep it next to the stove); several sizes of pastry brushes (I buy natural bristle paint brushes in the hardware store for this purpose); a wooden meat mallet; and a rubber mallet for whacking garlic cloves. A large salt shaker and a heavy duty pepper mill should be near the stove at all times, as well as two or three pairs of heavy duty tongs.

Machines

If your kitchen is well equipped with the tools I have described, you will find that cooking is a great pleasure. Unless you cook professionally for large groups of people, machines are, for the most part, superfluous. Too many of them deprive the cook of the joy of having his or her hands in the food. Kneading by hand is far more rewarding than kneading with a dough hook; chopping quickly and deftly with a chef's knife is much more satisfying than chopping with a food processor; and bread toasted in the oven tastes better than that toasted in a toaster. There are times, however, when mixers, blenders, and so forth make life a little easier. Add a heavy duty mixer, a blender and a food processor to the simple basics that I have listed, and there will be almost no limit to the beautiful food you will be able to turn out.

Stoves

The ideal stove is a gas stove; the flame is supple and can be regulated from highest to lowest in no time at all. With an electric stove, when a quick change of heat is needed in a recipe, have another burner ready at the second heat, and shift the pot.

It is very important to use your oven thermometer. Many inadvertent cooking disasters are the result of a poorly calibrated oven; if your oven is off by 50 degrees or more, you want to know about it. Make it your business to understand your oven very well; know where the hot spots are and shift the pans during baking to insure even baking.

Helpful Hints About Ingredients

Butter

Nothing compares with the taste of sweet, unsalted butter; use it for best flavor. Whipped butter has air whipped into it; it's fine for spreading on bread, but not very good for cooking.

Butter burns easily; to mitigate this problem, use clarified butter, or butter augmented with corn or peanut oil for sauteeing. Either method will keep the butter from burning over high heat. To clarify butter, heat it slowly in a heavy pan. Skim off the foam and let the sediment settle on the bottom of the pan. Slowly pour the butter through a strainer that is lined with several thicknesses of cheesecloth, discarding the sediment that is left behind in the pan. The clarified butter will keep in the refrigerator for months.

If you must curtail your use of animal fats for medical reasons, do not attempt to make hollandaise or bearnaise sauces with margarine—the results will be a mockery of the real thing. Those on restricted diets must steel themselves to total abstinence from such tempting pleasures.

Egg Whites and Yolks

Eggs are easiest to separate when cold, but they should be at room temperature for cooking. Separate them while cold, and then let them stand for an hour or so before using. The most convenient way to separate an egg (although your child will take one look and mutter "gross" as he shudders his way out of the kitchen) is to break the egg into your hand over a bowl. Let the white drip through your fingers into the bowl and deposit the yolk into another bowl. The yolks tend to form a skin when they are left whole at room temperature—to avoid this, stir them with a fork and then cover with plastic wrap.

Seasonings

Seasonings give life to food; without them, we merely feed our hungers; with them, we dine pleasurably. Part of the fun of cooking is in balancing flavors, deciding which herb goes with which food, adding judicious pinches of this and that to the pot, and then later watching the pleasure on the faces of friends and family as they eat what was so carefully prepared. Seasoning food properly is a matter of practice; the more you cook and taste, the easier it becomes to achieve a proper balance.

Salt: The salting of food is a highly individual affair. Some people crave it in large quantities, others are content with a mere sprinkling. And, of course, many must curtail their sodium levels for medical reasons. As a result, I rarely specify the amount of salt in a recipe. Salt according to your taste and according to good sense, but do not overdo it. In a dish that will cook for a long time—a stew, a stock or a soup, for instance—salt frugally at first; remember that the dish will cook down and the flavor will concentrate. If you undersalt, the seasoning can be corrected at the end, but it is harder to compensate for oversalting. If, however, you have done the worst and oversalted a soup or stew, haul out the potatoes and slice a few. Simmer the raw slices in the stew or soup, but do not let them cook to a mush or they will become incorporated into the dish. Discard the simmered slices, and a good deal of the saltiness will be discarded as well. If this is impractical because of the nature of the dish, make another batch of the recipe, with no salt at all. Combine the unsalted batch with the oversalted, and the seasonings should balance properly.

Some foods (sausages, meat loaves, pates, and so on) cannot be tasted before cooking. In this case, fry a tiny piece of the uncooked mixture and taste it, then correct the seasonings in the whole batch. Cold foods should be salted liberally; they soak up seasonings and will seem bland if not slightly overseasoned.

Pepper: Like salt, pepper is a matter of taste, so add it to please your taste when it is called for in a recipe. Do not use packaged ground pepper; use whole peppercorns and grind them in a mill as you need them. If you can't stand black specks in your food, keep a separate mill for white peppercorns to use in light colored food. White and black pepper are from the same berry. For black pepper, the berry is slightly underripe. White pepper is the mature berry with the outer husk removed. Green peppercorns are immature berries, and are available pickled in brine.

Cayenne pepper, that marvelously hot, ground red pepper, has had a name change. It is still available, but it is now called red pepper. Some companies specify "red pepper" on the label, and then "cayenne" in parentheses.

Dried Herbs: If you do not grow your own or live near an herb farm, fresh herbs are but a fond wish. Dried herbs are a necessary substitute in such cases, but use them with caution. They become old and musty very easily; buy them in small amounts, and throw them away when they begin to smell stale. Keep them in a dark, cool place. A shelf over the stove—although convenient—is the worst possible location. As a general rule, use three times as much fresh herb as dried, but be flexible and season according to your taste. Too much of a dried herb will give very unpleasant results, so be careful. To release the flavor components in dried herbs, rub them between the fingers before dropping them into the pot. Dried herbs are usually added early in the cooking process, fresh herbs towards the end.

Dried bay leaves are useful, but be cautious. California bay leaves, which grow on trees, are extremely pungent and should be used frugally. One half of a California bay leaf is usually sufficient for any dish. European or Turkish type bay leaves grow on bushes and are much milder. A whole bay leaf or even two or three are lovely in a stew, a pot of simmering beans, or a sauce. California bay leaves are labeled "California Laurels," and Turkish bay leaves are labeled "Bay Leaves."

Fresh Herbs: Fresh herbs used liberally in cooking bring a dimension of freshness and clear flavor never realized with the dry variety. For cooks who grow their own or who have access to an herb source, the summertime conversion from dried to fresh is exciting and satisfying. Should you decide to experiment with fresh herbs, consider the following:

Basil—It's hard to imagine a plate of summer tomatoes without a few accompanying sprigs of basil. Tomatoes and basil are soulmates—they flourish together in the garden and are ambrosial on the plate. And best of all, with basil in the garden, pesto—that wonderful rough green puree of pine nuts, olive oil, Parmesan cheese, basil leaves, and garlic—can be a weekly menu staple.

Coriander—Coriander (sometimes called cilantro or Chinese parsley) is an herb that tastes strange to those who have never eaten it. It looks like parsley but has an odd, almost musty flavor. The herb is an essential flavoring component of the cuisines of Mexico, India, and most Oriental countries; there is no substitute for it. The presence of a few garnishing sprigs of coriander on certain ethnic dishes is a pungent declaration of authenticity.

Parsley—Parsley is one fresh herb that is generally available, and it is wonderful. It imparts a welcome, fresh flavor to foods. Use it liberally; it looks and tastes good. There is no excuse for using dried parsley flakes when lovely fresh bunches of the herb are available in every supermarket.

Sorrel—On her way to the remote mountain farm that was to become her home, Millie stopped to gather some wild greens. "My wedding bouquet," she said, smiling shyly at her new husband. "Sorrel—it makes a nourishin' soup." The year was 1954, the movie, Seven Brides for Seven Brothers. In true Hollywood fashion, the bundle of greenery Millie clutched so tightly was not sorrel at all; it exhibited the short curly leaves that characterize parsley. In reality, sorrel's long feathery leaves are nothing at all like parsley; with its tart acidic edge and haunting, unfamiliar flavor, sorrel is unlike any other herb.

Very few people use sorrel or even know what it is. At dinner parties, it's fun to serve it in a sauce or a soup, and then to sit back, smiling enigmatically, as guests try to pinpoint the elusive and mysterious taste. Traditionally, the tart, green leaves are stripped from their ribs and stems and cut into fine shreds called chiffonade. Raw sorrel chiffonade imparts a lovely crunch as well as a bracing acidity; try it in a green salad, stirred into vichyssoise at the last minute, or folded into good ricotta cheese with some chopped parsley, sliced scallions, salt, and pepper. When the chiffonade is sauteed in a small amount of butter, it forms an intensely flavored, dark green puree that freezes well. The puree is wonderful in omelets and sauces, or simmered in cream as an interesting vegetable accompaniment to chicken or fish. Sorrel is easy to grow, even for those who lack green thumbs—it spreads like a weed in the yard.

Tarragon—To many cooks, tarragon means bearnaise sauce, but even if you decide to forego the labors and subsequent pleasures of bearnaise there is no need to miss out on the wonderful, sharp, licorice complexities of the herb. While fresh tarragon is available, use it with eggs and chicken, for which it has a special affinity, or anywhere else you see fit; it is a very versatile herb.

Spices: Spices are a collection of aromatic barks, seeds, roots, and buds that are used to season food. They should be bought in small quantities, kept in tightly closed containers in a cool spot, and used up within six months—when their oils turn rancid they are unusable. Sometimes spices (cinnamon sticks and cloves, for instance) can be used whole; they give their flavor to a dish, and then are discarded before the dish is eaten. Others are used in powder form—nutmeg and allspice are familiar examples.

Curry Powder: "You forgot to list the curry powder in the recipe for kofta curry!" exclaimed a confused reader, after an article on Indian food appeared on the Sunday magazine food page. No, I hadn't forgotten—curry powder, as we know it, is not used in Indian cookery. The use of commercial curry powder is tantamount to bottling a conglomeration of thyme, bay leaf, tarragon, and pepper, sprinkling it liberally over everything and calling it "French." Much better to buy small jars of individual spices and combine them in proportions that complement each particular recipe. Curry spice mixtures often begin with turmeric and continue with any or all of these: cinnamon, cloves, allspice, fennel, fenugreek, caraway, cumin, coriander, red pepper, and more. The curry spices are cooked in butter, or oil, early in the recipe, usually with the flavoring vegetables.

Chinese Five Spice Powder: This is a delightful, fragrant blend of seasonings that can be found in Oriental grocery stores and some specialty stores. If you cannot find it, a fair approximation can be made by blending equal parts of ground cloves, cinnamon, fennel, nutmeg, ginger, and Szechuan peppercorns.

Ginger: Ginger, although it looks like a vegetable, is classified as a spice. The fresh, knobbly root is now available in almost all supermarkets. Always peel it with a swivel-bladed peeler, and then grate it, slice it, or mince it. If you cannot find whole, fresh ginger root, leave it out of the recipe.

Other Flavoring Components of Food: **Onions,** alas, will make you weep. There have been many words of advice bandied among cooks concerning the tearful process of onion slicing and peeling; most of them are ineffective. I have tackled the onions when they were under water, slightly chilled, and partially frozen; I have peeled them near an open window, under the exhaust fan, and with a wooden kitchen match clenched between my teeth. Each time I was forced to exclaim tearfully, "This method (sniff, sniff) does not work!" Try wearing swim goggles when working with onions; it looks eccentric, but it keeps you tear-free.

Some people (dentists who cook, for instance) worry about removing the odor of onions from their hands. It will come off quite easily (as will garlic odors) with a generous application of lemon juice.

Green onions (scallions) are a delicate addition to both green salads and cooked dishes. A handful of thinly sliced scallions— both the white and green portions—mixed with a handful of chopped fresh parsley make a delicious and fresh tasting garnish. The white portion makes a good substitute for shallots, when shallots are overpriced or unavailable. Whole scallions, poached in butter, are an unusual and excellent vegetable accompaniment to meat dishes.

Leeks are a mild member of the onion family; they look like fat, overgrown scallions. Leeks are always loaded with sand and grit; trim them, slit them and wash them very well before using.

Vidalia Onions: During the months of May and June, Georgia becomes a state of onion eaters. We eat our famous sweet Vidalia onions out of hand, as we would apples—relishing big, crunching bites. The chemical balance of the soil in Georgia's Toombs County area makes Vidalia onions very special indeed—the juicy, amazingly sweet globes are responsible for the onion fever that hits us every year.

The season for Vidalias is short; by the third week in June, they are gone. Cooks who revel in seasonal foods ride out their bout of onion fever by eating onions every day until there is not a Vidalia left in the markets. Many people buy 50 pounds of the compelling things every year, and cook their way through them in short order. The onions are at their best when eaten during their brief season, but they can be stored if necessary. Some onion growers in Vidalia suggest putting them in the refrigerator where they will keep until Christmas. Unfortunately, cramming 50 pounds of globe onions into the average refrigerator leaves little room for the everyday necessities of life. If you plan to buy a quantity of Vidalias, but cannot spare the refrigerator space, keep them in a cool, dry, dark place instead; a basement, for instance. Spread them out on boards or burlap—never directly on concrete because concrete sweats and the moisture will quickly rot the onions. Check the cache of Vidalias often, and when you spot one that seems to be spoiled, throw it away at once. Lacking a basement, try filling pairs of clean, old pantyhose with the onions, tying a knot between each one. Hang the filled pantyhose in a cool, dark place. Should you forget they are there, the shock of unexpectedly encountering the bottom half of a large, lumpy monster will be intense, so remember where you put them. Under these conditions, they should keep well into the fall, and perhaps until Christmas.

Garlic: There is no other food that is as hated and as loved as garlic. To some it is the very essence of vulgarity and bad taste; to others, its perfume and powerful savor are essential and irresistible. I confess that I belong to the latter group. For me a world without garlic would be impossibly dull and bland. Unless you are a practicing vampire, I can see no reason for shunning the succulent little cloves; they are so useful and so interesting in all sorts of dishes.

To realize garlic's essential goodness and to keep vulgarity at bay, it is important to use it only in its natural form. Garlic salt and powder and granulated garlic are revolting; they impart a harsh, artificial, rancid flavor to foods. Many people who profess to hate garlic, are reacting to the ersatz quality of these processed flavorings; they appear with monotonous regularity in prepared foods of all kinds and in the cookery of some restaurants. When buying fresh garlic, look for large, heavy heads that have not begun to sprout, and contain no shriveled cloves. Keep them in a well-ventilated basket in your kitchen—there is no need to refrigerate them. Don't ever use a garlic press. That dangerous little gadget releases the garlic's volatile oils which react with the metal of the press. As a result, the garlic clove is reduced to an evil smelling mush. Throw away your press and use a kitchen mallet. Hit the clove lightly to loosen its papery skin, remove the skin and mince or dice the clove with a sharp knife. When sauteing the garlic bits, do not let them brown, or they will become bitter, unpleasant, and indigestible. Some cooks like to keep the cloves whole, impaled on toothpicks; when the dish is finished, and the garlic has given its all to the sauce, the cloves are fished out and discarded.

Horseradish: Horseradish root is considered a condiment, as are onions and garlic. The fresh root is an ugly looking object; it must be scraped of its rough covering and grated to be useful.

Grating horseradish is painful; you will emerge from a bout with the sharp spicy root with tears running down your face and a red, sniffy nose. If you can't find fresh horseradish or would rather not wrestle with it, some of the prepared horseradish mixtures that are sold in the dairy cases of supermarkets are quite good.

Citrus Zest: The zest of a citrus fruit is the aromatic outer peel, minus the bitter white layer underneath. A strip of orange or lemon zest is a delicious flavoring component for soups and stews, and the slivered zest, parboiled, is an excellent addition to relishes and some sauces. To remove the zest, use a swivel-bladed vegetable peeler; the bitter portion will stay behind.

Capers: A caper is the pickled berry of the caper bush. Capers come in jars, packed in brine or in vinegar; rinse them well before using. The little berries are pungent; never plan a menu that uses capers in more than one dish.

Cornichons: Cornichons are tiny French pickles available in jars from specialty food shops. They make a traditional garnish for slices of pate. Chopped cornichons are often used to flavor cold sauces such as tartar sauce and remoulade.

Dried Mushrooms: European style dried mushrooms are a splendid flavoring component for many soups, stews, and sauces. Sometimes, the only ones available are packaged in Korea, a cross cultural fact that causes confusion for cooks in search of the mushrooms. When all else fails, look for them in small, round plastic containers—labeled Kirsch or Bonaparte mushrooms—in Jewish delis or on supermarket shelves that are devoted to Jewish or Middle European food products. The mushrooms must be rinsed well before they are soaked, to rid them of grit and dirt; a small amount in a dish will go a long way.

Hot Peppers: Lovers of fiery food find the specialties of Hunan, Mexico, India and so on as soothing as mother's milk, as bracing as a walk through an autumn forest, and as nourishing as a dietician's dream. The strength of seasonings in such cuisines, however, does not always reach the longed for fiery heights. Three basic levels of heat are achievable at the cook's discretion. The first and mildest leaves a vague, piquant glow in the mouth— pleasant and pungent but not at all searing. The second level is deceptively gentle. After the first mouthful or so, just as the essential mildness of the dish seems disappointingly apparent, both tonsils burst into flames and several glasses of cold liquid are required to bring body temperature down. The final level is searingly and euphorically hot—the food almost sizzles on the fork as it sterilizes the air between plate and mouth. Food at this level causes the eyes to bulge and tear, the face to flush and sweat, and the sinuses to spontaneously clear. Many restaurateurs specializing in spicy cuisines tend to present the first level to their American clients—even to those who long for the exhilaration of blistering heat. The second and third levels are saved for after hours dining around the staff table. Restaurant owners and waiters seem to live in fear that a hapless customer will self-incinerate one day while consuming a dish of twice cooked pork, tandoori chicken, or salsa fria.

If the nervousness of such restaurateurs has frustrated your quest for edible fire, you can do as an Indian friend does and carry a bottle of Tabasco sauce in your pocket to be sprinkled liberally over all food that comes your way. Home cookery, however, provides a much more sensible and satisfying solution. In the privacy of your own kitchen, you can fling hot chili peppers into seething sauces and douse the hors d'oeuvre with hot chili oil. Please remember, however, that hot peppers are very potent indeed; always wash and trim chili peppers under cold water and cut away the seeds and ribs unless you want a super-fiery finished dish. After handling chilies, wash your hands well before rubbing your eyes, hugging your beloved, or cuddling the baby.

Wine: "I've never taken a drink in my life, and I don't intend to begin now!" snapped straitlaced Aunt Harriet as she firmly pushed away a plate of beautiful food. I was young, newly married, proud of my developing kitchen skills; she was elderly, ironspined, and fiercely tenacious about her abstinence. In vain did I plead that boeuf bourguignon was not the first fatal step in the journey to the gutter. That night, my husband, uncle and I feasted on the beef while Aunt Harriet ate a large dish of blameless but boring rice. The memory of Aunt Harriet's misplaced outrage has stayed with me over the years; as I cook, her specter occasionally looms over the stove. "Take that, Aunt Harriet," I murmur as I pour the entire contents of a bottle of wine into the stew pot.

Wine used in cookery flavors foods in a very special way; if you choose to cook with wine, never use a so-called "cooking wine"; it will be of poor quality. Use a good wine for cooking purposes, and then drink the remainder with the meal. Wines do not keep very well, but if you find yourself with leftover wine that you wish to use for cooking on another day, pour it into a small jar or bottle. Air is the enemy of wine, so fill the small bottle to the top and close it tightly. Dry vermouth makes a lovely cooking wine; it is fortified, so it will keep for long periods once it is opened. It can be used in most recipes that call for dry white wine, and even in some that call for dry red. Use a bit less of the vermouth; it will not be as subtle as a regular wine.

Chapter 2

Appetizers, Soups, Beverages

Appetizers

An International Assortment of Dips:

A dip or two with appropriate dippers to be served with drinks or wine is a sociable way to begin a party or a dinner, but there are many things that can be stirred, creamed, whisked or blended together to make a far more delicious mixture than any of the ubiquitous commercial concoctions. Sour cream laced with dehydrated onion soup, and little containers of clam dip are to be avoided at all costs. Crisp, raw vegetables cut into strips make refreshing, attractive and nutritious dippers, far superior to potato chips for communal dabbling. Almost any raw vegetable can be used for this purpose; some of the more obvious choices are carrots, green, and red peppers, radishes (trimmed and left whole), cucumbers, celery, and cherry tomatoes (left whole with stems on). A few less obvious but equally delicious choices are cauliflower and broccoli, (cut into flowerets), white turnip (peeled and cut into strips), zucchini and yellow squash, white radish, small white mushrooms, endive spears, snow pea pods, and whole scallions. Augment the vegetables with wedges of plain and whole wheat pita bread, both toasted and untoasted; good crackers; squares of dark peasant bread (many dips can be spread as well as dipped); and tortilla chips, if you plan to make a refried bean dip. Leftover vegetables can be turned into a gala vegetable soup on the next day, and leftover bread can be frozen or turned into bread crumbs.

Liptauer Cheese
Serves 8-10

10 ounces farmer cheese
1 tablespoon sweet Hungarian
  paprika
salt and pepper to taste
2 teaspoons caraway seeds

1 teaspoon dry mustard
1 teaspoon chopped capers
1 tablespoon finely chopped onion
½ cup sour cream

1. Put farmer cheese into mixer bowl. Beat in the paprika, salt, pepper, caraway seeds, mustard, capers, onion, and sour cream.
2. Continue beating at medium speed until the mixture forms a smooth paste. Scrape into a bowl and smooth top. Chill. Thrust a few butter knives into the Liptauer, and serve with squares of brown bread.

Refried Bean Dip
About 3 cups

1 can (1 pound) refried beans
1 cup shredded Cheddar cheese
½ cup chopped scallion, green
  and white parts

salt to taste
2 to 3 tablespoons jalapeno relish

Mix the refried beans, cheese, scallion, salt and jalapeno relish in a small saucepan. Cook slowly over low heat, stirring, until hot and bubbly and the cheese has melted. Keep warm. Serve with tortilla chips.

Guacomole
About 2 cups

Avocados are perfect for emotionally difficult times. Smooth, nourishing and silken against the roof of the mouth, they provide a voluptuous and tranquilizing gastronomic interlude. Try the following recipe as a dip with raw vegetables or tortilla chips, or spread on good bread. Guacomole has· the bite of hot peppers that I find soothing, but if you crave blandness, omit the peppers.

2 ripe avocados
juice of 1 lime
½ cup sour cream

salt and pepper to taste
3 tablespoons jalapeno relish

Cut avocados in half and scoop out meat. Mash in a non-metal bowl with remaining ingredients. It should be a very rough puree. Cover closely with plastic wrap and refrigerate until ready to use. (Eat as soon after preparing as possible).

Jean Leon's Mahammara (Lebanese Hot Pepper Dip)
About 1¾ cups

This is a family recipe from the owner of the Middle Eastern Baking Company in Atlanta, the first bakery of its kind in Georgia. The dip is a special treat for those who crave edible fire.

5 fresh red chili peppers, washed, stemmed, and seeded
2 medium tomatoes, peeled, seeded, juiced and chopped
½ cup diced onion
½ cup chopped walnuts or pecans
salt to taste
¼ teaspoon cumin
4 tablespoons olive oil
1 tablespoon pomegranate juice (available in shops specializing in Middle Eastern foods and health foods)

1. Place peppers in a blender or processor. Blend or process to a rough paste. Scrape into bowl.

2. Add remaining ingredients and mix well. Serve with wedges of pita bread.

Hummus Tahini (Middle Eastern Chickpea Dip)
About 3 cups

The women of the Saint Elias Orthodox Church in Atlanta are a dedicated band of extraordinary cooks. The following two cream salads are examples of their artistry.

2 cans (15½ ounces each) chickpeas (reserve ¼ of the liquid from 1 can of chickpeas—discard all remaining liquid)
6 tablespoons tahini (sesame seed paste—available in shops specializing in Middle Eastern foods)
¼ cup lemon juice or more to taste
3 cloves garlic
salt to taste
olive oil, paprika, and chopped parsley for garnish

1. Combine all ingredients, except garnish, in blender or processor. Blend or process to a smooth, creamy paste. Taste and add more salt or lemon juice to your taste. It should be the creamy consistency of thick mayonnaise. Thin with water or lemon juice if necessary.

2. Scrape into an attractive bowl. Color olive oil with a bit of paprika. Drizzle oil over the surface in a decorative pattern and sprinkle with chopped parsley. Serve with wedges of pita bread and raw vegetable dippers.

Baba Ganooj (*Middle Eastern Eggplant Dip*)
About 3 cups

3 large eggplants	*3 cloves garlic*
9 tablespoons tahini (sesame seed paste)	*salt to taste*
¼ cup plus 1 tablespoon lemon juice	*olive oil, paprika, and chopped parsley for garnish*

1. Preheat oven to 350 degrees. Pierce eggplants in several places with a fork. Bake them in the oven until soft and pulpy to the touch, about 1 hour. Remove peels and drain eggplant pulp in a colander until all juice has drained away. If the eggplant seeds seem tough, discard them.

2. Place eggplant pulp in blender or processor with all remaining ingredients except garnish. Blend or process to a thick, smooth paste. Taste and add more salt or lemon juice if necessary. Scrape into an attractive bowl. Color olive oil with a bit of paprika. Drizzle oil onto the surface of the eggplant in decorative swirls, sprinkle with parsley, and serve with wedges of pita bread.

Niko's Taramasalata
Serves 20

If Pegasus Airlines ever stops over in Atlanta, the whole Olympian crowd will surely take the time to visit Nick Letsos at Niko's Greek Restaurant for a little something to eat. Nick and Anna Letsos' restaurant is one of the best ethnic restaurants in Atlanta. Their creamy, lemony, taramasalata is irresistible and habit forming.

3 large Idaho potatoes	*1 small onion, grated*
1 10 ounce can tarama (fish roe)	*1 quart Greek olive oil*
juice of 4 lemons	*1 cup water*

1. Peel the potatoes and boil until tender. Drain.

2. Mash potatoes.

3. Place tarama in a mixing bowl. Add lemon juice, onion, olive oil, and potatoes to the mixing bowl. Beat at medium speed until mixture is smooth and creamy. If it is too thick, beat in one cup water. Serve to a crowd with wedges of ripe tomato, sprigs of parsley, and thick slices of French bread.

Ajada *(Potato and Garlic Dip)*
About 5½ cups

This is an unusual and garlicky dip; a Sephardic specialty from the women of the Or-Ve Shalom Temple Sisterhood in Atlanta. It is a close relative of the Greek Taramasalata.

4 Idaho potatoes
2 cloves garlic, crushed
juice of 3 lemons

2 eggs
salt to taste
¼ cup olive oil

1. Peel potatoes and boil until tender. Drain.

2. Mash fine or whip in mixer.

3. Beat in crushed garlic, lemon juice, eggs, salt, and oil gradually. Beat until of a slightly thicker consistency than mayonnaise.

4. Chill and serve with crackers.

Roquefort Dip
About 2 cups

¼ pound Roquefort cheese
juice of ½ lime
pepper to taste
½ cup mayonnaise (preferably
  homemade)

½ cup sour cream
½ teaspoon dried tarragon

1. With a fork, mash cheese with lime juice in a bowl. Add pepper.

2. With the fork, stir in the remaining ingredients. It should be a very rough mixture. Serve with raw vegetable dippers.

Pates

There are many types of pates, although at one time, the term applied only to a mixture of ground or chopped meats baked in a pastry covering. Now the term refers also to compressed loaves of baked, highly seasoned, ground and chopped meats, traditionally served in thin slices with a garnish of cornichons; and smooth, spreadable mixtures of chopped livers, fat, and seasonings. Either one makes an elegant beginning to a meal.

Chicken Liver Pate, Jewish Style
Serves 8

A friend's mother, a marvelous cook, went to Paris where she ate liver pate, enriched with duxelles. "Why, this is chopped liver with mushrooms in it," said Mrs. Levine. "If the French can do it, I can too!" This recipe is the traditional Jewish version, with Mrs. Levine's Parisian addition. It must not be made in a food processor or blender—the texture will be all wrong. I use a wooden bowl and chopper that belonged to my grandmother—similar bowls and choppers are available in most cookware shops.

2 tablespoons rendered chicken fat (see index for recipe)
2 medium onions, coarsely chopped
½ pound mushrooms, coarsely chopped
2 tablespoons rendered chicken fat
3 pounds chicken livers
5 hard-boiled eggs, mashed
3 to 4 tablespoons additional chicken fat
grebenes (see chicken fat recipe)
salt and pepper to taste

1. Heat chicken fat. Cook onions and mushrooms in hot fat until soft and all mushroom liquid is evaporated. Scrape onions, mushrooms and fat into a big wooden chopping bowl and set aside.

2. In the same skillet, melt 2 more tablespoons chicken fat. Saute chicken livers in the fat until just done all the way through. (Cut one open to check). Drain thoroughly in a colander. Trim the livers well.

3. With a hand chopper, in the big wooden bowl, chop the sauteed onions and mushrooms until very fine. Set them aside with their fat. With the same chopper, in the same bowl, chop the livers very fine. Add the mushrooms and onions back to the bowl.

4. Add the mashed eggs, additional chicken fat, and grebenes. Chop it all together until everything is well combined. Season to taste.

Put the mixture into a crock or non-metal bowl. Chill. Serve with crackers, rye bread or matzoh.

25

Ten Herb Pate
Serves 12

Nero Wolfe, Rex Stout's gourmandizing and corpulent fictional detective doted on ten herb sausage. My ten herb pate was inspired by Stout's formula for Wolfe's sausage; serve it in thin slices with Cumberland sauce (see index for recipe) and cornichons.

1½ pounds pork shoulder (Boston butt), fat and lean, ground
1 pound beef chuck, ground
½ pound ground veal
1 tablespoon bacon fat
1 clove garlic, minced
1 medium onion, minced
2 eggs, lightly beaten
¼ cup cognac
salt and pepper to taste
1 Turkish bay leaf or ½ California bay leaf, crumbled

⅛ teaspoon ground cloves
1 teaspoon fennel or anise seed
1 tablespoon chopped fresh parsley
1 teaspoon marjoram
½ teaspoon dried thyme
½ teaspoon dry mustard
¼ teaspoon mace
¼ teaspoon nutmeg
½ pound bacon

1. Preheat oven to 375 degrees. Place the ground meats in a bowl.

2. Saute garlic and onion in hot bacon fat until tender but not browned. Add to meats.

3. Add eggs, cognac, and all seasonings. Use your hands to mix it all together very well. Fry a tiny piece of the mixture in a skillet and taste it. Adjust seasonings to your liking. Remember that this pate should be quite spicy, and that chilling will mute the flavoring a bit.

4. Line a 9 x 5 x 3½ (2 quart) loaf pan with bacon strips, letting them extend up the sides of the pan and over the edge. Fill the pan with the meat mixture, pressing down to even it out, and to eliminate air spaces. Fold the overhanging bacon over the meat, adding a few more strips if necessary, to cover the top.

5. Place the loaf pan in a larger pan, containing 2 inches of boiling water. Place in the preheated oven and bake, uncovered, for about 1½ hours, or until the juices run clear.

6. Let the loaf rest in the pan for 15 minutes after its removal from the oven. It will have shrunk considerably and appear to be floating in its own fat.

7. Do not pour off the fat. Empty the water out of the larger pan. Leave the loaf pan in the larger shallow pan to catch any overflow. Cover the top of the pate with foil. Top with a brick or another

weight. Cool the pate, then refrigerate with weights in place. Next day remove the weights, and discard all solidified fat. Save the jellied meat juices to serve with the pate if desired. Do not disturb bacon strips. Wrap pate with plastic wrap or foil. Refrigerate for 2 or 3 days before serving so that flavors develop. Serve in thin slices, with the jellied juices or Cumberland sauce and cornichons.

Pain de Veau
Serves 8

This is a quick pate; it may be cooked in the morning, chilled for a few hours in the refrigerator, and served in the evening.

1 pound ground veal
¼ pound ground smoked pork hock, smoked pork shoulder, or ham (trim off fat before grinding)
1 tablespoon chopped fresh parsley
1 tablespoon chopped fresh tarragon

pinch cinnamon
pinch cloves
salt and pepper to taste
1 tablespoon melted butter
1 teaspoon Dijon mustard
1½ tablespoons additional melted butter

1. Preheat oven to 325 degrees.

2. In a large bowl, combine all ingredients except the additional melted butter. Mix it well with your hands. Fry a tiny piece in a skillet and taste for seasoning. Add more salt or pepper if necessary.

3. Form the mixture into the shape of a long loaf of French bread, about 12 inches long. Cover a baking sheet with foil. Place the veal loaf on the sheet. Sprinkle with additional butter.

4. Bake in the 325 degree oven for one hour, or until browned and cooked through.

5. Drain off fat. Cool on a rack, then refrigerate. Serve in thin slices with a French bread that is the same size and shape as the pate, and good mustard.

Pate with Chicken
Serves 12

2 chicken breasts, skinned and
  boned
salt and pepper to taste
¼ teaspoon nutmeg
½ cup cognac
1 pound good quality Italian
  sausage (sweet)
1 pound ground veal
1 pound ground beef chuck

1 tablespoon bacon fat
1 onion, finely chopped
2 eggs, lightly beaten
½ teaspoon tarragon
½ teaspoon thyme
¼ cup chopped parsley
salt and pepper to taste
¾ pound bacon
bay leaves

1. Trim chicken breasts of all fat and gristle. Cut into strips about ½ inch wide. Toss the strips with salt, pepper, nutmeg, and half the cognac. Marinate for several hours or overnight.

2. Preheat oven to 375 degrees.

3. Remove sausage from its casing. Place it in a bowl with the veal and beef.

4. Saute onion in hot bacon fat until soft but not browned. Add to meats.

5. Add eggs, tarragon, thyme, the remaining cognac, parsley, salt and pepper to meats. Use your hands to mix it all together very well. Fry a tiny piece in a skillet and taste for seasoning.

6. Line a 9 x 5 x 3½ (2 quart) loaf pan with bacon strips, letting them extend up the sides of the pan and over the edge. Place half the meat mixture in the bottom of the lined pan. Press down to eliminate air spaces. Place the chicken strips in rows over the meat. Cover with remaining meat and press down. Fold the over-hanging bacon over the meat mixture; use a few more strips if necessary to cover the top. Place bay leaves on top of the loaf.

7. Place loaf pan in a larger pan containing 2 inches of boiling water. Place in preheated oven and bake, uncovered, for 1½ to 2 hours, until the juices run clear.

8. Let the loaf rest in the pan for 15 minutes.

9. Do not pour off the fat. Empty the water out of the larger pan. Leave the loaf pan in the larger shallow pan to catch any overflow. Cover the top of the pate with foil. Put a brick or two on top of the foil. Cool the pate, then refrigerate with weights in place. Next day remove the weights, and discard all solidified fat. Save the jellied meat juices if desired. Do not disturb bacon strips. Wrap pate with plastic wrap or foil. Refrigerate for 2 or 3 days before serving. Serve in thin slices, with the jellied juices or with Cumberland sauce and cornichons.

Turnovers

Small, hot turnovers make excellent finger food; perfect for a first course or as one of a series of dishes on an international buffet. The two following turnover recipes are versatile; the lamb and mushroom fillings are good in both the phyllo pastry and the whole wheat pastry. For a change, see the recipe for spanikopita (see index). The spinach-cheese filling works well in phyllo turnovers; follow the filling and folding instructions for mushroom turnovers, but wrap loosely to allow for expansion of the egg-based filling.

Mushroom Turnovers
Approximately 20

1 recipe duxelles (see index for recipe)
¼ cup unseasoned bread crumbs

1 package phyllo leaves, thawed in refrigerator overnight
melted butter

1. Preheat oven to 375 degrees.

2. Stir the bread crumbs into the duxelles. Taste and adjust seasonings.

3. Place a slightly damp towel on a flat surface. Cover with a sheet of wax paper. Unwrap the phyllo leaves and place the whole stack on the wax paper. Cover with another sheet of wax paper and another damp cloth.

4. Remove one leaf and spread it out on your work surface. Butter it well with a large pastry brush. Fold the long sides in toward the middle as if you were folding a business letter, forming a strip about two inches wide. Brush with melted butter. Place a tablespoon of the mushroom mixture in the lower right-hand corner. Fold the corner up to form a triangle. Fold back down to form a new triangle. Continue folding back up and down until you have formed a compact, many layered triangle, (much like folding a flag). Butter the finished triangle well and place on an ungreased baking sheet.

5. Repeat this process with all the phyllo leaves and mushroom mixture.

6. Bake at 375 degrees for 20 minutes, or until the triangles are puffed and golden brown. Allow to cool 3 to 5 minutes before serving.

Note: the unbaked, filled triangles may be frozen; to bake, do not thaw, but add 10 minutes extra to the baking time.

Samosa *(Indian Lamb Turnovers)*
20 Samosas

Dough:

1½ cups whole wheat flour
1½ cups unbleached white flour
1 teaspoon salt

5 tablespoons clarified butter
approximately 1 cup cold water
additional clarified butter

Filling:

2 medium onions, chopped
2 cloves garlic, minced
1 thin slice ginger, minced
2 pounds ground lamb
salt to taste
1 teaspoon turmeric
1 teaspoon ground cumin

1 teaspoon ground coriander
¼ teaspoon red pepper flakes
1 Turkish bay leaf or ½ California
   bay leaf crumbled
½ teaspoon cinnamon
½ cup stock
vegetable oil

1. Combine flours and salt in a bowl. Add butter and rub with the fingers until the mixture resembles coarse meal.

2. Mix in about one cup water, a little at a time, until the particles adhere into a firm dough. Gather into a ball, turn out onto a lightly floured surface, and knead for about 10 minutes until dough becomes smooth and elastic. Brush lightly with butter, cover with a damp cloth, and set aside until needed.

3. Combine onions, garlic, ginger, and lamb in a wide, heavy skillet. Cook slowly until lamb is thoroughly cooked. Break up the meat with a wooden spoon as it cooks. Drain in a colander to remove all fat. Return meat and onions to skillet.

4. Add all spices to meat. Cook and stir over low heat until meat is coated with spices. Add stock, bring to a boil, reduce heat, and simmer, covered, for about 30 minutes or until the mixture is thick.

5. Preheat oven to 200 degrees.

6. Divide dough into about 20 equal pieces. Work with one piece at a time, keeping remainder covered with damp towel.

7. Roll a piece of dough into a ball. Flatten it on a lightly floured surface. With a rolling pin, roll the flattened ball into a circle about five inches in diameter. Place approximately two tablespoons of filling on the circle. Fold over, dampen edges, press edges together, and crimp with a fork. Cover with plastic wrap. Repeat.

8. Pour 3 inches vegetable oil into a wok or saucepan suitable for deep frying. Heat to 375 degrees. Fry samosas, 2 at a time, for 2 to 3 minutes, turning once, until they are lightly browned. Place them on a paper towel lined baking sheet in the oven to keep warm until all the samosas are done. Serve hot.

Other Appetizers

One of my favorite first courses is a selection of seasonal vegetables, lightly poached or raw according to their natures, served with bowls of mustard vinaigrette (see index for recipe). I like to serve this at the dining room table with a small bowl of the sauce in front of each person along with individual plates of beautifully arranged vegetables. Barely cooked baby carrots, poached scallions, and steamed asparagus are particularly nice served this way; each guest uses his or her fingers to dip the vegetables.

When Vidalia onions are in season, onion sandwiches are a perfect first course; spread crustless slices of good thin bread with homemade mayonnaise, sprinkle with some chopped fresh parsley, and top with paper thin slices of Vidalia onion. Cover with more crustless slices of mayonnaise-spread bread, and cut the sandwiches into strips. Pile them onto a platter garnished with bunches of watercress or parsley. Eat the sandwiches slowly and thoughtfully. You will not meet the taste again until next Vidalia season.

Stuffed Grape Leaves
30 stuffed leaves

30 grape leaves (available in jars, packed in brine)
½ cup raw rice, rinsed in cold water
½ pound ground lamb
salt and pepper to taste
water
3 cloves garlic
juice of 1 lemon
lemon wedges

1. Drain grape leaves. Rinse well in several changes of water and drain again. Spread leaves out on tray or wax paper, dull side up. Trim off any stems. Set damaged or torn leaves aside.

2. Mix rice, meat, salt and pepper and blend well. Place some of the mixture on a leaf. Roll leaf, tucking in ends as you roll, to form a neat parcel. Do not wrap too tightly as the rice will expand. Repeat until all leaves are filled.

3. To prevent scorching, line a heavy saucepan with a layer of damaged and torn grape leaves. Place filled leaves, in tight layers, in the pan. Sprinkle some salt on each layer. Push garlic down among rolls. Place an inverted plate on the top layer to prevent unrolling. Pour in water to the top of the plate. Bring to a boil, reduce heat, and simmer, covered, for about 1½ hours, or until rice is done and leaves are tender. Replenish water if it boils away.

4. With tongs, remove grape leaf rolls from the water, and arrange on a platter. Squeeze lemon juice over them, and serve with additional lemon wedges. May be served hot or cold.

Carpaccio
Serves 6

This version of an Italian raw beef dish is from La Grotta, Atlanta's excellent and elegant Northern Italian restaurant. Make it in the summertime when fresh herbs are available.

1½ pounds beef tenderloin
1 tablespoon fresh sage, finely chopped
1 tablespoon fresh rosemary, finely chopped
1 tablespoon fresh basil, finely chopped

1 tablespoon minced shallots
3 tablespoons Dijon mustard
juice of 2 lemons
2 tablespoons red wine vinegar
1½ cups olive oil
salt and pepper to taste

1. Trim the tenderloin of all fat, sinew, and skin and cut into very thin slices. Place in a deep dish.

2. In a bowl, whisk together the chopped herbs, shallots, mustard, the juice of 2 lemons, and the vinegar. Whisk in the olive oil in small drops. Season to taste with salt and pepper.

3. Pour over sliced tenderloin and marinate for 5 hours.

Roasted Garlic

This makes a very special first course for garlic lovers. The flavor of the cloves becomes gentle and sweet after baking, and the method of squeezing the puree onto the bread is great fun.

Whole heads of garlic
Toasted rounds of French bread

Butter

1. Preheat oven to 375 degrees.

2. Remove the papery outer covering of the garlic heads, but do not separate the cloves, and do not peel them. Place as many whole heads of garlic as there are people to be served on a large square of heavy aluminum foil. Fold up the foil so that the cloves are completely wrapped.

3. Bake in the preheated oven for 1 hour.

4. Serve each diner a head of garlic, several slices of toasted French bread and some sweet butter. The diner then butters the bread and separates the cloves. When the clove is squeezed the garlic puree pops out, like toothpaste from a tube. The puree, spread on the buttered bread, is utterly delicious.

Smoked Salmon in Horseradish Cream
Serves 6

½ cup sliced scallions, green and
   white parts
½ cup chopped parsley
1 tablespoon fresh dill, snipped,
   or ½ teaspoon dried
½ pound smoked Nova Scotia
   salmon, shredded

¼ cup prepared horseradish
2 tablespoons mayonnaise
¾ cup sour cream
pepper to taste

1. Combine scallions, parsley, dill, and salmon.

2. Whisk together the horseradish, mayonnaise, sour cream, and pepper. Add sour cream mixture to salmon mixture and toss it together well. Serve with slices of dark bread.

Soups

Stocks and Hot Soups

The soothing, gentle bubbling of simmering soup, its heady aroma and comforting nourishment, make it a dietary staple at any time of the year, but early fall seems to bring out my aggressive soup making tendencies. The soups I yearn for during crisp weather are those hearty concoctions in which a spoon will almost stand straight; they need only a loaf of crusty bread and perhaps a crisp green salad to make a perfect meal.

The basis for almost any hot soup is a strong, well made stock. Homemade chicken stock is a staple; make it in large quantities every once in a while, and freeze it to use as needed. For cooks in a hurry, water can replace the stock in some recipes, or better yet, a good canned product. (They are always called 'broth' on the label. Buy the brands that do not need diluting). It's best to avoid boullion cubes; their flavor is highly unsatisfactory. Vegetarians may use a vegetable stock made from carrots, onions, clean potato peelings, leeks, green pepper tops and seeds, whole, unpeeled garlic cloves; indeed anything except the strongly flavored vegetables such as cauliflower, cabbage, and broccoli. Learn to save bones, poultry carcasses, and vegetable scraps in a plastic bag or container in the freezer. When you have accumulated a sufficient amount, drag out your biggest pot and make a huge batch of stock.

Chicken Stock

5 pounds chicken parts and
   scraps, i.e., backs, necks,
   wings, gizzards (no livers)
   (you can add turkey wings and
   necks as well)
2 large onions, quartered
2 large carrots, unpeeled
2 leeks, trimmed and washed
   thoroughly to remove sand

2 ribs celery, leaves and all
1 Turkish bay leaf or ½
   California bay leaf
6 or 7 parsley sprigs
3 quarts cold water
salt and pepper to taste

1. Combine all ingredients, except salt and pepper, in a large stock pot and bring slowly to a boil. Reduce heat and simmer slowly, covered, for 2 or 3 hours, skimming off scum often. Add some salt and pepper after the first hour.

2. Strain through a cheesecloth lined strainer or colander into a container, pressing and squeezing down on the solids to extract all the juices. Discard solids.

3. Chill the broth thoroughly in the refrigerator, preferably overnight.

4. When chilled, the fat will have solidified on top of the broth. Remove and discard fat.

This stock (and the stocks below) will keep in the refrigerator for a week and a half if it is thoroughly boiled every 3 days. Better yet, freeze it in small quantities and use it as you need it.

Chicken Soup

To make a truly wonderful chicken soup, submerge a whole small chicken in some of your lovely, defatted chicken stock, add a carrot or two, an onion, a handful of fresh dill, a trimmed, cleaned leek and some parsley. Simmer gently, covered, until the chicken is tender and succulent, about 45 minutes. Skim frequently. Let the chicken cool in the stock, then pull the meat from the bones and cut it into chunks. Discard the skin, but save the bones for a future stock; they still have lots of goodness in them. Discard the onion, leek, and herbs. Skim most of the fat from the stock, and bring it to a boil. Slice the carrot and add it back to the stock along with the chicken chunks and some fresh chopped parsley and dill. Add salt and pepper to taste and a pinch of nutmeg if you like it, and you have one of the most powerful culinary panaceas of all times. It's the kind of utterly simple, yet deeply satisfying soup your kids will remember in fits of nostalgia, many years from now.

Beef Stock

1 veal shank
4 or 5 meaty beef bones
3 pounds beef shank
2 cups water
2 large onions, quartered
2 large carrots, unpeeled

2 cloves garlic, mashed
2 ribs celery
6 or 7 parsley sprigs
2½ quarts water
salt and pepper to taste

1. Preheat oven to 400 degrees.

2. Place the bones and meat in a large baking pan with 2 cups of water. Let them bake for about 1 hour, stirring frequently, until they are richly browned.

3. Transfer the meat and bones to a large stock pot. Add the remaining ingredients, except salt and pepper. Pour 1 cup of water into the baking pan. With a wooden spoon or spatula, scrape up all the brown particles on the bottom of the pan. Add to pot.

4. Bring contents of stock pot to a boil. Reduce heat and simmer, covered, for 2 or 3 hours, skimming often. Add salt and pepper after the first hour.

5. Strain through a cheesecloth lined strainer or colander into a container, pressing and squeezing down on the solids to extract all juices. Discard solids. (Slice the meat from the shanks for sandwiches or beef salad.)

6. Chill the stock thoroughly in the refrigerator, preferably overnight.

7. When chilled, the fat will have solidified. Remove and discard.

To make lamb stock, follow the above recipe but substitute lamb bones and lamb shanks for the beef.

Avgolemono Soup (Greek Egg-Lemon Soup)
Serves 6

4 cups well seasoned, clear, fat-
   free chicken stock or lamb stock
½ cup raw rice

4 eggs
¼ cup fresh lemon juice

1. Bring chicken stock to boil. Stir in rice. Reduce heat and simmer until rice is cooked. Remove from heat.

2. Beat eggs until light yellow and foamy. Beat in lemon juice. Beat 2 cups of hot stock into eggs. Then beat egg mixture into remaining stock.

3. Place over low heat and beat like mad for a minute or so, until soup is slightly thickened. Do not let it boil, or eggs will scramble. Serve at once.

Maritata
Serves 6

Maritata is the perfect remedy for temporary sufferers of broken hearts and shattered dreams. It's rich, smooth, and delicious— easily made and immensely consoling to eat.

6 cups good chicken stock
2 ounces vermicelli
¼ pound softened sweet butter
¾ cup freshly grated Parmesan cheese

4 egg yolks at room temperature
1 cup whipping cream

1. Bring stock to a boil. Add vermicelli and cook uncovered 5 to 7 minutes or until noodles are cooked but al dente.

2. In a bowl, blend the butter with the cheese and egg yolks, then gradually beat in the cream.

3. Beat some of the hot stock into the cream mixture, then slowly pour this mixture back into the hot stock stirring constantly. Serve immediately.

Chinese Hot and Sour Soup
Serves 3-4

¼ cup shredded lean pork
1 teaspoon dry sherry
1 teaspoon cornstarch
4 cups chicken stock
¼ cup dried wood ears, soaked for 15 minutes and drained
¼ cup sliced mushrooms
¼ cup shredded bamboo shoots
½ cup shredded bean curd
¼ teaspoon M.S.G. (optional)

2 tablespoons cider vinegar
1 tablespoon soy sauce
½ teaspoon white pepper, or to taste
cornstarch paste (3 tablespoons cornstarch dissolved in ½ cup water)
2 eggs beaten
1 tablespoon minced scallions
1 teaspoon sesame oil

1. Mix the pork, sherry, and 1 teaspoon cornstarch.

2. Bring the stock to a boil. Stir in the pork mixture. Boil for 1 minute, then add wood ears, mushrooms, and bamboo shoots. Boil for 1 minute more.

3. Add the bean curd, M.S.G., vinegar, soy sauce, and pepper. As soon as the soup boils again, add the cornstarch paste and stir until the soup thickens. Stir the beaten eggs into the boiling soup to form "egg flowers."

4. Remove from heat immediately. Taste, and add a bit more pepper or vinegar to achieve the hot and sour taste that suits you. Garnish with scallions, sprinkle with sesame oil, and serve.

Garlic Soup
Serves 6

Be brave and try garlic soup. The taste is mild, haunting, and surprising.

40 cloves of garlic
boiling water, to cover
2 tablespoons olive oil
1 small onion, chopped
1 small green pepper, chopped
1 large can (1 pound 12 ounces)
  plum tomatoes, undrained and
  chopped

4 cups chicken stock
¼ teaspoon allspice
⅛ teaspoon ground cloves
¼ teaspoon tarragon
salt and pepper to taste
1 egg yolk
6 slices Italian or French bread,
  toasted

1. Boil the unpeeled garlic cloves for 2 minutes in enough water to cover. Drain, rinse in cold water, and peel. Hit each garlic clove very lightly with a kitchen mallet or the side of a wide knife. (They shouldn't be pulverized, just lightly flattened).

2. Heat the oil in a deep pot. Cook the onion, green pepper, and garlic over very low heat for 10 to 15 minutes, until soft but not browned. Add the tomatoes, stock and seasonings. Bring to a boil, reduce heat and simmer uncovered for 20 minutes.

3. Pour the soup through a fine sieve into a bowl. With a wooden spoon or spatula, press down very hard on the solids to extract all juices. Return the strained soup to the pot.

4. Beat the egg yolk in a small bowl. Gradually beat about ¼ cup hot soup into the yolk, then gradually add the yolk mixture into the soup, beating constantly. The egg should not flake, making an egg-drop effect, but should be smoothly incorporated into the stock. Cook gently for 1 to 2 minutes more. Do not boil or the soup will curdle.

5. Spread the reserved vegetable solids on the toasted bread and serve them separately with the soup.

Split Pea Soup, Indian Style
Serves 6

2 tablespoons clarified butter
2 onions, chopped
2 cloves garlic, minced
1 slice peeled ginger root, ¼ inch
   thick, minced
1½ teaspoons turmeric
1½ teaspoons ground coriander
½ teaspoon dry mustard
1 teaspoon ground cumin
salt to taste

2 cups quick cooking dried split
   peas
5 cups water or stock
1 large can (1 pound 12 ounces)
   tomatoes, undrained and
   mashed with the hands
1 small can (3 ounces) chopped
   green chilies
cayenne pepper

1. Heat butter in a deep pot; saute onions, garlic, and ginger root until limp.

2. Add spices and stir until onions are well coated.

3. Add remaining ingredients and mix well.

4. Simmer, covered, for an hour, or until mixture is thick and cooked but the peas have not lost their shape. If the soup thickens too much, thin it with a bit of water or stock. Taste and correct for seasonings. Add some cayenne to spice it up according to your taste. Serve hot.

Mushroom Barley Soup, Jewish Style
Serves 8

2 quarts water or stock
½ pound fresh mushrooms,
   quartered or eighthed
1 1-ounce container European-
   style dried mushrooms, rinsed
   (snap any large mushrooms
   into halves or quarters)
1 onion, cut in half, then sliced
   into thin half-moons

½ cup coarsely grated carrots
½ cup dried baby lima beans
½ cup coarse barley
salt and pepper to taste
½ cup browned onions (see index
   for recipe)
¾ cup milk

1. Combine all ingredients, except browned onions and milk, in a large, heavy pot. Bring to a boil, then reduce heat and simmer, covered, until the barley and limas are very tender and the soup is very thick, about 2 hours.

2. Stir in the onions and milk and simmer 10 to 15 minutes more. Correct seasonings and serve or cool and refrigerate. Reheat just before serving. (This soup tastes delicious on the second and third day.)

Mushroom Soup
Serves 6-8

4 tablespoons butter
2 pounds mushrooms, coarsely
  chopped
2 cloves garlic, minced
½ cup sliced scallions

salt and pepper to taste
½ teaspoon tarragon
5 cups chicken stock
½ cup Madeira
½ cup whipping cream

1. Heat butter in a deep, heavy pot. Add mushrooms, garlic, and scallions and stir to coat mushrooms with butter. Cook, stirring occasionally for 15 minutes, or until mushrooms have exuded quite a bit of liquid.

2. Add salt, pepper, and tarragon. Add stock and bring to a boil. Reduce heat and simmer for ½ hour.

3. Add Madeira. Simmer for 5 minutes more. Stir in cream. Taste and adjust temperature and seasoning. Serve at once.

Chili-Bean Soup
Serves 6-8

If you have a leftover ham bone, cook it with this soup for wonderful flavor.

¼ pound bacon, diced
1 onion, chopped
1 clove garlic, minced
1 tablespoon chili powder
½ teaspoon ground cumin
1 pound dried baby lima beans

3 quarts water or stock
1 can (1 pound 12 ounces) plum
  tomatoes, drained and chopped
3 tablespoons brown sugar
salt and pepper to taste
½ cup fresh chopped parsley

1. Cook bacon slowly in a deep, heavy pot until cooked but not crisp. Remove with a slotted spoon and set aside.

2. To the fat in the pot add onion and garlic. Cook until tender.

3. Add chili powder and cumin to onions. Stir over very low heat until the onions are coated with the spices.

4. Add the beans and water or stock. Bring to a boil, reduce heat and simmer, partially covered, for 1 to 1½ hours, or until the beans are just tender.

5. Stir in the tomatoes, brown sugar, salt, pepper, and reserved bacon. Simmer until beans are very tender, approximately 1 hour.

6. Stir in parsley. Taste and correct seasoning. Serve at once, or cool and refrigerate for later reheating. This soup improves with age, but it will thicken dramatically overnight. To reheat, thin with a bit of water or stock.

The Masselli's Escarole Soup
Serves 8

10 cups chicken stock
1 chicken, about 2½ pounds
1 large onion, quartered
3 or 4 sprigs fresh parsley
1¼ pounds extra lean ground beef
2 large eggs, lightly beaten
2 tablespoons chopped fresh parsley

3 cloves garlic, chopped
salt and pepper to taste
4 tablespoons freshly grated Romano cheese
½ cup unseasoned bread crumbs
1 head escarole, washed well
Additional grated Romano cheese

1. In a deep, heavy pot, simmer the chicken, onion, and parsley in the stock, until the chicken is tender and succulent, about 45 minutes. Let cool slightly.

2. Meanwhile, in a bowl, combine beef, eggs, parsley, garlic, salt, pepper, cheese, and breadcrumbs. Knead it all together and form into 30 small meatballs. Set aside.

3. Trim bottom from head of escarole, separate the stalks, and break each stalk in half.

4. Skim most of the fat from the stock and discard onion quarters and parsley sprigs. Skin chicken and pull the meat off the bones in chunks. Discard skin, fat, and gristle, and save bones for a future stock.

5. Put escarole in the stock, cover, and bring to a boil. Add meatballs when soup returns to a boil. Reduce heat and simmer, covered, for 10 to 15 minutes. Meatballs should be just done—check by breaking one open.

6. Put chicken chunks in the soup, and let them heat through.

Pass additional Romano cheese and serve with hunks of crusty bread and butter.

Onion Soup with Calvados
Serves 6

Do not ruin this soup with generous applications of croutons and melted cheese. It's just fine as it is.

3 tablespoons butter
1 tablespoon vegetable oil
6 cups thinly sliced onions
1 tablespoon flour
2 quarts rich chicken stock,
  brought to a boil

½ cup dry white vermouth
salt and pepper to taste
½ teaspoon thyme
3 tablespoons Calvados

1. Heat butter and oil in a deep, heavy pot that can be covered. Stir onions into hot fat, cover pot, and cook over low heat for 15 minutes.

2. Uncover pot, and raise heat slightly. Cook over moderate heat, stirring frequently for 40 to 50 minutes or until onions are deeply browned.

3. Sprinkle in flour and stir over low heat for 3 minutes.

4. Whisk in boiling stock. Add vermouth, salt, pepper, and thyme. Simmer, partially covered, for 40 minutes. Stir occasionally.

5. Skim the surface of the soup. Adjust seasoning. Stir in Calvados. Serve at once, very hot.

Potato-Tarragon Soup
Serves 6

2 tablespoons butter
2 leeks, trimmed, cleaned, and
  sliced
4 cups chicken stock
1 pound baking potatoes, peeled
  and coarsely diced

salt and pepper to taste
½ tablespoon chopped fresh
  tarragon (½ teaspoon dried)
2 tablespoons freshly grated
  Parmesan cheese

1. Heat butter in a heavy pot. Saute leeks until limp, but not browned.

2. Add stock, potatoes, salt and pepper to leeks. Simmer until potatoes are very tender. With a wooden spoon, crush some of the potatoes against the side of the pot.

3. Stir in tarragon and cheese. Serve at once. Pass a bowl of additional grated Parmesan at the table.

Liz Terry's Potato Soup
Serves 6-8

2 tablespoons rendered chicken fat
  (see index)
1 onion, diced
1 stalk celery, diced
3 cups diced boiling potatoes
1 cup chicken stock
1 pound mushrooms, cleaned,
  trimmed, and sliced

½ pound fresh spinach, chopped
salt to taste
pinch cayenne pepper
6 tablespoons butter
6 tablespoons flour
3 cups hot chicken stock
1 cup milk

1. Heat chicken fat in a deep, heavy pot. Saute onions and celery until transparent.

2. Add potatoes and stock. Cover and cook until tender.

3. Stir in mushrooms, spinach, salt and pepper.

4. Melt 6 tablespoons butter in a saucepan. Whisk in flour. Stir and cook over low heat for 2 to 3 minutes. Whisk in the 3 cups of hot stock. Bring to a boil. Stir into potato mixture. Add milk. Adjust heat and seasonings. Serve piping hot.

Peasant Soup
Serves 8

3 tablespoons olive oil
2 large onions, coarsely chopped
2 cloves garlic, minced
3 carrots, sliced
1 small white turnip, diced
1 can (1 pound 12 ounces) plum
  tomatoes, undrained and
  mashed with the hands
5 cups chicken stock
½ cup dry red wine
½ teaspoon dried oregano,
  crumbled

½ teaspoon dried basil, crumbled
1 Turkish bay leaf or ½ California
  bay leaf
4 meaty ham hocks
2 10-ounce packages frozen
  chopped turnip greens or
  collard greens, defrosted
½ cup orzo, or any small pasta
1 pound can chick peas, well
  drained and rinsed
salt and pepper to taste
½ cup fresh chopped parsley

1. Heat the oil in a deep, heavy pot that can be covered. Cook the onion and garlic in the oil until soft but not browned.

2. Add the carrots, turnip, tomatoes, stock, wine, oregano, basil, bay leaf and ham hocks. Bring to a boil, then partially cover, reduce heat and simmer 1½ to 2 hours until everything is tender.

3. Remove the ham hocks and cut the meat off the bones in chunks. Return the meat to the pot. Discard the fat, bones, and rind.

4. Stir in the greens, orzo, and chick peas. Simmer an additional ½ hour or more, until the greens are tender and the orzo is cooked. Add salt and pepper to taste. Stir in parsley.

Serve at once or allow to cool, then refrigerate and reheat gently at serving time.

Squash Soup in Squash
Serves 6

This is the most dramatic of soups. Each squash forms a mini tureen for each diner.

6 acorn squash of equal size and
   shape
4 tablespoons butter
2 onions, chopped
¾ cup bread crumbs
salt and pepper to taste

⅛ teaspoon nutmeg
1 cup grated Gruyere cheese
¼ cup grated Parmesan cheese
6 cups hot chicken stock
butter
1 cup warmed whipping cream

1. Preheat oven to 400 degrees.

2. Cut a very thin slice off the bottom of each squash so that it sits on a level bottom. Be careful; there must be no leaks in the squash, and the bottom must remain thick. Cut a "cap" off the top of each squash. Scrape out the seeds and the fibers.

3. Heat butter, cook onions until tender. Add the crumbs and stir until the butter is absorbed. Turn off heat, stir in salt, pepper, nutmeg, and cheeses.

4. Divide the crumb-cheese mixture equally among the 6 squash. Add stock so that each squash is ⅞ full. Place caps back on each squash.

5. Butter a baking pan that can hold the six squash snugly. Put the covered squash in the pan in the 400 degree oven for 45 minutes to 1 hour, or until the soup is simmering and the interiors of the squash are beginning to get tender.

6. Reduce oven temperature to 300 degrees and bake an additional 15 to 20 minutes, or until interiors of squash are quite tender. Remember, the outside of the squash must not lose its shape.

7. Stir some cream into each squash, adjust seasonings, and serve each guest a squash in a soup bowl at once. The diner spoons out the stock along with the tender squash flesh.

Cold Soups

Cool, refreshing, and fragrant, cold soups are as much a culinary tradition of summer as steaming hot, bubbly ones are of winter. There are wonderful examples of such soups in almost every culture, although the most familiar to Americans are vichyssoise and gazpacho. The less familiar ones—cold cherry and blueberry from Hungary, schav and borscht from Russia—often cause confusion. One evening years ago, during my stint as chef in a small restaurant, a customer called me to his table after he had finished his meal. He was feeling expansive, as well fed, pampered customers always do, but there was a seed of displeasure there, too. "The veal," he said, kissing his fingertips and rolling his eyes towards heaven, "It was the best I have ever eaten. And the zucchini with walnuts . . ." Words failed him; the zucchini was just too remarkable to talk about, apparently. "But the soup," he beckoned me closer and dropped his voice to a horrified whisper, "The soup was ICE COLD!"

His distress was quite unwarranted, of course; the cold cherry soup was a traditional Hungarian recipe, and I was very proud of its chilly, pink, creamy, winy, glory. To avoid such misunderstandings at your own dinner table, always explain these soups to your guests before serving. Present them in clear glass bowls to show off their brilliant color, and announce firmly. "The soup is *supposed* to be cold!"

Tomato Soup, Hungarian Style
Serves 6

4 pounds summer tomatoes
2 onions, chopped
½ cup fresh parsley
slivered zest of ½ lemon
1 tablespoon sweet Hungarian
* paprika*

1 tablespoon sugar
salt and pepper to taste
juice of 1 lemon
sour cream

1. Peel, seed, and juice the tomatoes. Chop them coarsely into a large, non-metallic pot. Add the onions, parsley, lemon zest, paprika, sugar, salt, and pepper. Bring to a simmer, and simmer for 5 to 7 minutes. Stir in the lemon juice.

2. Put the soup into the blender in batches and flick the blender on and off. This soup should be lumpy; *not* a puree. Pour into a glass bowl and chill.

3. Serve with a dollop of sour cream on top of each bowlful.

Tomato Soup, Mexican Style
Serves 4

Use the freshest, juiciest, ripest summer tomatoes for this one.

*4 cups peeled, seeded, and
  chopped summer tomatoes*
*¼ cup canned chopped green
  chilies, drained*
¼ cup red wine vinegar
2 tablespoons olive oil
*2 tablespoons chopped fresh
  parsley*

2 cloves garlic, minced
*1 tablespoon fresh oregano,
  chopped*
1 teaspoon fresh thyme, chopped
1 tablespoon fresh basil, chopped
salt and pepper to taste

Combine all ingredients. Chill.

Avocado Tomato Soup
Serves 6

2 avocados
juice of 1 large lime
2 cups clear, fat-free chicken stock
½ cup canned, crushed tomatoes
*1 can (3 ounces) chopped green
  chilies*

1 cup sour cream
salt and Tabasco sauce to taste
1 cup cubed avocado
chopped fresh coriander leaves

1. Peel and cube avocados. Put in blender with lime juice and 1 cup of stock. Blend until very smooth. Scrape into a large bowl.

2. With a whisk, stir in remaining stock, crushed tomatoes, chilies, sour cream, salt, and Tabasco. Cover with plastic wrap right over the surface of the soup. Chill for an hour or so.

Do not make this soup a day in advance or it will turn an unattractive olive drab color. Garnish each bowl of soup with a few cubes of avocado and a sprinkling of coriander.

Heinz Sowinski's Strawberry Soup
Serves 6

1 pint strawberries, hulled
2 cups sour cream
1 cup buttermilk

1 tablespoon honey (or to taste)
fresh strawberries, sliced
fresh mint

1. Place strawberries, sour cream, buttermilk, and honey in blender jar. Blend briefly—the soup is best if a few flecks of strawberry remain so don't overblend. Pour into a glass bowl.

2. Garnish each serving with strawberry slices and a sprig of mint.

Note: more honey can be added to taste, but remember, this should be a tart soup, not a milkshake.

Blueberry Soup
Serves 6

6 cups blueberries, fresh or frozen
2 cups water
1 lemon, sliced (remove seeds)
1 cinnamon stick

⅓ cup granulated sugar
1 cup half and half
additional fresh blueberries
   (if available)

1. Combine first 5 ingredients in a non-metal saucepan. Bring to a boil. Reduce heat and simmer for 10 minutes. Cool.

2. Remove lemon and cinnamon stick, and puree soup, in batches, in the blender. This soup should be very smooth and velvety.

3. Chill thoroughly. Just before serving, stir in half and half. If fresh blueberries are available, garnish each bowlful with a few.

Cherry Soup
Serves 6

3 cups cold water
1 cup sugar
1 cinnamon stick
4 cups (2 cans) tart cherries
   canned in water, drained

1 tablespoon arrowroot
½ cup cold whipping cream
¾ cup cold dry red wine

1. Combine water, sugar, and cinnamon stick in a 2 quart non-metal pot. Bring to a full rolling boil.

2. Add drained cherries to boiling water.

3. In a small cup or bowl, mix arrowroot with 2 tablespoons cold water. Mix to a paste.

4. Beat arrowroot into the cherries and water. Stirring constantly, bring the soup to just below the boil.

5. Immediately reduce heat to low and simmer about 2 minutes, stirring all the while, until soup is no longer cloudy and has thickened slightly.

6. Pour into a glass or ceramic container. Cool, and then chill in the refrigerator.

7. Just before serving, stir in cream and wine.

Vichyssoise
Serves 6

2 tablespoons butter
1 bunch scallions, sliced, green
   and white parts
2 leeks, trimmed, cleaned, and
   sliced

4 cups clear, fat-free chicken stock
4 medium baking potatoes, peeled
   and coarsely diced
salt and pepper to taste
2 cups half and half

1. Heat butter in a heavy pot. Saute scallions and leeks until limp.

2. Add stock, potatoes, salt, and pepper. Simmer until potatoes are very tender. Cool. Skim off fat.

3. Push the soup through a fine sieve, or puree it through a food mill (a blender will make the mixture pasty).

4. Pour into a glass bowl. Stir in half and half. Taste and adjust seasonings. Chill.

5. If desired, just before serving, stir in 2 cups of sorrel chiffonade (see index) for sorrel vichyssoise, or 2 cups of chopped watercress for watercress vichyssoise.

Schav
Serves 4-6

Schav, a sorrel soup of Russian-Jewish and Polish-Jewish origin, is one of the best summer soups in the world. It's elegant, mysterious because of the sorrel flavor, and extremely refreshing.

1 pound sorrel, cut into
  chiffonade (see index)
1 onion, cut in half and sliced
  into paper-thin half moons
4 cups clear, fat-free, chicken
  stock or water
1½ tablespoons sugar
3 tablespoons lemon juice
salt to taste

½ cup sour cream, at room
  temperature
2 eggs, at room temperature
sour cream
sliced scallions, green and white
  parts
peeled, seeded cucumbers, chopped
chopped radishes

1. Combine sorrel, onion, and stock or water in a nonreactive pot. Bring to a boil, reduce heat, and simmer for 15 minutes.

2. Add sugar, lemon juice, and salt, and simmer for 10 to 15 minutes more. Turn off heat.

3. Beat sour cream and eggs together. With a whisk, slowly beat 2 cups of the hot soup into the egg-cream mixture. Slowly pour the mixture back into the soup pot, beating vigorously all the while.

4. Taste, and add more salt, sugar, or lemon juice according to your taste, but remember that this soup should be tart.

5. Chill the soup. Serve it cold—taste again for seasonings just before serving. Top each bowl of soup with a dollop of sour cream and a sprinkling of scallions, cucumbers, and radishes.

Borscht
Serves 8

10 beets, peeled and coarsely
   grated
4 summer tomatoes, peeled,
   seeded, and chopped
3 leeks, cleaned, trimmed, and
   chopped (see note)
9 cups water

¼ cup tomato paste
½ cup lemon juice
⅓ cup sugar
salt to taste
3 eggs at room temperature
sour cream

1. Combine beets, tomatoes, leeks, and water in a heavy pot that can be covered. Bring to a boil, reduce heat, and simmer for 1 hour, partially covered.

2. Add tomato paste, lemon juice, sugar, and salt. Simmer for an additional ½ hour. Remove from heat.

3. Beat the eggs. Beat in some of the hot soup, a little at a time. Then beat the egg mixture back into the soup.

4. Heat gently for a few minutes, stirring constantly, but do not let it boil or even simmer or the eggs will scramble. Taste carefully and add additional lemon juice, sugar, or salt if necessary. The soup should be tart, but not unpleasantly so.

5. Cool, and then chill.

Serve with a dollop of sour cream on top of each serving.

Note: to trim leeks, cut off tip and "beard." Cut off and discard most of green portion, leaving just one inch of green. With a sharp knife, slash through part of the white bulb and up through the remaining green portion. Wash leeks well under cold running water, holding them apart at the slash to wash away sand. Then chop and proceed with the recipe.

Beverages

Aperitifs

Wine and food lovers tend to avoid pre-dinner cocktails for the damage they do to the tastebuds, but a drink or two with hors d' oeuvre is a civilized custom. An aesthetically pleasing aperitif will delight your gastronome friends. My favorite aperitif is Kir, a mixture of well chilled dry white wine and creme de cassis (black currant liqueur). In France, where it originated, Kir (pronounced Keer) is traditionally prepared by adding 1 part creme de cassis to 4 parts dry white Burgundy. These proportions result in a drink that is oversweet to many palates; the proportions may be changed to a tablespoon of creme de cassis per glass of wine, or even a few drops per glass. A dry white California jug wine is perfect for Kir, or if the budget permits, a French dry white, but never use a really fine wine for Kir; it would be sacrilege. The cassis is available in many forms, from a nonalcoholic black currant juice concentrate to extremely fine and expensive creme de cassis from France. The taste will differ, of course, with the wine and the quality of the cassis, but the resulting Kir is always delicious and satisfying. Chilled dry vermouth can be substituted for the white wine to make vermouth cassis; if you use such a vermouth, make sure that it is an imported one—domestic vermouths tend to be off balance. A cold, young Beaujolais mixed with a few drops of creme de cassis makes a Cardinal, a robust aperitif that stimulates the tastebuds nicely.

Jep Morgan's Mint Julep

Jep Morgan grows herbs for all of Atlanta at Morgan Farms, his herb farm in Kennesaw. His mint julep is the perfect drink for a hot, Georgia summer afternoon.

4 sprigs of fresh mint　　　　　　*shaved ice*
1 teaspoon powdered sugar　　　*additional fresh mint for garnish*
2½ ounces Kentucky bourbon
*　whiskey*

1. Mash the mint and sugar together in a 12 ounce silver goblet or Tom Collins glass.

2. Pour bourbon into the glass and fill with shaved ice. Stir gently until glass is frosted.

3. Decorate with sprigs of mint. Serve with straws and sip decorously.

Paul Masselli's "Pop's Wine"

Use a jug wine for this. (Paul's grandfather used his homemade wine).

Cut up some ripe peaches. Put into a big pitcher or jug with the wine. Cover well and let stand for 12 hours. Serve as is, peaches and all. Serve over crushed ice or not, as you wish.

Festive Champagne Punch
20 punch cup servings

This is excellent for weddings and other big parties.

1 fifth Chenin Blanc, chilled   ¼ cup lemon juice
2 fifths Champagne, chilled   1 cup orange liqueur
¼ cup sugar

Combine all ingredients. Serve from a punch bowl. Float a large block of ice in the bowl.

Sangria
24 half-cup servings

2 fifths of dry red jug wine   1 cup orange liqueur
4 cups fresh orange juice

Combine and chill. Serve in wine goblets with crushed ice.

Chapter 3

Eggs, Cheese

Eggs

Omelets

Omelets are the faithful standbys of experienced cooks. With a carton of eggs on hand, all sorts of lovely, eggy dishes can be ready for guests or family on short notice. Unfortunately, although short-order type omelets—flat, tough, and dry—are easy to make, classic omelets represent a challenge to novice cooks. An aura of mystery surrounds their production; but the rules of classic omelet making are simple and easily understood. Once mastered, they enable the cook to turn out fluffy, creamy omelets time after time with no trouble at all. A good omelet pan is vital to the whole operation; it should have a fool-proof, non-stick lining, and gently sloping sides. Season it according to the manufacturer's instructions, and wipe it clean after each use. Do not put it in the dishwasher, and never, under any circumstances, scour it. Keep it safe on a wall hook out of the range of scratches and gouges. If the lining becomes marred, the omelet will stick.

If you are trying out your omelet pan for the first time, remember that omelet making is largely a matter of practice. By the third or fourth try, a lovely, creamy, perfectly formed omelet is usually achieved, but the first few attempts often result in eggs in the burners of the stove or even on the opposite wall. Don't be discouraged; just mop up and try again. The knack of keeping the eggs in the pan is quickly learned and like bicycle riding, once you've mastered it, you have it forever. Be careful not to overcook the eggs. Once the omelet is cooked, it must be served and eaten. If made to wait, it will toughen. Serve it on a warm, not hot, plate.

Classic Omelet 1
Serves 1 or 2

3 eggs, at room temperature
1 tablespoon water
salt and pepper to taste
pinch of herb of your choice
  (tarragon, basil, etc.)
1 tablespoon butter
¼ cup hot filling (chopped
  vegetables, meat or
  combination; try cooked
  chicken, ham, bacon,
  mushrooms, potatoes, onions,
  peppers, unsalted nuts,
  avocados, croutons, etc.)

1 to 2 tablespoons grated cheese,
  if desired (Swiss, Parmesan,
  Cheddar, Jack, Fontina, etc.)

1. Break eggs into bowl. Add water, salt, pepper, and herbs. (Add salt sparingly; too much tends to harden the egg protein).

2. With a fork, beat the eggs 30 to 35 strokes, just enough to blend whites and yolks well. Overbeating results in a thin mixture.

3. Melt butter in a 6 to 8 inch non-stick omelet pan. Tilt the pan to coat it with butter. When butter is hot and the butter foam is subsiding, pour in eggs. The heat should be moderately high.

4. Let eggs set for 2 or 3 seconds. Then, with a wooden or nylon spatula, quickly but gently slide the eggs toward the center of the pan. Do this very quickly all around the pan, forming large soft curds. Then grasp the handle of the pan and shake the pan rapidly toward and away from you, using sharp, definite movements. The omelet will form an oval of fluffy, softly scrambled eggs in an envelope of coagulated egg.

5. In 10 to 15 seconds, when the omelet is set and cooked but still creamy and soft in the center, and not at all browned on the bottom, spoon filling down the center and sprinkle with grated cheese, if used.

6. Slide the omelet out onto a warm plate that is tilted against the pan. When half out of the pan, let the omelet fold closed over the filling, to rest on the plate. Serve at once. (The whole operation will have taken less than a minute).

Classic Omelet 2
Serves 1 or 2

In this method, the eggs and the filling are more intimately combined. Try this after you have thoroughly mastered method number 1.

1½ tablespoons butter
4 to 6 tablespoons filling
3 eggs, at room temperature
1 tablespoon water
salt and pepper to taste (easy on
*   the salt)*

pinch herbs of your choice
3 tablespoons grated cheese
*   (optional)*

1. Melt butter in a 6 to 8 inch non-stick omelet pan. When hot, add chopped vegetables and meat and saute until hot.

2. Break eggs in bowl with water, salt, pepper, and herbs and with a fork, beat 30 to 35 strokes. Throw eggs into hot pan right over filling. Continue as in Omelet 1, step 4. Serve hot.

Frittatas
Serves 4

If you want to feed omelets to several people at once without going to the trouble of making them one at a time as you must with the classic omelet, try frittatas.

A frittata is a round, cushiony filled omelet, Italian in origin. The technique of preparation is somewhat different from the classic methods outlined above, and the eggs are sometimes allowed to become delicately brown. Frittatas are traditionally served in wedges; they may be eaten hot, warm or cool. Cool, they make wonderful picnic food. Cooked potatoes, sliced, sauteed zucchini, leftover pasta, or cooked artichoke hearts make splendid frittata fillings, but as with the classic omelet, almost anything goes. Use a larger omelet pan, of a similar non-stick, sloping design.

4 tablespoons butter or olive oil *pinch of herbs, if desired*
8 eggs *1 cup cooked filling*
3 tablespoons water *grated cheese, if desired*
salt and pepper to taste

1. Preheat broiler.

2. Heat butter or oil in a 10-inch, non-stick omelet pan or skillet.

3. With a fork, beat eggs with water, salt, pepper, and herbs. The yolks and whites should be blended, but do not overbeat. Stir in filling.

4. Tilt the pan so it is coated with butter or oil—pour the egg mixture into the hot pan. Cook over medium heat, without stirring, for a few moments, until the eggs begin to set on the bottom.

5. With a wooden or nylon spatula, lift the edge of the omelet away from the pan, tilt the pan so that the uncooked egg flows beneath the cooked portion. Continue doing this all around the pan, until the frittata is almost completely set, but still soft in the center and runny. If cheese is used, sprinkle it evenly over the top at this point.

6. Slide under the broiler for a minute or two until the eggs are set and the cheese melted. Slide onto a warm serving plate. The frittata will look like a golden cushiony pancake. Cut into wedges to serve.

Piperade Omelet
Serves 6

This is a classic Basque open faced omelet, suitable for any meal, and extremely attractive to serve. If you grow basil, the fresh leaves make a perfect garnish.

Piperade Mixture

3 tablespoons olive oil
2 large onions, thinly sliced
2 large green peppers, thinly sliced into long strips
3 cloves garlic, minced
1 large (1 pound 12 ounces) can tomatoes, well-drained, cut into strips

salt and pepper to taste
½ teaspoon basil (1 tablespoon fresh)
3 slices boiled ham, cut into thin strips
½ cup fresh parsley, chopped

1. Heat the oil in a large, heavy skillet. Saute onions, peppers, and garlic in the oil until soft but not browned.

2. Add the tomatoes, raise heat and cook 2 or 3 minutes, until tomatoes start to render their juices.

3. Add salt, pepper, and basil. Lower heat and simmer until the mixture is thick and chunky.

4. Add ham and parsley to the vegetable mixture and set aside.

Omelet

10 eggs
salt and pepper to taste
4 tablespoons olive oil

¼ cup grated Parmesan cheese
basil leaves, if available

1. With a fork, beat eggs with salt and pepper until well blended.

2. Heat oil in a 10 to 12 inch omelet pan. When hot, throw in eggs and let set for 2 or 3 seconds. With a wooden or nylon spatula, quickly and gently slide the eggs toward the center of the pan, forming large, fluffy, creamy curds. When the eggs are done, but still soft, unbrowned and slightly runny, spread on the hot piperade mixture. Sprinkle with cheese, garnish with basil leaves, and serve right out of the pan with crusty bread.

Souffles

Souffles are dramatic, gossamer, golden creations, although the thought of making one fills many novice cooks with fear and trembling. A souffle's spectacular appearance, and the blissful sighs that greet it as it emerges from the kitchen in all its airy glory, make souffle cookery very gratifying indeed. Ignore all the stories you have heard about their unpredictability and their penchant for collapsing at a footstep; souffles are really quite easy to make, once the rules are understood.

Beaten egg whites folded into an egg yolk-enriched base—usually a thick sauce or a pureed fruit or vegetable—cause the magical rising of the souffle in the oven. If you can afford the cost in time and money, buy a large copper lined bowl for beating the egg whites. When the egg whites are beaten with a balloon wire whisk in the copper bowl, they will yield up to a third more volume than in an ordinary bowl, but copper bowls are expensive and a chore to keep clean and shiny. You will achieve good results in an ordinary bowl with a pinch of salt and a pinch of cream of tartar added to the egg whites. An electric mixer with a whisk attachment works well, too. Always have your bowl and whisk meticulously clean; the slightest trace of egg yolk or grease will prevent the whites from expanding. The whites must be at room temperature or the volume will be diminished, and the souffle will be a paltry one. Beat them until they hold firm peaks when the beater is withdrawn. Do not overbeat or they will turn grainy and clumpy and lose some of their airy, light quality. When adding the beaten mass of whites to a stiff souffle base, stir some of the whites in first to lighten the base, then fold the remainder in gently; be careful because overfolding will result in loss of volume. The volume of the batter, after the beaten whites have been folded into the base, depends upon the beating and folding experience of the cook. If the batter fills the souffle dish up to seven-eighths full, a collar is not needed. If the batter reaches the top of the dish, fashion a collar of folded wax paper around the dish to increase the height of the dish and to avoid overflow as the souffle rises. Butter the inside of the collar and secure it tightly with string and tape. Collared or not, bake the souffle in the center of the bottom oven shelf. (Make sure there is plenty of head room). Some recipes call for the souffle dish to be set in a larger pan of hot water—I prefer the crust that forms around the souffle when it is baked right on the oven shelf with no protective water bath. A slightly undercooked souffle yields a runny center that serves as a sauce for the surrounding firm areas. Each diner gets a bit of the crust, a bit of the firm part, and some of the runny center.

If you prefer, the souffle can be baked for an extra few minutes so that it is uniform all the way through. While the souffle is baking, you may peek at it now and then if you feel the need to, but do not slam the oven door, or you will be serving your guests a pudding. Of course, being stuck with a pudding is not the worst fate in the world; should the souffle fall or rise imperfectly for some reason, unmold it onto a pretty plate, surround it with sour cream, whipped cream or a sauce, and explain to your guests that an elegant pudding was what you had in mind all the time.

Blue Cheese Souffle
Serves 4-6

softened butter
1 to 2 tablespoons fine bread
  crumbs
4 tablespoons butter
1 small onion, minced
3½ tablespoons flour
1 cup hot milk

5 egg yolks, at room temperature
5 ounces blue cheese, crumbled
salt and pepper to taste
7 egg whites, at room
  temperature
pinch of salt
pinch of cream of tartar

1. Preheat oven to 350 degrees.

2. Butter a 1½ quart souffle dish with softened butter. Sprinkle in crumbs and tilt dish to coat the bottom and sides.

3. Melt butter in a saucepan. Saute onion until tender and golden. Whisk in flour. Stir over low heat for about 3 minutes.

4. Whisk in the hot milk. Stir and cook over a very low light for a few minutes until thickened. Scrape into a bowl and cool.

5. Whisk in the egg yolks, one at a time, and the cheese. Season with salt and pepper, but allow for the saltiness of the cheese.

6. With a clean balloon whisk, in a clean bowl, beat the egg whites with the salt until they begin to get foamy. Add cream of tartar, and increase beating speed. Beat until the whites are greatly expanded in volume and hold firm peaks when the whisk is withdrawn, but do not let them get dry or grainy.

7. With a rubber spatula, stir ⅓ of the whites into the blue cheese mixture. Dump the remaining whites over the blue cheese mixture. Fold them together with a large rubber spatula, using an under-over motion and turning the bowl as you fold. 15 to 20 strokes should be sufficient. Do not overfold.

8. Spoon souffle mixture into prepared dish. Place in the center of preheated oven for 30 to 35 minutes. A cake tester inserted through one of the side cracks will emerge almost clean. The center will be slightly runny—if you prefer a firmer souffle, bake it for 5 minutes more. Serve at once.

Chocolate Souffle
Serves 4-6

softened butter
1 to 2 tablespoons sugar
3 squares semi-sweet baking
chocolate
1 cup milk
4 tablespoons butter
3 tablespoons flour

⅓ cup sugar
2 teaspoons orange liqueur
5 egg yolks, at room temperature
7 egg whites, at room
temperature
pinch of salt
pinch of cream of tartar

1. Preheat oven to 350 degrees.

2. Butter a 1½ quart souffle dish with softened butter. Sprinkle in sugar and tilt dish to coat the bottom and sides.

3. Melt chocolate with milk in a saucepan.

4. Heat butter in a heavy pot. Whisk in flour. Stir over low heat for 3 to 4 minutes, but do not let the roux get brown.

5. Whisk in hot milk-chocolate mixture and the sugar. Whisk and cook over low light until thick. Scrape into a bowl and cool slightly.

6. With the whisk, stir in liqueur and the yolks, one at a time.

7. With a clean balloon whisk, in a clean bowl, beat the egg whites with the salt until they begin to get foamy. Add cream of tartar, and increase beating speed. Beat until the whites are greatly expanded in volume and hold firm peaks when the whisk is withdrawn, but do not let them get dry or grainy.

8. With a rubber spatula, stir ⅓ of the whites into the chocolate mixture. Dump the remaining whites over the chocolate mixture. Fold them together with a large rubber spatula, using an under-over motion and turning the bowl as you fold. 15 to 20 strokes should be sufficient. Do not overfold. It is all right if a few white streaks show.

9. Spoon souffle mixture into prepared dish. Place in the center of preheated oven for 30 to 35 minutes. A cake tester inserted through one of the side cracks will emerge almost clean. The center will be slightly runny—if you prefer a firmer souffle, bake it for 5 minutes more. Serve at once with whipped cream or vanilla ice cream.

Mushroom Souffle
Serves 4-6

softened butter
1 to 2 tablespoons bread crumbs
5 tablespoons butter
1 pound mushrooms, chopped
1 bunch scallions, trimmed and
*   sliced, green and white parts*
½ cup European-style dried
*   mushrooms, rinsed and soaked*
*   in hot water for at least 1 hour*
3 tablespoons Madeira

salt and pepper to taste
1 tablespoon flour
½ cup sour cream, at room
*   temperature*
5 egg yolks, at room temperature
7 egg whites, at room
*   temperature*
pinch of salt
pinch of cream of tartar

1. Preheat oven to 350 degrees.

2. Butter a 2 quart souffle dish with softened butter. Sprinkle in crumbs and tilt dish to coat the bottom and sides.

3. Melt butter in a wide heavy skillet. Saute the mushrooms and scallions in the butter until the mushrooms begin to exude their liquid. Chop the soaked dried mushrooms and add them to the skillet, along with their soaking liquid and the Madeira. Simmer briskly until the mixture is almost dry. Season liberally with salt and pepper.

4. Whisk the flour into the sour cream. Stir the sour cream into the mushrooms. Simmer gently until the mixture is thick, and the flour has lost its raw taste.

5. Scrape the mixture into a bowl and cool slightly. Beat in the egg yolks, one by one.

6. With a clean balloon whisk, in a clean bowl, beat the egg whites with the salt until they begin to get foamy. Add cream of tartar, and increase beating speed. Beat until the whites are greatly expanded in volume and hold firm peaks when the whisk is withdrawn, but do not let them get dry or grainy.

7. In this case, it is not necessary to lighten the base with ⅓ of the beaten whites. Simply fold the whites into the mushrooms with a large rubber spatula, using an under-over motion and turning the bowl as you fold. Do not overfold. A few white streaks won't hurt.

8. Spoon souffle mixture into prepared dish. Place in the center of preheated oven for 35 to 45 minutes. A cake tester inserted through one of the side cracks will emerge almost clean.

Potato Souffle
Serves 6

2 large baking potatoes
1 tablespoon butter
2 onions, chopped
softened butter
1 to 2 tablespoons Parmesan
   cheese
2 tablespoons sour cream

2 tablespoons butter
salt and pepper to taste
½ teaspoon thyme
6 egg yolks, at room temperature
8 egg whites, at room
   temperature
pinch cream of tartar

1. Preheat oven to 350 degrees.

2. Cook potatoes in boiling salted water until tender.

3. Heat butter in a small skillet; saute onions until browned.

4. Butter a 1½ quart souffle dish. Sprinkle in Parmesan cheese and turn to coat the bottom and sides of dish with cheese.

5. Peel potatoes while still hot. Put through a ricer into a bowl. Beat in sour cream, butter, salt, pepper, and thyme. Be *very* generous with salt and pepper. Beat in sauteed onions. Cool slightly.

6. Beat egg yolks, one at a time, into potatoes.

7. In a large, clean bowl, with a clean balloon whisk, beat egg whites. When they begin to get foamy, add cream of tartar and increase beating speed. Beat until they hold firm peaks, but do not let them get dry or clumpy. With a rubber spatula, beat ⅓ of beaten whites into the potatoes. Dump the remaining whites over potato mixture. Fold them together with the spatula using an under-over motion, and turning the bowl as you fold. Do not over fold; a few white streaks won't hurt.

8. Spoon mixture into the prepared souffle dish. Bake in the center of the preheated oven for 40 minutes. The center of the souffle will be very slightly runny. Serve at once.

Carrot Souffle
Serves 6

¼ cup grated apple
2 tablespoons lemon juice
5 egg yolks, at room temperature
½ cup sugar
1 cup grated carrots, tightly
   packed

¼ cup cream sherry
6 tablespoons flour
6 egg whites, at room
   temperature
pinch of cream of tartar

1. Preheat oven to 375 degrees.

2. Toss the grated apple with the lemon juice. Set aside.

3. Beat the egg yolks and the sugar until light, fluffy, and lemony. Stir in the apple, carrots, wine, and flour. Beat well to avoid lumps.

4. Begin beating the egg whites in a very clean bowl. As they get foamy, add the cream of tartar and increase beating speed. Beat until stiff peaks are formed when the beater is withdrawn.

5. Gently fold the egg whites into the carrot mixture with a rubber spatula. Do not overfold; a few white streaks in the mixture won't hurt.

6. Lightly spoon the mixture into an oiled 1½ quart souffle dish. Bake until beautifully puffed and golden, about 35 minutes. Serve at once.

Liqueur Souffle
Serves 4-6

In this method, the whites are folded into yolks that are not augmented with starch of any kind. The souffle is as airy and fragile as a flavored cloud. Try it when you have mastered the preceding methods.

softened butter
1 to 2 tablespoons sugar
5 egg yolks, at room temperature
½ cup sugar
4 tablespoons liqueur of your
    choice: rum, Cointreau, pear
    brandy, etc.

7 egg whites, at room
    temperature
pinch of salt
pinch of cream of tartar

1. Preheat oven to 400 degrees.

2. Butter a 2 quart souffle dish with softened butter. Sprinkle in sugar and tilt dish to coat the bottom and sides.

3. Beat the yolks with the sugar until light, fluffy, and lemony. Stir in the liqueur.

4. With a clean balloon whisk, in a clean bowl, beat the egg whites with the salt until they begin to get foamy. Add cream of tartar, and increase beating speed. Beat until the whites are greatly expanded in volume and hold firm peaks when the whisk is withdrawn, but do not let them get dry or grainy.

5. Gently fold the whites into the liqueur mixture with a rubber spatula. Do not overfold; a few white streaks in the mixture won't hurt.

Lightly spoon the mixture into the prepared dish. Bake until beautifully puffed and golden, about 15 to 20 minutes. Serve at once.

Bread Puddings

Whenever I ask people to share interesting recipes with me (and I do ask, everywhere I go), the subject of bread pudding seems to come up. People, from Canada to Mexico, remember with fondness a bread pudding of one sort or another that was served to them regularly in childhood by a mother or grandmother or aunt. There are bread puddings of all kinds; they can be served at breakfast, as a main supper dish, or for dessert. They can be as spectacular as a souffle, while lacking a souffle's temperament; they can be reminiscent of a quiche, but there is no need to take time rolling out pie dough.

A bread pudding can be put together early in the day and refrigerated until an hour or so before baking time. Then let the pudding come to room temperature and bake. It will rise to a golden puffy airiness.

If you serve one of the following recipes to your family, you may be starting a tradition of your own. Many years from now, one of your offspring may reply to the badgering of a nosy recipe collector, "Ah, I remember a bread pudding . . ."

Main Dish Bread Pudding
Serves 6

¼ cup diced onion
2 tablespoons butter
1 package frozen chopped spinach,
    thawed and squeezed as dry as
    possible
5 to 7 stale crusty rolls

6 tablespoons butter
3 eggs
2 cups half and half
salt and pepper to taste
¼ teaspoon nutmeg

1. Preheat oven to 350 degrees.

2. Saute onions very gently in 2 tablespoons butter. When onions are limp, add the spinach and cook for 1 minute. Set aside.

3. Cut rolls into ½ inch strips and place in a 1½ quart souffle dish or a 10 inch quiche dish. Melt remaining butter and pour over rolls, turning rolls so they soak up all the butter.

4. Add spinach and onions to bread and mix thoroughly. Mix together eggs, half and half, salt, pepper, and nutmeg, and pour over bread. Bake at 350 degrees for 30 to 45 minutes, (the longer time in the souffle dish) or until a knife inserted near the center comes out clean.

Breakfast Bread and Butter Pudding
Serves 6

6 ounces day-old soft rolls, cut
   into chunks, about 1 inch
   square
¼ pound butter, melted

4 eggs
½ cup sugar
2 cups half and half
1 teaspoon cinnamon

1. Preheat oven to 350 degrees.

2. Place the chunks of bread on the bottom of a 1½ quart souffle dish or 10 inch quiche dish.

3. Pour the melted butter over the bread.

4. Beat the eggs. Beat in the sugar, half and half, and cinnamon. Pour this mixture over the bread. Let it soak for 20 minutes.

5. Bake uncovered for 45 minutes to 1 hour, (the longer time in the souffle dish) or until the custard is set. (A knife inserted in the center will come out clean). The custard will emerge from the oven puffed and golden, but will almost immediately deflate a bit. Serve at once.

Luncheon Bread and Cheese Pudding
Serves 6

6 ounces day-old French or Italian
   bread, cut into 1 inch chunks
¼ pound butter, melted
½ cup thinly sliced scallions,
   green and white parts
½ cup freshly chopped parsley
½ teaspoon thyme

½ cup grated sharp Cheddar
   cheese
½ cup grated Swiss cheese
4 eggs
2½ cups whole milk
2 tablespoons Dijon mustard
salt and pepper to taste

1. Preheat oven to 350 degrees.

2. Place bread in the bottom of a ceramic 1½ quart souffle dish or a 10 inch quiche dish.

3. Pour the melted butter over the bread. Scatter the scallions, parsley, thyme, and grated cheeses over the butter soaked bread.

4. Beat the eggs. Beat in the milk, mustard, salt and pepper. Pour the egg mixture over the bread. Push the bread down in the mixture. Let soak for at least 20 minutes.

5. Place in 350 degree oven for 45 minutes to 1 hour (the longer time in the souffle dish) or until a knife inserted in the center comes out clean and the pudding is puffed and golden. Serve at once.

Chocolate Bread Pudding
Serves 6

Chocolate bread pudding is fail-safe and very souffle-like in texture. Its airiness combines with the haunting rich taste qualities of hot melted fudge brownies; its intense chocolatiness will instantly banish the screaming meanies.

6 ounces day-old plain soft rolls,
   such as Parker House, cut into
   chunks, about 1 inch square
¼ pound butter, melted

4 eggs
1 cup sugar
½ cup unsweetened cocoa, sifted
2 cups half and half

1. Preheat oven to 350 degrees.

2. Place the chunks of roll in a 1½ quart souffle dish.

3. Pour the melted butter over the rolls. Beat the eggs. Beat in the sugar, cocoa, and half and half. Pour this mixture over the bread. Let it stand for 20 minutes. Push the bread down into the chocolate mixture as it soaks.

4. Bake uncovered for 45 minutes to 1 hour, or until the custard is set. (A knife inserted in the center will come out clean). The pudding will emerge from the oven beautifully puffed. Serve immediately with vanilla ice cream or whipped cream.

Crepes

Crepe cookery has become an all-American pastime it seems, although the thin pancakes originated in Europe; most notably France and Hungary. But thanks to the proliferation of crepe restaurants in American cities, and a few very popular crepe cookbooks, just about every kitchen enthusiast has tried his or her hand at making the delicate things.

There is a knack to making crepes, but it is easily mastered; and once mastered, crepes are as easy to make as pancakes from a mix. The best way to learn is to arm yourself with a crepe pan and a bowl of batter and get to work. By the time you have made two or three batches of crepes, the knack is mastered and you are an expert.

The question of what sort of a pan to use is an interesting one. Lately, there has been a flood of gadgets on the market designed, it seems, to complicate a very simple process. It is best to ignore the crepe pans that cook upside down, that plug in, or that otherwise obfuscate what should be a very simple design. The ideal crepe pan is 8 inches in diameter, has gently curving sides, and has a dependable non-stick surface. Butter is used to coat the pan even though the surface is non-stick, but very little is needed. That little bit of butter will make a world of difference in the taste of the finished crepe. The more accomplished you become, the thinner your crepes will be, and the more of them you will produce from a single batch of batter. The heat of the pan is critical, and this is learned by trial and error. The first crepe of a batch is usually a test one; it tests the heat of the pan. If it fails, don't fret. Throw it away, adjust the temperature, and go on to the next one. You will probably find that the rest will be perfect.

The following recipe is for an all purpose crepe, suitable for main dishes or for dessert. It will freeze and reheat beautifully, so when the mood is on you, make up a stack to squirrel away for a rainy day. With a tidy sum of crepes to work with, a meal can be as elaborate or as simple as you wish it to be. The easiest thing to do with crepes is to make an inventory of your leftovers and subject them to merciless scrutiny. Goulash or stew type things are delicious if you dice the meat and roll them with their sauce into a crepe. Top with sour cream and heat through in the oven. Leftover turkey or chicken can be folded into a well made mornay sauce and rolled up in a similar fashion, this time using a bit more mornay sauce to top the crepe.

Crepes for dessert are delicious, too. The simplest crepe dessert possible is also one of my favorites. Simply take a hot crepe, brush it with clarified butter that has cooked slowly until it has taken on a nut-like flavor, sprinkle it with a bit of granulated sugar, fold into quarters and serve. The crunch of the sugar, the nuttiness of the butter, and the tenderness of the crepe all contribute to the goodness of this simple dessert.

Crepes can also be stacked for a main dish or a dessert. Place them one by one in a cake pan. Spread each crepe with a filling before adding another. The filling can be jam, whipped cream, pastry cream, or grated chocolate for dessert. For a main dish, try duxelles or finely chopped cooked ham mixed with sour cream and eggs. Whisk ½ tablespoon of flour into ½ cup of room temperature sour cream and spread it on top of the ham and duxelle stack. Top the dessert stack with dots of softened butter. Bake the stacks in a preheated 350 degree oven for ½ hour or so. Serve these concoctions by cutting them into wedges like a cake.

Crepes
16-18 crepes

1 cup all-purpose flour (spoon flour lightly into a one cup measure until cup is overflowing. Level off with a knife)
pinch of salt
2 whole eggs

2 egg yolks
2 tablespoons butter, melted and cooled slightly
3 tablespoons brandy
¾ cup milk
½ cup water
melted butter

1. Put flour and salt in container of electric blender. Add eggs and yolks and blend, stopping to scrape the sides of the blender jar frequently.

2. Add butter, brandy, milk, and water. Blend well. Let the batter stand for at least an hour before using.

3. Use a heavy, non-stick 8-inch omelet or crepe pan. Have melted butter and a pastry brush on hand and a bowl containing the batter. Heat pan until very hot. Use the pastry brush to coat the pan with melted butter.

4. Use a ladle or scoop that holds about ¼ cup. Ladle batter into the hot pan. Immediately tilt pan so batter covers bottom and sides. Pour any excess batter back into the batter bowl.

5. Cook over high heat for about a minute. When batter begins to bubble a bit and come away from the sides of the pan, grasp the edge of the crepe and flip it over.

6. Cook the second side for about 10 seconds. Slide crepe onto wax paper.

7. Continue until batter is used up. Crepes may be refrigerated or frozen. Stack them between sheets of wax paper.

Cheese

Cheese Saganaki *(Flaming Greek Cheese)*

1 pound soft Kasseri or Kefalotiri
   cheese
3 tablespoons melted butter

2 tablespoons good brandy
½ lemon

1. Preheat broiler.

2. Cut cheese into ¼ inch thick slices. Place on a flat baking dish and brush with melted butter.

3. Broil 4 to 6 inches from heat until cheese is bubbly and light brown. Remove from heat.

4. Warm brandy in a ladle and pour it over the hot cheese. Ignite at once (avert your face). When the flames begin to die down, squeeze the lemon juice over the cheese and serve at once with bread.

Fried Cheese
Serves 8

4 eggs
4 tablespoons water
1 cup flour
2 cups bread crumbs

salt and pepper to taste
8 rindless slices Fontina, Swiss,
   or Port-Salut, ¼ inch thick
vegetable oil

1. Beat the eggs with water in a soup plate.

2. Place flour in a similar plate and bread crumbs in another. Season both with salt and pepper.

3. Dip slices of cheese in flour and shake off the excess. Dip the slices into the egg wash, then bread crumbs. Dip in egg and bread crumbs again—make sure the slices are thoroughly coated with the crumbs, especially around the edges.

4. Pour an inch of oil into a skillet and heat until hot but not smoking. Fry the coated cheese slices a few at a time, turning once with tongs, until golden brown and crisp. Drain on paper towels and serve at once. When the slices are cut into with a fork, the melted cheese oozes out in a most delicious way.

Swiss-Onion Cheese Tart
Serves 8

This is very like a quiche, but the cheese mixture is poured directly into the raw crust. No need to partially bake the crust first. To succeed, the tart must be made with real Swiss cheese. If you don't feel like wrestling with pie dough, leave it out and call the dish onion-cheese custard.

4 tablespoons butter
1 large onion, cut in half and
   sliced into thin half moons
   (use a Vidalia when in season)
1 unbaked, unsweetened pie shell
   for a 10 inch quiche dish
   (see below)

9 ounces Swiss Emmenthaler
   cheese, grated
9 ounces Swiss Gruyere cheese,
   grated
4 large eggs
2 cups half and half
salt and pepper to taste

1. Preheat oven to 400 degrees.

2. Heat butter in a wide heavy skillet. Saute onion until limp but not browned.

3. Fill unbaked pie shell with half of the cheese. Spread sauteed onions over cheese and cover with remaining cheese.

4. Beat eggs. Stir in half and half and salt and pepper to taste. Pour over onions and cheese.

5. Bake in preheated oven for 45 minutes, until the custard is browned and set.

6. Let sit for 10 minutes or so before cutting and serving.

Pie Crust

2 cups unbleached all-purpose
   flour
¼ pound cold butter
pinch salt

2 cold egg yolks
5 tablespoons ice water

1. Sift the flour onto a cool working surface. Make a large well in the middle of the heap of flour.

2. Whack the butter a couple of times with a rolling pin to soften it up a bit. Place the butter in the well with the salt, egg yolks, and water.

3. With the cool fingertips of one hand, begin mixing the water, yolks, and butter together. Gradually work in the flour, using the cool fingertips of both hands to form large crumbs. If the dough seems too dry, add up to 1 tablespoon more cold water, but be careful; this dough should be soft and pliable but not at all sticky.

4. Gather the dough into a ball. Lightly and briefly knead it using the heel of your hand in a pushing, flattening motion—the palm will be too warm. When it is smooth and very pliable, form it into a compact ball, wrap very well with plastic wrap and chill for at least ½ hour, up to 3 days.

5. Lightly butter a 10 inch quiche pan or tart pan. Lightly flour your work surface. Unwrap chilled dough and flatten it. Lightly flour the top of the dough. Roll it out, rolling from the center and using quick, light strokes, giving the dough scant quarter-inch turns as you roll.

6. When it is ⅛ inch thick, roll the pastry over the rolling pin, and unroll it over the quiche dish. Fit it gently into the pan. Trim the edges, leaving a one-inch overhang.

7. Fold the overhang into the dish and press it to the sides of the dish all around, forming a double thickness. Wrap the dish in plastic wrap and chill.

Spinach Cheese Pie *(Spanikopita)*
Serves 12

Frozen phyllo leaves are available in many supermarkets and specialty food shops. Once thawed and unwrapped, they must be kept moist under damp towels or they will dry out and become impossible to work with.

3 *packages frozen chopped*
  spinach, thawed
4 *tablespoons olive oil*
4 *onions, chopped*
1 *pound Feta cheese, crumbled*
1 *pound Ricotta cheese*
6 *eggs, beaten*

freshly ground pepper
¼ *teaspoon nutmeg*
½ *cup bread crumbs*
1 *package phyllo leaves, thawed*
  slowly in refrigerator
melted butter

1. Preheat oven to 350 degrees.

2. Drain thawed spinach in a colander. Squeeze it as dry as possible.

3. Heat oil in a wide heavy enameled or glass-ceramic skillet. Saute onions in the oil until limp and transparent. Add spinach and stir to combine it with the onions and oil. Cover skillet and let spinach steam over moderate heat for 5 minutes, or until tender.

4. Mix Feta, Ricotta, eggs, pepper, and nutmeg. Stir in spinach mixture and bread crumbs. Taste and add salt if necessary, but Feta is salty, so salt may not be needed. Set filling aside.

5. Lightly brush a long shallow baking pan, such as a lasagna pan, with melted butter. Unwrap phyllo leaves. Place a damp towel on your work surface. Cover with wax paper. Keep unused leaves on the wax paper. Cover with another sheet of wax paper and another slightly damp cloth so that the leaves will not dry out. Stack 10 sheets of phyllo into the baking dish, one at a time, brushing each with melted butter before adding another. Brush leaves so that they are thoroughly coated with butter.

6. Spread spinach mixture over the leaves. Top with 10 more sheets of phyllo, again brushing each sheet with butter. Trim edges all around pan with kitchen scissors.

7. Bake at 350 degrees for 1 hour, until puffed and golden. Cut into squares and serve.

Chapter 4

Main Dishes

Fish and Shellfish

"When I was a kid, we ate shrimp *every night*,"said a friend who grew up on the coast of Florida. "We were too poor to eat anything else." Now that she has reached affluent middle age, she refuses to have anything to do with the succulent little crustaceans. To her, they will always represent low-class food, the food her father foraged for when there was no money for the store.

My childhood was also spent near the sea, on a small sandy island. The smell and sound of the sea were constant and comforting, but the myriad edible creatures that lurked within that sea were of no interest to me then. Local fishermen used clams and shrimp for bait. The thought of eating one was shocking—I would as soon have eaten a worm. Mussels were smelly things, stuck onto the jetties where I played on the beach at low tide, and crabs were strange, menacing creatures that nipped the toes of anyone who walked barefooted across the sands. Tuna fish sandwiches with lots of mayonnaise were the extent of my culinary seafood encounters.

When I reached adulthood and left the island, I was far removed from my intimacy with the sea. Its creatures kept turning up, though, in restaurants and markets, and people I respected doted on them. I began to appreciate the bounty of the sea with the same fervor that my friend began to ignore it. Fresh seafood, I learned, just cooked through and seasoned intelligently, is lovely food. But old and overcooked seafood are awful; in such circumstances, I prefer to ignore it, too.

To cook seafood properly, cook it quickly. Clams and mussels should be steamed only until they open, oysters should be cooked until they are just warmed through, and shrimp until they turn

71

pink and begin to curl. Finny fish should be cooked very briefly. Do not "cook until it flakes" as many recipes direct. Rather, cook it until it turns opaque and just barely begins to flake, so that it retains that faint sweet taste and moisture of the sea or the stream.

It is imperative that your fish be fresh; all the careful timing and clever seasoning in the world will do nothing for fish that is past its prime. When buying fish and other seafood, keep the following rules in mind:

1. If it smells fishy, don't buy it. Fish and shellfish should have a faint, clean odor of the sea or stream. Any trace of fishiness means old fish—leave it in the store!

2. The fish should be firm. Poke it with your finger—if the flesh springs back it is fresh; if the dent remains, the fish is not for you.

3. Sunken, milky, filmed eyes belong to fish that have been dead for quite a while, or carelessly stored. Only buy fish with bright, bulging, staring eyes, however disconcerting that stare may be.

4. Crab meat should feel dry, not slick or slimy. Whole crabs and lobsters should be alive when you buy them.

5. If the proprietor of the fish market does not let you poke, prod, and smell his or her wares, leave and find another market.

Tarragon Trout in Parchment
Serves 4

½ pound clarified butter
10 cloves garlic, minced
2 tablespoons chopped fresh
  tarragon (2 teaspoons dried)
1 tablespoon chopped fresh parsley

4 squares cooking parchment
4 small fresh trout of equal size,
  cleaned and washed
salt and pepper to taste

1. Melt butter in a heavy pan. Let butter simmer slowly for 20 to 30 minutes. Add garlic. Simmer over low heat for 10 minutes. Do not let the garlic brown. Remove from heat and stir in herbs. Refrigerate for several hours, until the butter solidifies. (It will keep for weeks in the refrigerator, well covered.)

2. Have ready 4 pieces of cooking parchment, each big enough to enclose a trout.

3. Preheat oven to 450 degrees. Place a flat baking sheet in the oven.

4. Dry trout. Lay them on their side on your work surface. With a ruler, measure the thickness of the fish at its thickest point. (Make sure you measure its depth, not its length.) Jot down the inches of thickness.

5. Salt and pepper the fish on the inside and outside. Place an equal sized chunk of hardened garlic-herb butter in the cavity of each fish.

6. Place each fish on a square of parchment, near the bottom edge. Fold the parchment over the fish. The outer edges of the parchment should be even. Crimp the parchment closed over the fish by folding down the upper left hand corner. Start a second fold, so that it incorporates a bit of the first fold. Continue folding and crimping all around until the fish is well secured and no steam or juices can escape.

7. Place the packages on the hot baking sheet in the oven. Cook for 10 minutes for each inch thickness of the fish plus 4 extra minutes for the parchment. For instance, if the fish measured 1 inch, it would cook for a total of 14 minutes. The parchment will puff up and turn brown as the fish cook.

8. Serve each person an unopened package on a plate. As each diner cuts his or her package open with a sharp knife, a cloud of fragrant steam arises to perfume the air and delight the company.

Red Snapper in Parchment
Serves 6

6 squares cooking parchment
6 red snapper fillets, about ½
   inch thick
6 cloves garlic, minced

juice of 3 lemons
3 tablespoons butter
salt and pepper to taste

1. Preheat oven to 450 degrees. Place a baking sheet in the oven.

2. Have ready 6 pieces of cooking parchment, each large enough to completely enclose one fillet.

3. On each piece of parchment, place a red snapper fillet, skin side down. Top each fillet with one minced garlic clove, the juice of ½ lemon, ½ tablespoon butter, salt, and pepper.

4. Fold the parchment over the fish and seal each package well by crimping, as explained in the previous recipe. There must be no openings for juices or steam to escape.

5. Place the 6 packages on the baking sheet in the preheated oven. Bake for 9 minutes. Serve each diner a package to open at the table. The fish will be opaque and just beginning to flake, but still moist and succulent.

   Note: in both the preceding recipes heavy duty foil may be substituted for the parchment, although it won't be as elegant and as much fun. With foil, add 1 extra minute cooking time.

Mr. Ma's Braised Whole Red Snapper
Serves 4

Frank Ma, proprietor of the Hunan Restaurant in Sandy Springs is a passionate cook and a walking compendium of Chinese food lore. When we get together, the air crackles with ingredients, measurements, techniques, and food folklore. His braised fish is often served as the grand finale at his family's Chinese New Year's banquet. The wholeness of the fish reflects hope for the whole of the New Year and the fish itself is a pun. "Yu," the character for fish, also means remainder. Eat the fish at the New Year and good things will not come to an end. Something will remain.

1 *whole red snapper, cleaned and*
  scaled, about 2 pounds
4 *to 6 tablespoons peanut oil*
2 *to 3 thin slices ginger*
2 *pieces star anise*
4 *scallions chopped*
¼ *cup soy sauce*
2 *tablespoons dry sherry*
2 *tablespoons sugar*
salt to taste

½ *teaspoon M.S.G. (optional)*
2 *cloves garlic, sliced*
water
approximately 1 tablespoon
  cornstarch paste (3 tablespoons
  cold water, 1 tablespoon
  cornstarch blended to a paste)
½ *teaspoon sesame oil*
2 *scallions, chopped*

1. Score fish, cutting diagonally into the fish, on both sides.

2. Heat oil in wok until very hot. Hold the fish by the tail and lower it into the hot oil. Let brown for a minute on each side.

3. Lower heat. Add ginger, star anise, scallion, soy sauce, sherry, sugar, salt, M.S.G., garlic, and enough water to just cover fish. Bring to a boil, reduce heat and simmer gently, covered, until fish is just done, 15 to 20 minutes.

4. When done, the fish is very fragile. With a wide spatula, lift it out of the stock very gently and place on an attractive serving platter. Turn flame up under wok. Stir and boil sauce for a few minutes. Stir in cornstarch paste. Stir over medium heat for a minute or so until thickened and glossy. Add a bit more cornstarch paste if necessary, but don't overdo it. Taste and adjust seasonings. Pour over fish.

5. Sprinkle sesame oil and chopped scallion over sauced fish. To serve, put the platter in the center of the table, and let the diners pick pieces of fish right off the bone with their chopsticks.

Variation Braised whole fish with vegetables—Add chopped Chinese cabbage, dried black mushrooms, soaked, drained, and sliced, and snow pea pods to fish in step #3.

Swordfish with Sorrel Hollandaise
Serves 2

This is a lovely dish; the succulent white fish and the tart, golden, green-flecked sauce make a stunning combination. Be very careful not to overcook the swordfish—it must not lose its wonderful, characteristic juiciness.

4 tablespoons butter
2 tablespoons vegetable oil
1 large, fresh swordfish steak, 1 inch thick
salt and pepper to taste

2 teaspoons sorrel puree (see index)
hollandaise sauce (see index)
steamed or boiled new potatoes, unpeeled

1. Heat butter and oil in a heavy skillet, wide enough to hold the swordfish.

2. Salt the swordfish steak lightly on both sides, and grind on a good amount of pepper.

3. Over medium heat, cook the swordfish for 5 minutes on one side, then turn carefully with a spatula and cook for 5 minutes on the other side.

4. Baste the fish with the pan juices, reduce the heat, cover the skillet, and cook gently for 5 to 10 mintues longer, until the fish is done. Uncover occasionally to baste with the pan juices. The fish is done when it feels firm and springy, not soft and pulpy.

5. Cut the steak into 2 equal portions. It should be opaque inside with just the faintest translucence in the center. Do not overcook, or it will become dry and boring.

6. Stir the sorrel puree into the freshly made hollandaise sauce. Serve the swordfish on hot plates. Put a few potatoes on each plate. Spoon some sorrel hollandaise onto each piece of fish, and some of the pan juices over the potatoes. Pass the rest of the hollandaise separately. Any leftover fish is delicious served cold on the next day, with sorrel mayonnaise (see index).

Dailey's Swordfish au Poivre
Serves 4

Swordfish au Poivre is a best seller at Dailey's, one of Atlanta's Peasant restaurants. It was created by Elaine Reader, the Peasant Corporation's talented young recipe developer.

½ cup mustard cognac sauce*
2 tablespoons black peppercorns, crushed
2 tablespoons pink peppercorns, crushed

4 10-ounce swordfish steaks, center cut
½ cup clarified butter

1. Spread a small baking sheet with half the mustard sauce.

2. Combine the 2 peppercorns and sprinkle half of them over the mustard.

3. Press the swordfish steaks down onto the pan so sauce and pepper adhere.

4. Brush topside of fish with remaining sauce. Sprinkle with remaining pepper. Allow to marinate 1 hour or more in the refrigerator. Preheat oven to 375 degrees.

5. Film 1 large or 2 medium skillets with clarified butter. Sear fish about 30 seconds on each side until peppers form a crust.

6. Transfer steaks to oven and cook 15 to 20 minutes until just cooked.

*The mustard cognac sauce that Dailey's serves with this fish is a trade secret. You will achieve excellent results by substituting ½ cup Dijon mustard, blended with 1 tablespoon oil and a scant 1 tablespoon honey.
Note: Pink peppercorns are available at food specialty and "gourmet" shops.

Heinz Sowinski's Halibut on Eggplant, Beurre Blanc
Serves 4

1 medium eggplant
4 4-ounce center cut halibut steaks
acidulated water (water mixed with lemon juice)
salt and pepper to taste
flour
1½ tablespoons butter
1½ tablespoons oil
3 tablespoons butter

2 large shallots, chopped
1 fresh basil leaf, chopped
1 cup peeled, seeded, juiced and diced tomatoes (if the fresh tomatoes available are poor, substitute seeded, drained, and chopped canned plum tomatoes)
beurre blanc (see below)

76

1. Preheat oven to 375 degrees.

2. Peel the eggplant. Slice into four, even, ¼-inch thick slices, the long way. Trim the slices to fit the fish steaks. Save the excess eggplant for another use.

3. With a sharp, thin knife, remove skin from halibut steaks. Carefully separate the meat of the fish steaks from the center bone— each steak will yield 2 "fingers" of meat. Set aside.

4. Dip the eggplant slices into acidulated water; dry thoroughly. Season with salt and pepper. Dip into flour, and shake off excess. Heat butter and oil in a heavy skillet until very hot. Saute eggplant slices quickly, about 2 to 3 seconds on each side. Place on a baking sheet.

5. Heat 3 tablespoons butter; saute shallots until tender. Toss in the basil, the chopped tomatoes, and a bit of salt and pepper.

6. Place an equal amount of the tomato mixture on each eggplant slice, and top each with 2 "fingers" of halibut. Spoon 1 tablespoon Beurre Blanc over the fish on each eggplant slice.

7. Place in the 375 degree oven and cook for 10 to 15 minutes, until the fish *just* turns opaque. DO NOT OVERCOOK! Serve at once.

Beurre Blanc, Heinz's Way

¾ *cup sherry wine vinegar*
2 shallots, chopped
juice from 1 lime
¼ *cup Chablis*
¼ *pound butter, softened*

heaping teaspoon of chopped
  chives
dash Tabasco sauce
salt and pepper to taste

1. Combine vinegar, shallots, lime juice, and Chablis in a small saucepan. Bring to a boil. Simmer briskly until reduced by half. Cool.

2. Whip the softened butter with an electric mixer until fluffy. Whip in the cooled sherry vinegar reduction. Whip in chives. Season with Tabasco, salt and pepper. Store in the refrigerator until ready to use. (This will keep for weeks, and is excellent on veal and light fish.)

Dailey's Sea Trout Phyllo
Serves 4

This is another creation from the Peasant Corporation's Elaine Reader.

¼ cup clarified butter
4 8-ounce boneless sea trout fillets
6 ounces carrots, shredded
6 ounces onions, grated
2 teaspoons fresh garlic, finely minced

salt and pepper to taste
12 sheets phyllo pastry
½ cup egg wash
hollandaise sauce (see index for recipe)

1. Film a large skillet with clarified butter and heat until very hot. Sear fish 30 seconds (or longer depending on thickness) on each side until fish is barely opaque. Remove fish from skillet; reduce heat to low. Saute carrots and onions in the same skillet.

2. Season fish with garlic, salt, and pepper, and cover with vegetables.

3. Preheat oven to 375 degrees.

4. Brush 3 sheets of phyllo with melted butter, and stack them. Continue making buttered stacks of 3 phyllo leaves for each fillet.

5. Wrap each fillet in phyllo, lengthwise, enclosing it completely. Shape the phyllo so that it resembles a whole fish (rounding the top and pinching it 2 inches from the bottom for the tail). Brush each phyllo fish with egg wash.

6. Bake 15 to 20 minutes until golden. Serve with hollandaise.

Note: beat 1 egg and 2 tablespoons water for egg wash.

Sauteed Scamp
Serves 4

"Scamp is the Cadillac of the groupers," declared the fish man in a Hilton Head seafood market. "It's one of the best fish in the world." He was right, and this simple recipe is the best way to prepare it. (It's a lovely way to cook sole, flounder, and red snapper fillets, too.)

4 fillets of scamp
flour
salt and pepper to taste
6 tablespoons butter
2 tablespoons corn oil

2 cloves garlic
juice of 1 lemon
¼ pound butter
chopped parsley
lemon wedges

1. Dry fillets well with paper towels. Season flour with salt and pepper and spread on a platter. Dip the fillets into the flour.

2. Heat the butter and oil in two heavy skillets. Add garlic. When

hot, saute the fillets, 2 to a pan, for 1 minute on each side until lightly browned.

3. Reduce heat. Cook gently, basting with the pan juices and turning once with a wide spatula, until the fish is opaque and just barely beginning to flake (3 to 4 minutes on a side).

4. Transfer fish to a hot serving platter. Squeeze the lemon juice over the fish. Discard garlic cloves and pour out cooking fat. Place the stick of butter in one of the skillets. Heat until foamy. Pour over fish. Sprinkle with parsley and serve at once with lemon wedges.

Kedgeree
Serves 6

The coziest type of British murder mystery sequesters the detective and his suspects in an ancient, murder-prone manor house. Tradition demands that a storm be raging outdoors, while indoors, the guests, one by one, are polished off ingeniously by the elusive murderer. In the warm and fragrant dining room, the detective and his rapidly dwindling complement of suspects breakfast opulently every morning on a magnificent array of classic English breakfast foods; grilled kidneys, bacon, sausage, acres of scrambled eggs, a joint or two of mutton and the inevitable kedgeree.

Kedgeree is an Anglicized version of an Indian fish pilaf; it usually contains rice, curry powder, fish, and hard-cooked eggs. It can be absolutely dreadful, or—as in this case—quite good.

4 tablespoons unsalted butter
4 tablespoons thinly sliced
  scallions, green and white parts
1½ tablespoons Madras curry
  powder
pinch cayenne pepper
4 tablespoons flour

2 cups half and half, scalded
salt and pepper to taste
½ pound thinly sliced smoked
  salmon
2 cups hot cooked rice
3 hard-cooked eggs, peeled and
  coarsely chopped

1. Melt the butter in a heavy saucepan. Saute scallions in hot butter until limp. Stir in the curry powder and cayenne and cook gently over low heat for a few moments.

2. Whisk in flour. Cook, stirring constantly, for 3 or 4 minutes. Whisk in half and half. Stir and cook until smooth and thickened. Add salt and pepper. (Be easy on the salt; the smoked salmon will be quite salty.) Simmer gently over low heat for 5 minutes, stirring occasionally.

3. Cut salmon slices into 1-inch pieces. Fold salmon and rice into sauce. Gently fold in chopped eggs. Pour mixture into an attractive serving dish. Sprinkle with fresh chopped parsley and serve.

Crab Meat

If you were ever a child at the seashore, and had your tender juvenile bottom nipped by an unfriendly crab as you sat making drip castles at the ocean's edge, take heart! Crab meat is one of life's great pleasures. It is available in fish markets in 1 pound containers; no claws, no shells. Just lovely white meat for cold dishes and hot dishes as well. It is already cooked, so in hot dishes be sure to cook it long enough to heat it through only; overcooking will toughen it.

Marinated Mushrooms with Crab
Serves 6

The longer the salad is marinated, the more "cooked" the mushrooms will seem to be.

*1 cup crab meat, picked over
  carefully*
*1 pound mushrooms, trimmed
  and sliced*
*1 cup sliced scallions, green and
  white parts*
1 clove garlic, finely minced
½ cup chopped parsley

½ cup olive oil
3 tablespoons white wine vinegar
*½ teaspoon dried tarragon
  (1½ teaspoons fresh)*
*½ teaspoon dried dill
  (1½ teaspoons fresh)*
salt and pepper to taste

1. Place crabmeat in a bowl. Add mushrooms, scallions, garlic and parsley, toss lightly to combine.

2. Mix remaining ingredients in screw top jar. Shake vigorously.

3. Pour mixture over crab and mushrooms. Toss gently but thoroughly.

4. Allow to chill and marinate in the refrigerator at least 1 hour or more.

Crab, Hunan Style
Serves 4-6

This searingly hot dish is only for those who long to scour their tastebuds with fiery spices.

½ pound fresh mushrooms, trimmed, cleaned, and sliced thin
1 cup fresh crab meat, picked over
1 cup scallions, sliced thin
1 clove garlic, minced
1 teaspoon minced fresh ginger root
1 teaspoon shredded fresh green chili pepper

2 teaspoons dry sherry
salt and pepper to taste
1 teaspoon five-spice powder
1 tablespoon chili paste with garlic
1 tablespoon hot chili oil
1½ teaspoons sesame oil

1. Toss the first 6 ingredients together.

2. Combine remaining ingredients. Pour over crab-mushroom mixture and toss well to combine. Chill. Serve as part of a Chinese dinner.

Gratin of Crab and Macaroni
Serves 6

2 tablespoons butter
3 scallions sliced, green and white parts
1 clove garlic, minced
1 8-ounce box seashells, cooked al dente
½ cup half and half, at room temperature
1 cup grated Emmenthaler

1 cup grated Gruyere
salt and pepper to taste
2 cups crab meat, picked over carefully
2 tablespoons grated Parmesan cheese
2 tablespoons fine bread crumbs
2 tablespoons butter

1. Preheat oven to 400 degrees.

2. Melt the butter, saute the scallions and garlic until soft. Reserve.

3. While the macaroni is cooking, stir the half and half into the grated Emmenthaler and Gruyere cheeses.

4. Place the drained, hot seashells in a warm mixing bowl, stir in the sauteed scallions and garlic with their butter, the cream-cheese mixture, and the salt and pepper. Toss with 2 spoons to thoroughly coat the pasta. Toss in the crab. Combine well.

5. Pour the mixture into a baking dish. Combine the Parmesan and bread crumbs and sprinkle it over the top. Dot with the remaining butter. Bake in the preheated oven for 10 to 15 minutes, until the cheese is completely melted and everything is hot.

Crab Meat Breakfast
Serves 2

This simple but marvelous dish is my ritual Sunday morning breakfast during vacations spent in a vintage 1930 beachfront cottage on Hilton Head. It seems to taste best within sight and sound of the sea.

2 English muffins, split and
   toasted
2 cups fresh crab meat, picked
   over carefully
1½ cups hot mornay sauce (see
   index for recipe)

1½ cups grated Swiss cheese
4 tablespoons grated Parmesan
   cheese
4 strips bacon, partially cooked

1. Preheat broiler. Place toasted muffin halves on a baking sheet.

2. Combine crab and mornay sauce.

3. Divide the sauced crab meat among the muffin halves. Cover with cheeses. Cut each bacon strip in half, and place 2 halves in a crisscross on top of each crab meat covered muffin.

4. Place under the broiler until browned and bubbly. Serve at once.

Shrimp and Capers
Serves 6

6 tablespoons olive oil
¼ cup sliced scallions, green and
   white parts
2 cloves garlic, minced
2 pounds jumbo shrimp, shelled
4 anchovy fillets, rinsed, drained,
   and chopped

2 tablespoons capers
3 tablespoons chopped parsley
juice of 1 lemon
¼ cup chopped fresh parsley
lemon wedges

1. Heat oil in a wide heavy skillet; saute scallions and garlic until tender but not browned.

2. Add shrimp, anchovies, capers, parsley, and lemon juice. Toss and cook for about 5 minutes or until the shrimp turn bright pink and are just done. Sprinkle with parsley, garnish with lemon wedges, and serve at once.

Shrimp and Eggplant
Serves 6 as a main course, 8 as a first course

3 medium eggplants
salt
6 tablespoons olive oil
2 large onions, coarsely chopped
2 cloves garlic, minced
2 stalks celery, coarsely chopped
1 green pepper, coarsely chopped
½ cup freshly chopped parsley
¼ cup tomato puree
½ teaspoon dried rosemary, crumbled

½ teaspoon fennel seeds
1 Turkish bay leaf or ½ California bay leaf, crumbled
salt and ground red pepper to taste
1 pound shrimp, peeled and coarsely chopped
6 to 8 tablespoons bread crumbs
6 to 8 tablespoons butter

1. Preheat oven to 350 degrees.

2. Cut the stem ends off the eggplants and cut the eggplants in half lengthwise. Sprinkle cut sides with salt and let stand ½ hour. Rinse, drain, and dry with paper towels.

3. Brush cut sides with a bit of oil. Place eggplants on an oiled baking sheet, cut side up, in the preheated oven and bake until golden and very tender, about 45 minutes.

4. Meanwhile, heat 4 tablespoons oil in a wide heavy skillet. Saute onions, garlic, celery and green pepper until limp and tender.

5. Stir in parsley, tomato puree, rosemary, fennel, bay leaf, salt, and pepper. Cook over moderately high heat, stirring, until almost all liquid has cooked away.

6. Stir in shrimp. Cook and stir until shrimp *just turn pink.* Do not overcook!

7. When eggplant is tender, scoop out the pulp and place it in a colander over a bowl to drain. If the seeds seem hard, discard them. When thoroughly drained, chop the pulp coarsely. Raise oven heat to 400 degrees.

8. Stir chopped eggplant pulp into shrimp mixture. Taste and adjust seasonings, adding more salt and red pepper as needed. The mixture should be piquant.

9. Spoon mixture into 6 individual casseroles if you are serving it as a main dish or 8 scallop shells if you are serving it as a first course. Dot with breadcrumbs and butter. Place in the preheated oven until heated through and lightly browned, about 15 minutes. Serve at once.

Shrimp With Feta, Greek Style
Serves 6

3 tablespoons olive oil
2 large onions, coarsely chopped
2 large cloves garlic, minced
½ cup freshly chopped parsley
1 tablespoon chopped fresh dill (or
    ⅓ the amount dried)
pepper to taste
pinch sugar

2 large cans (1 pound 12 ounces
    each) tomatoes, drained and
    chopped
2 pounds large shrimp, shelled
    and deveined
¾ pound Feta cheese, crumbled
juice of 1 lemon

1. Preheat oven to 450 degrees.

2. Heat olive oil in a heavy skillet. Saute onions and garlic until limp but not browned. Stir in parsley, dill, pepper, and sugar.

3. Add tomatoes. Bring to a boil, then reduce heat and simmer until quite thick and chunky, about ½ hour. Taste and add more sugar if the tomatoes are particularly acidic. Add no salt as the cheese will contribute a salty flavor.

4. Pour tomato sauce into a baking dish. Arrange shrimp in a single layer over sauce. Sprinkle with Feta cheese.

5. Put in the oven for about 15 minutes or until the shrimp are pink and cooked and the cheese is softened. Squeeze the lemon juice over the top and serve at once.

Barbecued Shrimp
Serves 6

Barbecued shrimp are typical of New Orleans cuisine, although New Orleans cooks tend to overcook the shrimp, thereby rendering them extremely flavorful but tough. I have found that overnight marination of the shellfish gives them excellent flavor; on the next day they can be cooked briefly enough to remain tender.

½ pound butter
½ cup olive oil
juice of ½ lemon
1 teaspoon paprika
2 teaspoons rosemary leaves,
    crushed
2 bay leaves, crumbled
½ teaspoon cayenne pepper
½ teaspoon oregano, crushed

1 to 2 dashes Tabasco sauce
salt and pepper to taste
1 to 2 dashes Lea & Perrins
    Worcestershire sauce
4 large cloves garlic, peeled and
    lightly crushed
3 pounds shrimp (approximately
    20 per pound), unpeeled

1. Gently heat butter and olive oil in a heavy skillet. Add all remaining ingredients except shrimp. Simmer gently, stirring occasionally, for about 15 minutes. Remove from heat and let cool for about ½ hour.

2. Spread shrimp out in a large, shallow roasting pan. Pour butter-spice mixture over the shrimp, and turn them so that they are thoroughly coated. Refrigerate for several hours, or overnight.

3. Preheat oven to 400 degrees.

4. Place the shrimp, in the roasting pan, in the oven. Bake, stirring occasionally, until the shrimp are pink, about 15 minutes. Do not overcook! Serve in soup bowls with crusty bread for mopping up the sauce. Have empty plates on the table for the litter of shrimp shells, and lots of big napkins—the shrimp are best peeled and eaten with the hands and it gets messy.

Coquilles Saint-Jacques Baumaniere
Serves 4

Diane Wilkinson is a woman of considerable charm and culinary talent. Many of the dishes she presents at her Atlanta cooking classes are collected during her far ranging travels. She collected this scallop dish recently, while in France. She advises serving it as a first course or expanding it into a main course by tossing in a variety of cooked vegetables, (snow peas, baby carrots, onions, diced white turnip).

1 pound scallops	*5 tablespoons whipping cream*
2 teaspoons chopped shallots	*8 tablespoons butter at room*
1⅓ cups Noilly Prat vermouth	*temperature*
⅛ teaspoon dried tarragon	*salt and white pepper to taste*
(2 teaspoons fresh)	

1. Remove pearly membrane from side of each scallop. Rinse scallops. Cut in half horizontally if thick.

2. Lightly butter a pan wide enough to hold scallops in 1 layer. Sprinkle pan with shallots. Top with scallops and vermouth. Cook over high heat, 2 minutes per side, or just until springy to the touch.

3. With a slotted spoon, place scallops in a covered bowl to keep warm. Add tarragon to pot and boil down to 2 tablespoons liquid. Add any accumulated juices from scallops to the pan. Add cream and boil just until thickened.

4. Let pan cool a minute and whisk in butter by tablespoons over low heat. Season to taste. Toss scallops in sauce and serve.

Halpern's Pasta and Seafood Salad
Serves 6

Halpern's, on the lower level of Lenox Square, is Atlanta's food wonderland; an enormous bazaar of fresh produce, seafood, meat, and poultry, not to mention the best hot pastrami sandwich and hamburger in the city. Lynne Halpern's pasta-seafood salad is one of her large repertoire of interesting salads; it is perfect for those who make their own pasta, or for those who patronize the excellent pasta and cheese shop, also on Lenox Square's lower level.

½ pound tomato pasta (red)
½ pound spinach pasta (green)
1 pound cooked, peeled, and
   deveined tiny bay shrimp
½ pound lightly steamed bay
   scallops
1 leek, trimmed, thoroughly
   cleaned and chopped

2 cups mayonnaise (homemade,
   preferably)
¼ cup tomato paste
salt and white pepper to taste
1 teaspoon dry mustard
½ teaspoon tarragon (2 teaspoons
   fresh)

1. Cook pastas to the al dente stage. Drain, rinse, drain and cool.

2. Toss in the shrimp, scallops, and chopped leek.

3. Whisk together the remaining ingredients. Add to pasta-seafood mixture and combine thoroughly. Chill for several hours.

Steamed Mussels
Serves 6

3 quarts mussels
1 cup white wine
½ cup water
1 large onion, chopped
2 scallions, sliced, green and
   white parts
4 sprigs parsley

freshly ground black pepper
4 sprigs of fresh thyme or
   ½ teaspoon of dried
3 tablespoons butter
2 tablespoons chopped parsley
3 tablespoons butter

1. Scrub mussels well with a wire brush and remove their "beards." Discard any mussels that feel abnormally heavy; they are probably full of mud.

2. Place wine, water, onion, scallions, parsley, pepper, thyme, and 3 tablespoons butter in a large pot. Bring to a boil.

3. Add the mussels to the pot. Bring back to a boil. Cover the pot.

4. Reduce heat. Let the mussels steam over low heat, just until they open, about ten minutes. Discard any mussels that do not open.

5. Immediately divide mussels among four warm, deep soup bowls. Quickly strain the stock through several layers of damp cheesecloth into a saucepan. Bring to a boil. Stir in remaining butter and parsley. If the stock seems bland, add some salt, but it may not be needed.

6. Pour the stock over the mussels and serve at once with plenty of crusty bread for soaking up the juices. Have large napkins available, and a big empty bowl for shells.

Poultry

Chicken

There is a classic American recipe that begins with "You take some chicken breasts" and ends with a hour and a half of cooking time under a blanket of canned cream of mushroom soup. The mere thought of such cookery makes me want to lie down in a darkened room with a cold cloth on my head. Chicken breasts are perfect for elegant little dinner parties, but they must be cooked very quickly and sauced intelligently. They have a remarkably creamy and delicate texture when cooked properly; overcooking will make them pulpy and uninteresting. For best results, the breasts must be skinned and boned meticulously. Supermarket meat shelves carry chicken breasts that are already skinned and boned, but they are usually carelessly done. You can do a much better job yourself, and end up with the lagniappe of the skin and bones, which are perfect for simmering into stock.

It is not nearly as difficult to skin and bone the breasts as it may seem. Have the whole breasts split in two at the market. At home, pull off the skin with your fingers, then gently begin to pull the meat away from the bones. Use a small sharp knife to cut and scrape the meat from the smaller bones. You will find that some of the work can be done without the knife. When the skin and bones have been removed, pull off the small "fillet" under the larger piece. Trim each piece, large and small, of every bit of fat, remaining skin, cartilage, and connective tissue. Pull and scrape out the long white vein in the small fillet. The larger pieces are the cutlets; they can be sauteed for a minute or two in butter and finished off in the oven with cheese, wine, cream, or anything you can think of except canned cream soups. The small fillets can be cubed and quickly stir fried. Both the fillets and the cutlets will cook in a matter of minutes; they are done when they feel firm and springy, not soft and mushy. If they are impossible to test by poking because they are buried in sauce or melted cheese, cut into a piece. If no trace of pink remains, it is done.

The rest of the chicken takes longer to cook. The legs and thighs are delicious in braised dishes, especially when they are marinated first, and then the marinade is used as part of the cooking liquid. When cooking legs, thighs, and breasts together as in coq au vin, for instance, remove the breasts when they are just done and keep warm. When the legs and thighs are done, the breasts may be added back for a brief warm-through.

When roasting whole chickens, avoid cooking them to a dry, well-done death. In my opinion, a very slightly under-done roasted chicken—that is, one with just a trace of pink around the bone—is sheer heaven. Experiment with cooking times and you will see how succulent a simple, small roasted chicken can be.

Chicken and Avocado in Cream
Serves 4

3 cups whipping cream
2 cloves garlic, peeled and lightly flattened
juice of 2 limes
2 to 4 drops of Tabasco sauce
salt and pepper to taste

2 ripe avocados
lime juice
8 chicken cutlets
salt and pepper to taste
pinch of cinnamon
4 tablespoons butter

1. Preheat oven to 325 degrees.

2. In a deep, heavy saucepan, boil the cream with the garlic over high heat until reduced by half and thickened. Discard garlic cloves. Stir in lime juice, Tabasco sauce, and salt and pepper to taste. Set aside with a piece of plastic wrap directly over the surface of the sauce.

3. Halve the avocados. Remove the pit and the skin. Cut into chunks and sprinkle with lime juice to prevent darkening. Set aside.

4. Sprinkle chicken breasts with salt, pepper, and cinnamon. Heat butter in two wide skillets. Place chicken in skillets and saute gently for 1 minute on each side. They must not touch each other in the pan and they must not brown. They will just begin to turn white.

5. Place the breasts on an attractive ovenproof platter and place in the oven for 7 to 10 minutes only, or until *just* done. Do not let them overcook! Chicken cooked in this manner has an extraordinary, tender, creamy texture. They are done when they feel firm and springy, not soft and mushy.

6. While the chicken is in the oven, turn the avocado chunks in the hot butter remaining in the chicken skillet, just to warm them slightly.

7. When the chicken is done, place some chunks of warm avocado on each breast. Mask with the hot cream sauce. Serve with wild rice (see index for recipe) and spoon some sauce on the wild rice also. Eat slowly and consideringly . . . savour every sensual bite. This dish is quite an experience.

Ron Cohn's Chicken Sari
Serves 4

Ron Cohn is the chef-proprietor of Hal's, a very special restaurant in Atlanta. All of Ron's cookery is imaginative and delicious, but when he is in a Hungarian mood, he scintillates. Chicken Sari is named for Ron's Hungarian grandmother, and is a speciality of his restaurant.

4 chicken breasts, skinned and deboned, split, and trimmed of fat and gristle
¾ cup flour
1½ teaspoons salt
1½ teaspoons Hungarian paprika
¼ cup finely chopped onions

4 tablespoons butter
2 tablespoons flour
1 cup hot chicken stock
⅔ cup milk
1½ tablespoons Hungarian paprika
1½ cups sour cream

1. Coat each chicken breast half in a mixture of the ¾ cup flour, 1½ teaspoons salt, and 1½ teaspoons Hungarian paprika.

2. Cook onions in 2 tablespoons butter until transparent. Remove onions from pan.

3. Brown chicken pieces lightly in butter. Set aside in the skillet.

4. Melt 2 tablespoons butter in a saucepan. Add 2 tablespoons flour. Heat until the mixture bubbles, stirring constantly. Remove from heat and gradually add chicken stock. Return to heat and bring to a boil and cook for 1 to 2 minutes. Add, stirring constantly, milk and paprika.

5. When heated, remove from heat, beat with a wire whisk. Beat in sour cream. Mix in onion.

6. Pour the sauce over chicken. Cook over low heat, stirring 3 to 5 minutes, but do not boil. Cover skillet, turn off heat, and let stand for one hour. Reheat before serving.

Chicken Kiev
Serves 4

In preparing Chicken Kiev, the temptation is to step up the seasonings. Resist the temptation; avoid adding scallions, herbs, lemon juice, or anything else to the butter filling. Part of the charm of the dish is its buttery blandness.

1½ sticks butter, creamed
4 chicken breasts, split
salt and pepper to taste
flour

3 eggs, beaten with 1 tablespoon
water and some salt
3 cups unseasoned bread crumbs
corn oil

1. Cut butter in 8 equal sized "finger" shaped pieces. Wrap in plastic wrap and freeze.

2. Bone and skin chicken breast halves; remove every trace of fat and gristle. Remove small fillets and save for another purpose (stir-fry dishes, for instance). Place trimmed, cleaned breast halves, smooth side up, on a sheet of wax paper; cover with another sheet.

3. Pound breasts with a kitchen mallet until they have increased in size and are of a uniform thickness, about ⅛ of an inch.

4. Peel off paper; salt and pepper the breasts on both sides. Place a stick of frozen butter on one of the breasts. Trim the butter down to fit if the breast is small. Roll the breast around the butter, tucking in the ends securely. Press it firmly all around. Chicken is gelatinous, so the meat should stick together nicely; toothpicks are not necessary. Repeat until all the breasts are stuffed.

5. The flour, beaten eggs, and bread crumbs should each be in shallow bowls on your work surface. Toss some salt and pepper in with the crumbs. Dip the chicken packages into the flour first. Make sure the ends especially are well coated. Then dip it into the egg mixture and finally into the crumbs. For good measure, dip into the egg and crumbs again. Place the coated chicken on a platter or a rack and refrigerate for an hour or more, or place in the freezer for about ½ hour.

6. Heat 3 to 4 inches of oil to 350 degrees in a saucepan suitable for deep frying. Fry the chicken packages, 4 at a time, for 5 to 6 minutes each. Drain on paper towels and serve at once with rice, kasha, or wheat pilaf. The first cut into the chicken should be made with a sharp knife and with care. With luck, the butter will come squirting out in a golden fountain. If the chicken waits, the butter gets absorbed into the chicken meat and no squirting oc-

curs. This is no disaster, however; the Chicken Kiev will still taste rich and blandly delicious.

Heinz Sowinski's Breast of Chicken with Stilton Cheese Sauce
Serves 4

2 cups white Burgundy
4 shallots, chopped
1 cup whipping cream
beurre manie (1 teaspoon softened butter kneaded with 1 teaspoon flour, until the two are thoroughly amalgamated)

4 whole chicken breasts
salt and pepper to taste
4 sprigs fresh thyme
2 leaves fresh basil
4 tablespoons softened butter
8 ounces aged Stilton cheese, crumbled

1. Combine wine and shallots in a saucepan. Bring to a boil, reduce heat and simmer for ten minutes.

2. In another saucepan, bring the cream to a boil. Stir in the wine-shallot mixture. Whisk in the beurre manie, a little bit at a time. Simmer, stirring frequently, for 35 to 40 minutes. The mixture should be thick enough to heavily coat a spoon.

3. Preheat oven to 400 degrees.

4. Meanwhile, skin and bone the chicken breasts, but do not split them. Cut away the "fillet" from beneath each breast half and save for another use (stir-fry dishes, for instance). Carefully trim away all traces of fat, skin, gristle, and connective tissue. Spread the breasts on a sheet of wax paper. Cover with another sheet of wax paper. Pound the breasts lightly with a kitchen mallet until they are of an even thickness. Season on both sides with salt and pepper. Place them with the skinned side down. Put a sprig of thyme and a half leaf of basil on each breast. Starting with a long edge, roll up each breast into a long, sausage-like shape. Place, seam side down, on a baking sheet, and smear each breast with 1 tablespoon of softened butter.

5. Bake the rolled breasts in the 400 degree oven for 15 minutes. They should be *just* done. DO NOT OVERCOOK! Remove them from the baking sheet to a serving platter and cover loosely with foil. Keep them warm, but do not allow them to continue cooking or they will become dry.

6. Add the drippings from the cooked chicken breasts to the cream sauce. Stir in the crumbled Stilton cheese. Simmer gently for 20 minutes, stirring occasionally. Season to taste with salt and freshly ground pepper. Strain and smooth the hot sauce by rubbing it through a fine sieve. Spoon some of the sauce over each rolled chicken breast. Pass the rest of the sauce separately.

Chicken Gruyere
Serves 6

2 cups heavy cream
juice of 1 lemon
salt and pepper to taste
6 tablespoons butter

12 chicken cutlets
2 cups grated Gruyere cheese
1 cup minced boiled ham

1. Preheat oven to 375 degrees.

2. In a deep saucepan, boil cream, stirring frequently, until reduced by half. Stir in lemon juice. Add salt and pepper to taste. Set aside with a piece of plastic wrap directly over the surface of the cream.

3. Heat the butter in 2 heavy, wide skillets. Saute the chicken cutlets for a minute or so on each side until they turn white. Do not brown them.

4. Place a layer of cheese and ham in a shallow, wide baking dish. Place chicken cutlets in one layer on the cheese and ham. Sprinkle with salt and pepper and cover with remaining ham and cheese. Pour some thickened cream over each cutlet.

5. Place in the preheated oven for 10 minutes until just done. The chicken should be creamy and tender, and the cheese melted. Cut into a piece to check for doneness. If not quite done, return to the oven for a minute or so.

Sweet Chicken Curry
Serves 4-6

6 boned, skinned, trimmed
  chicken cutlets and fillets
juice of 1 lemon
2 tablespoons flour
salt to taste
1 teaspoon turmeric
1 teaspoon ground cumin
1 teaspoon ground coriander
½ teaspoon red pepper flakes
½ teaspoon sugar
½ bay leaf, crumbled

½ teaspoon cinnamon
¼ cup clarified butter
2 onions, coarsely chopped
2 cloves garlic, minced
1¼-inch thick slice ginger,
  minced
3 tablespoons clarified butter
½ cup chicken stock
½ cup plain yogurt
2 tablespoons tomato paste
½ cup yellow raisins

1. Cut the cutlets and fillets into 2-inch squares. Toss pieces in a bowl with lemon juice, then toss with the flour and all the spices. Set aside.

2. Heat butter in a wide heavy skillet. Saute onions, garlic, and ginger until brown. Scrape into a stove-top casserole.

3. Heat additional butter in the same skillet. Stir and fry the chicken and spices in the hot butter for 2 to 3 minutes, until lightly browned but not cooked through. Add the spice-coated chicken and its juices to the onions in the casserole.

4. Pour the stock into the skillet. Bring to a boil and boil briskly for one minute or so, scraping the bottom of the skillet with a wooden spoon or spatula to dislodge any browned particles.

5. Reduce heat, add yogurt, tomato paste and raisins to stock, stir to combine. Simmer, stirring, until thickened. Add to casserole. Stir to combine chicken, onions, and sauce.

6. Cut into a piece of chicken. If not quite done, bring contents of pot to a simmer. Simmer over lowest heat for a few minutes until chicken is *just* cooked through. Serve at once or serve at room temperature. Serve with Rice Pulao and Yogurt Cucumbers.

Saute of Chicken and Vegetables
Serves 6

3 tablespoons butter
3 tablespoons olive oil
2 green peppers, cut into 2-inch strips
2 large onions, slivered (cut onions into quarters, then eighths, and separate petals)
2 cloves garlic, minced
1 pound fresh mushrooms, quartered
3 large fresh summer tomatoes, skinned, seeded, juiced, and cut into eighths

2 tablespoons butter
2 tablespoons olive oil
12 well-trimmed chicken fillets, cut into 2-inch lengths
½ cup dry sherry
salt and pepper to taste
½ cup fresh parsley, chopped
¼ cup fresh basil, chopped

1. Heat butter and oil in heavy skillet. Saute vegetables over high heat, turning and tossing constantly. Do them in batches, about a minute or 2 for each batch, starting with the peppers. Vegetables should be very crisp, and the tomatoes should not lose their shape. As vegetables are done, transfer to an attractive serving dish and keep warm.

2. Heat remaining oil and butter. Add chicken and saute over high heat, tossing and turning constantly with wooden spatula for a minute or so, until *just* cooked through. Add to vegetables.

3. Add sherry to pan. Over high heat, scrape up browned particles with wooden spatula and reduce sherry to about half. Add to chicken-vegetable mixture. Add salt and lots of pepper.

4. Stir to combine. Stir in parsley and basil and serve immediately.

Tarragon Chicken
Serves 2

1 small frying chicken, split
   in two
½ cup flour
salt and pepper to taste
2 tablespoons butter
2 tablespoons peanut oil

¼ cup Applejack or Calvados
½ cup imported vermouth
2 tablespoons chopped fresh
   tarragon (½ tablespoon dried)

1. Remove, or have the meat man remove, the backbone of the chicken. Save it for stock.

2. Season flour with salt and pepper and spread it out on a platter.

3. Dry chicken thoroughly and dredge in the flour.

4. Heat butter and oil in a deep, heavy skillet. Cook the chicken halves over medium heat, turning frequently, until a deep, golden brown, about ½ hour in all. While chicken is cooking, preheat oven to 450 degrees.

5. When chicken is golden, remove and place in a shallow baking dish. Pour out fat and the large, loose bits of browned flour.

6. Pour Applejack or Calvados and vermouth into skillet. Boil briskly for 1 minute, scraping up browned particles with a wooden spoon. Remove from heat. Stir in tarragon.

7. Pour the tarragon mixture over chicken. Bake in preheated oven for 10 to 15 minutes, or until just done. Serve at once with pan juices.

Grilled Chicken
Serves 6

1 cup olive oil
2 cloves garlic, minced
½ teaspoon cinnamon
½ teaspoon allspice
½ teaspoon tarragon
½ cup wine vinegar

1 scallion, sliced, green and white
   parts
salt and pepper to taste
6 chicken legs
6 chicken thighs

1. Combine all ingredients except chicken in a deep glass or enameled bowl. Add the chicken and stir to coat the chicken pieces with the marinade. Marinate at room temperature for several hours, or overnight in the refrigerator, turning the pieces every so often.

2. Preheat charcoal grill and let the coals form a glowing bed. Grill the chicken, basting frequently with the marinade and turning frequently until it is tender and juicy on the inside and crisp on the outside. This can also be cooked in the oven broiler.

Consuelo's Chicken Adobo
Serves 6

Connie Richardson's cooking speciality is the traditional foods of her native Philippines. This is Connie's version of what is considered the national dish of the Philippines.

½ cup soy sauce
6 tablespoons wine vinegar
5 cloves garlic, peeled and
    smashed
6 Turkish bay leaves
2 tablespoons sugar
15 peppercorns

6 chicken legs
6 chicken thighs
water
1 teaspoon sesame oil
3 large onions, sliced thin
3 cloves garlic, minced

1. Combine first six ingredients. Arrange chicken in a wide, shallow pottery or glass bowl. Pour the vinegar-soy mixture over the chicken. Add water so marinade almost covers it. Turn chicken to coat it with the marinade. Let marinate for several hours at room temperature, or 24 hours in the refrigerator. Turn the chicken a few times during this period.

2. Brush a wide heavy skillet with sesame oil. Heat.

3. Drain the chicken and dry on paper towels. Reserve the marinade. Fry the chicken, skin side down, in the hot skillet. The chicken will render its own fat. Turn and fry until richly browned on both sides, but not cooked through. Remove chicken from skillet.

4. To the fat in the skillet, add onions and garlic. Saute, scraping browned particles from the skillet with a wooden spoon, until golden brown.

5. Return chicken to skillet. Strain marinade over chicken. Bring to a simmer, cover and simmer until chicken is cooked through, 25 minutes or so. Remove chicken. Cover it and keep it warm.

6. Boil pan juices in the skillet until reduced somewhat and thickened. Pour the juices into a jar and place in the freezer for 15 minutes or so. When the fat in the jar has risen to the top, skim it off and discard. Recombine chicken and sauce and reheat gently. Traditionally, this should be warm or at room temperature, not steaming hot.

This dish may be made a day or two in advance. The flavor improves dramatically day by day. Just scrape off any congealed fat and discard, then reheat gently.

Claudette's Coq Au Vin
Serves 6-8

Claudette in her kitchen is a sight that would send any Brueghel or Hogarth running for his paints and brushes. Larger than life, her face rosy and shiny from the steam, her robust laugh ringing out above the sounds of chopping, simmering, and kitchen gossip, she attacks her pots and pans with the same huge enjoyment she brings to all of life. Her food is marvelous; she has the knack of taking the simplest ingredients and making them into something wonderfully savory. Her cookery is, I think, a very special type of women's cookery. Many French chefs claim that women will always be inferior cooks, and some militant feminists say that women don't belong in the kitchen anyway; one look at Claudette, chattering away in fractured English while smashing garlic, flinging chickens into wine, and in general having the time of her life will convince you of the essential nonsense of these views. Claudette is a womanly cook; her food is soothing and nourishing; a sort of earth mother cuisine, but above all it is delicious. I believe that if Claudette took it into her head to saute cardboard, we would polish it off with gusto and ask for seconds.

Claudette has a restaurant in Decatur. I particularly like her chicken and fish dishes, because, unlike many other cooks, she knows when to stop cooking. As a result these dishes are never dry and overcooked. She shared the secret of her coq au vin with me; overnight marination of the partially cooked chicken in the wine sauce produces a bird in which the flavor of the wine penetrates right to the bone.

1 package pearl onions, peeled
½ pound bacon, diced
½ cup clarified butter
3 small chickens, quartered
½ cup cognac
1 pound mushrooms, sliced

⅓ cup flour
5 Turkish bay leaves
1 teaspoon thyme
salt and pepper to taste
6 cups red Burgundy

1. In a heavy skillet, brown onions slowly with the bacon in the butter. With a slotted spoon, remove bacon and onions to a Dutch oven or flame-proof casserole.

2. Add chicken to skillet and brown in batches. Place browned chicken in the casserole with the bacon and onions.

3. Heat cognac, pour into casserole, and flame. (Stand back and keep your face averted.)

4. When the flames have died down, toss in the mushrooms and let cook for a few minutes. When the mushrooms have started

to render some of their juice, stir in the flour. Add remaining ingredients except wine. Cook and stir for a few minutes and then stir in the red wine. At this point—STOP!

5. Let the casserole and its contents cool and then refrigerate. The next day let it come to room temperature and bring to a simmer. Cook, covered, about 30 minutes, and check breasts; they should be just done. Remove and keep warm. Cook remaining chicken for 10 minutes or so, until just done. Add breasts back, rewarm briefly, and serve.

Garlic Chicken
Serves 6

Garlic is at its best and most surprising when used in great quantity. There are many famous recipes that use 50 or 60 cloves at once. (Remember: a clove is one section, a bulb or a head is the whole thing.) The amount of garlic may seem shocking, but the taste of the finished dish is mild, delicious, and unexpected; the garlic cooks gently to become something quite different from its usual self. In most cases, if you don't tell, your guests will not guess that garlic is the major component of the next two dishes.

60 large cloves garlic
boiling water to cover
3 tablespoons olive oil
6 chicken legs
6 chicken thighs (the chicken
* pieces may be skinned if you*
* wish)*

1 cup chopped parsley
1 teaspoon dried tarragon
salt and pepper to taste
½ teaspoon ground allspice
¼ teaspoon cinnamon
1½ cups dry white wine

1. Preheat oven to 375 degrees.

2. Boil the unpeeled garlic cloves in water to cover for 2 minutes. Drain and peel.

3. Place all ingredients including garlic in a heavy pot that can be covered. Combine everything very well with your hands. Seal the pot very tightly with foil. Place the cover over the foil. The pot must be very well sealed so that no juices or steam can escape.

4. Place the tightly covered pot in the oven for 1½ hours. Do not open the pot during this time.

5. Serve with good bread to mop up the juices and the garlic.

Chicken Roasted with 60 Cloves of Garlic
Serves 4

60 cloves garlic
boiling water to cover
¼ pound butter, at room
   temperature
¼ cup fresh chopped parsley
½ teaspoon dried tarragon
salt and pepper to taste

1 whole chicken, about 3½
   pounds
2 tablespoons olive oil
2 large onions, peeled, halved,
   and sliced into thin half moons
1 cup chicken stock

1. Preheat oven to 350 degrees.

2. Boil the garlic cloves in water to cover for 2 minutes. Drain and peel.

3. Mash the softened butter with the herbs, salt, and pepper. Fold in the peeled garlic.

4. Stuff the chicken with the garlic butter. Sew up the chicken cavity or plug it with a ball of foil. Fold the wings back, but it is not necessary to truss the bird.

5. Brush the chicken with the oil, sprinkle with salt and pepper, and place it breast up on a rack in a small roasting pan. Scatter the onion slices on the bottom of the roasting pan and pour in ½ cup of stock.

6. Roast the chicken in the preheated oven until done, about 1½ hours. Baste frequently (every 10 to 15 minutes) with the pan juices. Add a bit more chicken stock if necessary. The chicken is done when a thermometer inserted into the breast reads 170 to 175 degrees. Let chicken stand for 15 minutes when done.

7. Skim some of the fat from the pan juices. Pour in the remaining ½ cup of stock and place the roasting pan directly on a stove burner. Bring it to a boil, scraping with a wooden spoon to dislodge any browned bits. Boil until reduced by about ⅓ and very flavorful. Skim off as much fat as possible, correct seasonings, and serve in a sauceboat with the chicken and the garlic.

Chilaquiles
Serves 6

Mexican housewives make many versions of this dish; it's a delicious way of using up stale corn tortillas. The hot peppers in this version are a compromise—the proper chilies are often difficult to find. Even so, the finished dish is pungent and satisfying.

1 chicken, about 3 pounds
well-seasoned chicken stock
2 tablespoons peanut or safflower
   oil
1 large onion, chopped
4 pickled hot cherry peppers,
   coarsely diced
2 fresh jalapeno peppers, coarsely
   diced (wash and trim under
   cold water first)

1 large can (35 ounces) Italian
   plum tomatoes, drained
2 cloves garlic
salt to taste
3 cups tortilla chips
2½ cups good, mild Cheddar
   cheese, grated
sour cream, at room temperature

1. Cook chicken, in stock to cover, until it is tender and succulent, about 45 minutes.

2. Let chicken cool in the double-rich stock, then skin, bone, and shred chicken meat. Set aside, covered. Strain stock, skim off fat, and set aside.

3. Heat oil in a heavy pot. Saute onion until limp and cooked but not brown.

4. Place the pickled peppers, jalapenos, tomatoes, and garlic in the blender jar. Blend to a smooth sauce. Pour into skillet with onions. Cook over gentle heat for a few moments.

5. Add two cups of the reserved stock, and salt to taste, to the onion-tomato-pepper mixture. Simmer, uncovered, for 45 minutes, or until thick and pungent. At this point, the sauce is so hot it will amost remove the enamel from a saucepan, or melt a spoon. When it is mixed with the other ingredients, however, its piquancy becomes somewhat diluted.

6. Preheat oven to 325 degrees.

7. Layer ⅓ of the tortilla chips, ⅓ of the sauce, ⅓ of the shredded chicken, and ⅓ of the cheese in a 1½ quart shallow baking dish. Repeat twice more, ending with cheese.

8. Place pan in the oven and cook, covered, for 35 minutes. Uncover, and cook for 10 minutes more, until browned and bubbly. Serve with cooling dollops of sour cream.

Roast Chicken, Chinese Style
Serves 4

1 whole chicken, 3½ to 4 pounds

Marinade

¼ cup scallions, sliced
2 thin slices, peeled ginger root, minced
1 clove garlic, minced
2 tablespoons peanut oil
¼ cup soy sauce

¼ cup pale dry sherry
½ teaspoon Chinese five-spice powder
1 teaspoon salt
1 teaspoon sugar

Stuffing

3 tablespoons peanut oil
1 pound mushrooms, sliced
2 thin slices fresh ginger root, minced

1 cup scallions, thinly sliced, green and white parts
salt and pepper to taste

Basting Sauce

¾ cup chicken stock
2 tablespoons soy sauce
½ cup sherry

1 tablespoon sugar
¼ teaspoon Chinese five-spice powder

Final Thickening

1 tablespoon cornstarch

3 tablespoons water

1. Preheat oven to 350 degrees.

2. Combine marinade ingredients. Rub the chicken thoroughly inside and out with the mixture. Let marinate for at least 2 hours, turning occasionally.

3. Meanwhile, heat oil. Add mushrooms, ginger root, scallions, salt and pepper, and toss and turn them in the hot oil until limp. Set aside to cool.

4. Combine the basting ingredients in a roasting pan.

5. Stuff the marinated chicken with the cooled mushroom-scallion mixture. Plug the opening with a ball of foil and place the chicken on a rack in the roasting pan. Add any marinade that has drained off the chicken to the roasting pan.

6. Roast the chicken in the preheated oven until done, 1 to 1½ hours. Baste frequently. The chicken is done when a thermometer inserted into the breasts reads 170 to 175 degrees. Let chicken stand for 15 minutes when done.

7. Slice all of the chicken meat into small slices, including the legs, thighs, and wings, and place it with the stuffing on a serving dish. Keep warm. Save the bones for stock.

8. Skim as much fat as possible from the liquid in the roasting pan and discard. Place the skimmed liquid in a saucepan.

9. Combine cornstarch and water and blend well. Add to the contents of the saucepan and heat over moderate heat, stirring constantly. When thickened and hot, pour over chicken and mushrooms and serve at once.

Liz Terry's Chicken Thighs with Cold Sauce
Serves 6

Liz Terry is the chef and proprietor of Elizabeth's, a charming restaurant in Savannah. Her cold chicken with its unusual sauce is an inspired dish for an elegant picnic.

6 chicken thighs　　　　　　　　　*½ cup sour cream*
6 finger-sized pieces of ham
bearnaise sauce (see index for
*　recipe)*

1. Preheat oven to 400 degrees.

2. Bone the chicken thighs by slitting along underside and slipping meat from bone. Replace the bone with finger size piece of ham. Place in a shallow baking dish.

3. Bake at 400 degrees for 45 minutes until browned and done. Cool the chicken and drain the cooking juices.

4. Meanwhile, make bearnaise sauce. Cool slightly.

5. Fold the sour cream and bearnaise together. Coat the chicken with the sauce.

Chicken Normande
Serves 4-6

1 tablespoon butter
1 onion, chopped
¼ teaspoon thyme
¼ teaspoon tarragon
1½ cups dry white wine
1½ cups chicken stock
6 tablespoons butter
2 tablespoons corn oil

2 chicken legs
2 chicken thighs
2 chicken breasts
salt and pepper to taste
⅓ cup Calvados or Applejack
1 tablespoon orange liqueur
1 cup whipping cream

1. Heat butter in a saucepan, saute onion until tender. Add thyme, tarragon, wine, and stock and bring to a boil. Simmer briskly until reduced by half. Set aside.

2. Melt the butter and oil in a deep, wide heavy skillet. When very hot, place the legs and thighs, skin side down, in the pan. Brown them over moderately high heat, turning them with tongs. After about 15 minutes, when they are golden brown, remove them to a dish.

3. Using a bit of fresh oil and butter if necessary, brown breasts in the same manner, starting skin side down. The breasts should brown about 10 minutes. Remove them to the dish with the rest of the chicken and drain all fat from the skillet.

4. Turn burner under skillet to high. Return all chicken to the skillet and season with salt and pepper. Pour Calvados or Applejack over the chicken and flame it—stand back! Shake the pan until the flames subside. Remove chicken to dish once again. Do not drain skillet.

5. Pour the stock-wine mixture into the skillet and bring to a boil. Boil for 3 to 4 minutes, scraping up all browned bits from the bottom of the pan. Add orange liqueur and cream. Boil, stirring until thickened and reduced to about 2 cups. Taste and season. Skim off any fat.

6. Return chicken to skillet. Turn to coat with sauce. Bring to a simmer.

7. Simmer very slowly, covered, for ½ hour. Uncover every 10 minutes to baste the chicken with the pan juices.

8. At the end of ½ hour, check breasts. They should be just done. Remove to a plate. Cover skillet and simmer legs and thighs 10 minutes or more, or until done. Return breasts to skillet and turn in the sauce for a moment to reheat. Arrange all chicken on a heated serving platter.

9. Skim as much fat as possible from sauce. Taste and adjust seasoning. Pour the sauce, through a fine sieve, over the chicken. Rub the onions in the sauce through the sieve with a rubber spatula. Each piece of chicken should be coated with the fragrant, rich sauce. Serve at once.

Frank Ma's Pon Pon Chicken
Serves 6

Pon pon chicken, sometimes called hacked chicken, is a spectacular, spicy, Chinese chicken salad. As with all Chinese food, it tastes best when eaten with chopsticks. Serve it at a picnic with almond curd to follow (see index for recipe) to cool the fire.

3 pounds chicken thighs
4 cups water
1 tablespoon Chinese sesame seed paste (available in Oriental markets)
1 tablespoon peanut butter
¼ cup soy sauce

½ teaspoon M.S.G.
1½ teaspoons sugar
2 teaspoons chili oil (available in Oriental markets)
salt to taste
scallions
fresh coriander leaves (optional)

1. Place chicken and water in a deep pot. Bring to a boil. Let boil, covered, for 15 minutes. Remove chicken from pot and let cool on a platter. Save the stock for another use.

2. In a small bowl, combine all remaining ingredients except scallions and coriander. Stir it well.

3. When the chicken is cool enough to handle, remove skin, bones, and all fat and gristle. Shred the chicken with a chef's knife or a cleaver.

4. Pour the sauce over the chicken. Toss it all together very well. Taste and add more chili oil, if you like it super-hot. Garnish with scallions and coriander and serve.

Chicken-Berry Salad
Serves 6

This salad is the essence of summer. Serve it at very special summer luncheons.

3 whole chicken breasts, split
water to cover
1 pound fresh berries (mixed
  berries; use blueberries,
  blackberries, strawberries,
  raspberries, or whatever you
  can find)
½ pound seedless grapes

fresh mint leaves
1 cup mayonnaise, homemade
  if possible
juice of ½ lemon
½ teaspoon honey
2 tablespoons heavy cream
salt and pepper to taste

1. Place chicken breasts in deep skillet. Cover with water and bring to a boil. Immediately lower heat and simmer, covered, for 8 to 10 minutes or until just done.

2. Remove chicken from stock. Save the stock for future soups. When cool, remove skin and pull meat off bones. Cut chicken into strips.

3. Gently toss the chicken with the fruit. Arrange on an attractive platter. Garnish with mint.

4. To make dressing, combine the remaining ingredients. Pass the dressing separately.

Dailey's French Charcoal Duck
Serves 6

This duck, from Dailey's in Atlanta has wonderfully juicy meat and a crisp, flavorful skin.

3 ducklings, 4½ to 5 pounds (fresh, if available; if frozen, defrost and remove giblets before using)
1 pound butter, melted
6 cloves fresh garlic, peeled and crushed

3 bay leaves
1½ teaspoons thyme
¼ cup honey
1 tablespoon salt
½ teaspoon white pepper

1. Place the ducks on a rack in a roasting pan and roast 20 minutes at 425 degrees.

2. Prick the skin with the tines of a fork to release fat. Reduce oven temperature to 300 degrees.

3. Combine butter, garlic, bay leaves, thyme and honey in a saucepan and heat until melted; stir to combine.

4. Roast the ducks two more hours, basting every 20 minutes with the butter mixture.

5. When the ducks are done (a thermometer will register an internal temperature of 180 degrees), sprinkle evenly with salt and pepper; cool.

6. Split duck in half. Grill (½ duck per serving) over charcoal until heated through.

7. Ladle two ounces reserved butter mixture over each serving.

Roast Turkey with Chestnut Dressing

My traditional Thanksgiving turkey is a gleaming, golden, fragrantly moist bird; bursting with chestnuts, redolent of thyme and cognac, crackling with crisp skin, and altogether magnificent. In spite of its magnificence, however, tradition was abandoned at one point in my gastronomic life as—in the name of experimentation—I committed all sorts of bizarre mayhem on my holiday birds. For several years they were, respectively, marinated in soy sauce, sherry and five spice powder; barbecued on a revolving spit; stuffed with buckwheat groats and dried apricots or boned and wrapped around pate. Each of these turkeys was interesting and unusual—sometimes even amazingly delicious—but they never matched the glory of my original bird. The urge to cook exotic turkeys has vanished with the years, and the magnificent golden, chestnut stuffed bird now appears again with reassuring and eagerly anticipated regularity, year after year. If you wish to make it a tradition of your own, serve it with a complement of dramatic and delicious vegetables.

Buy a large bird, as they are juicier and tastier, and leftovers are the best part of Thanksgiving anyway. Thanksgiving isn't Thanksgiving without turkey sandwiches at midnight in the kitchen, and turkey hash for dinner the next day.

Dressing for 15 to 18 pound turkey

1 pound bulk sausage meat
2 large onions, chopped
1 large can cooked, shelled
   chestnuts, drained and rinsed
1 cup fresh chopped parsley
1 teaspoon thyme

5 ounces French bread, torn into
   pieces and toasted lightly in the
   oven
milk
salt and pepper to taste
½ cup cognac

1. Brown sausage and onions in a heavy skillet. Break up meat as it cooks. Drain off all fat.

2. Mash chestnuts and add to meat and onions. Add parsley and thyme.

3. Moisten toasted bread with milk. Squeeze out excess. Place in a large bowl with chestnut mixture. Add salt, pepper, and cognac. Toss it all together.

Turkey

15 to 18 pound turkey (for best results, try to find a fresh bird that has not been frozen or prebasted)	*softened butter* *stock* *onions* *cognac*

1. Have the fresh turkey at room temperature. Remove giblets and use to make turkey stock (see index for directions). Save the liver for another use. Wash turkey inside and out and rub it inside with a cut lemon. Rub entire outside with some softened butter. Preheat oven to 325 degrees.

2. Stuff the body cavity with prepared dressing, just before you are about to cook it. Do not stuff too full because the dressing will expand during roasting. Plug up opening with a ball of foil, or skewer and lace closed.

3. Stuff the neck cavity with stuffing. Secure the flap of skin with a skewer. Any remaining stuffing can be baked separately with a generous amount of stock in a casserole. Secure the wings to the body with skewers. Do not truss legs (this is very unconventional, and the bird will not be quite as easy to carve as if it were trussed, but the heat will penetrate to the thighs more efficiently if the legs are left free).

4. Place turkey, breast down, on a rack in a roasting pan in the preheated oven. Put some stock and a small amount of cognac in the pan. Slice several onions into the pan. Roast, breast down, for a little more than half the cooking time. Then turn breast up for remainder of time. Baste the bird with stock and a bit of cognac every 20 minutes or so. Replenish stock as it evaporates.

5. When a thermometer inserted into the thickest part of the breast registers 170 to 175 degrees, the turkey is done. (Use a Bi-therm, if possible.) An overcooked bird is dry and tasteless, so check the temperature carefully. An 18 pound bird will be done in about 4½ hours, but turkeys are unpredictable. Depend on your thermometer; use the clock only as a guide. When finished, let the turkey rest for ½ hour.

6. Skim all fat from roasting pan and place pan on stove. Add stock if necessary and ½ cup cognac. Boil down rapidly, stirring, and scraping up the browned bits. Strain the gravy or not, as you wish. Serve with turkey and dressing.

Meat

Beef

Tournedos in Claire's Chemise
Serves 6

When I was teaching cooking classes, I had one particular class made up of the most lovable, enthusiastic students imaginable. Not the least of their charm was their creativity in taking what I taught them and galloping on with it to new heights of culinary discovery. During classes on Hungarian and Greek cookery, we used phyllo pastry for strudels, little triangular tarts, and big layered savory pies. My class was immediately ready to wrap everything remotely edible in the thin papery stuff. One student, Claire Coppage, suggested beef Wellington, wrapped in phyllo dough.

Now, beef Wellington is not my favorite dish; in fact, I think it's silly. The combination of foie gras, pastry, and beef never seems quite right; if the pastry is perfect, then the beef tastes steamed and overdone. If the beef is just right, then the pastry is soggy.

I decided to try individual filet mignon steaks wrapped in phyllo, but the meat took on that steamed taste typical of some beef Wellington productions. In fact, it was like eating very expensive, very bad pot roast. Finally, I hit on the idea of cooking the various components separately and putting them together at the last minute for a glorious presentation. Eureka! A brilliant success. The dish is named in honor of the student who inspired it.

6 filet steaks, 1 inch thick
6 strips bacon
5 sheets phyllo dough, stacked
melted butter
2 tablespoons butter

1 tablespoon oil
salt and pepper to taste
1 recipe duxelles (see index)
1 recipe bearnaise sauce (see index)

1. Preheat oven to 400 degrees.

2. Trim each steak of all fat and gristle; it should be a neat round of meat, about 2 inches in diameter. Wrap each steak in a strip of bacon and secure it with a toothpick. Set aside.

3. Cut the stack of 5 phyllo sheets in half. Butter a baking tray. Layer the 10 pieces of phyllo on the baking tray, brushing each piece well with melted butter before adding another. Butter top

sheet. With a sharp knife, cut the batch of buttered phyllo pastry into 6 equal parts.

4. Place baking tray in hot oven. Bake for about 15 minutes, or until pastry is golden brown and puffed.

5. Meanwhile, heat butter and oil in a wide heavy skillet. (Use two skillets if necessary). Dry steaks well. Saute steaks for about 3 minutes per side—they should be well-browned outside and red and juicy inside. When done, remove from pan. Discard toothpicks and season steaks well with salt and pepper. Discard bacon.

6. Place a portion of phyllo pastry on each of six hot plates. Remove top 2 or 3 layers of each and set aside. Place a generous tablespoon of duxelles on each phyllo base. Place steak on duxelles. Cover with bearnaise sauce. Replace phyllo cover. Serve at once.

Beef Provencal
Serves 6

¼ cup olive oil
2 large onions, chopped
6 cloves garlic, chopped
2 fresh tomatoes, skinned, seeded, juiced, and cut into eighths
⅔ cup halved and pitted black Greek olives
½ cup tomato puree
¼ cup tomato paste
1 tablespoon chopped fresh basil
1 teaspoon chopped fresh oregano

½ teaspoon sugar (more or less to taste, depending on acidity of tomatoes)
salt and pepper to taste
½ cup chopped parsley
¼ cup olive oil
3 pounds well-trimmed beef tenderloin, cut into 1-inch cubes
½ cup additional chopped parsley

1. Heat ¼ cup olive oil in a wide, heavy skillet. When it is hot, add the onion and garlic and cook until very tender but not browned.

2. Add fresh tomatoes and olives. Bring the mixture to a simmer and stir in the tomato puree, tomato paste, basil, oregano, sugar, salt, pepper, and chopped parsley. Cook this sauce gently for 5 to 10 minutes. Set aside.

3. Heat remaining olive oil in another wide, heavy skillet. When hot, add beef and stir-fry for a minute or two until the cubes are well browned but still quite rare inside.

4. Add beef to sauce and toss together. Sprinkle with chopped parsley. Serve at once. For a picnic, this dish may be made in advance, and served cooled or at room temperature. Don't serve chilled, or the flavors will disappear.

Stuffed Beef Roll, Italian Style
Serves 6-8

1 large well-trimmed flank steak
(2 pounds if possible)
freshly ground pepper to taste
1 pound ground veal
1 egg, lightly beaten
¼ cup bread crumbs
4 tablespoons freshly ground
Parmesan cheese
3 tablespoons chopped fresh
parsley
1 teaspoon dried basil or 1
tablespoon fresh, chopped
salt and pepper to taste
6 thin slices prosciutto
4 ounces Provolone cheese, cut
into 1-inch strips

¼ cup olive oil
3 tablespoons olive oil
2 large onions, chopped
4 cloves garlic, minced
2 large cans (1 pound 12 ounces)
plum tomatoes, drained and
chopped
1 can (6 ounces) tomato paste
1 bay leaf
½ teaspoon dried basil
salt and pepper to taste
1 cup dry red wine
beef stock
½ cup chopped fresh parsley

1. Butterfly the flank steak as follows: slit it down the long end with a very sharp knife. Cut it very carefully almost all the way through until you can open it flat like a book.

2. Spread out the butterflied steak on a sheet of wax paper on your work surface. Sprinkle with freshly ground pepper. Cover with another sheet of wax paper. Pound the steak gently with a kitchen mallet or the side of a wide knife, until it is about ¼ of an inch thick. Set aside.

3. In a bowl, combine the veal, egg, bread crumbs, Parmesan cheese, parsley, basil, and salt and pepper; use your hands or a wooden spoon to mix it very well. Set aside.

4. Spread the slices of proscuitto over the surface of the butterflied flank steak. Spread the veal stuffing over it. Place the strips of Provolone over the stuffing, pushing them in. Starting from the long edge of the flank, roll it up like a jelly roll, into a long sausage-like shape. Tie the roll securely crosswise in several places with kitchen string. Secure both ends with wooden toothpicks and tie it once lengthwise.

5. Heat ¼ cup olive oil in a wide heavy skillet. Dry the beef with paper towels. Brown it well on all sides in the hot oil, using tongs to turn it.

6. Meanwhile, prepare sauce: heat 3 tablespoons olive oil in a deep pot that can be covered. The pot must be large enough to hold the beef roll. Cook the onions and garlic in the hot oil until

limp. Add the tomatoes, tomato paste, bay leaf, basil, salt and pepper. Bring to a boil, then reduce to a simmer.

7. Preheat oven to 325 degrees. When the beef is thoroughly browned, put it in the pot with the tomato mixture. Drain the oil out of the skillet, and pour in the red wine. Bring the wine to a boil, and boil for 2 to 3 minutes, scraping up the browned particles on the bottom of the skillet with a wooden spoon. Pour the wine into the pot with the beef. Add stock, so that the sauce comes almost to the top of the beef roll. Simmer in the oven for 1 to 1½ hours, until the beef is tender. Adjust oven temperature during this time, so that the contents of the pot remain at a simmer.

8. When done, remove meat and let stand for 5 to 10 minutes. Skim fat from sauce. Cut string from beef and discard. Carve beef roll into ½-inch slices and arrange on a platter. Spoon some sauce on each roll and sprinkle with parsley. Pass the rest of the sauce separately. Serve with potato gnocchi (see index).

Hungarian Beef Rolls
Serves 6

2 pounds well trimmed flank steak
Hungarian paprika
salt and pepper to taste

½ pound bacon, each slice cut in half
1 tablespoon bacon fat

1. Slice the flank steak, against the grain, into slices about ¼ inch thick.

2. Spread wax paper over your work surface. Place the beef slices on the paper. Cover with another sheet of wax paper. With a kitchen mallet or the flat side of a wide knife, gently pound the pieces until they are about ⅛ inch thick. Remove top sheet of paper. Sprinkle upper surface of each slice with paprika, salt and pepper.

3. Roll each slice into a sausage like shape. Wrap with a piece of bacon and secure with a toothpick.

4. Melt bacon fat in a wide, heavy skillet. When sizzling, add the beef rolls and brown quickly over high heat on all side. When browned, pour into a colander over a bowl to drain away all fat. Return rolls to skillet.

5. Cover and cook over very low heat for 10 minutes, shaking pan frequently. Serve at once.

Beefsteak with Tarragon
Serves 4

This recipe works well with any steak; rib-eye, filet, sirloin, etc. I have used flank here because it is one of the most delicious cuts of beef. It has wonderful flavor and excellent, slightly chewy texture.

1 well-trimmed flank steak, about
   1½ pounds
salt and pepper to taste
2 tablespoons butter
½ cup dry red wine

2 tablespoons chopped shallots
1 tablespoon chopped fresh
   tarragon
1 tablespoon unsalted butter

1. Sprinkle flank steak with salt and pepper.

2. Heat a heavy, wide skillet. When hot, sear seasoned steak until sealed and well browned on both sides (about one minute per side).

3. Reduce heat and add butter. Cook 3 to 5 minutes on each side. For best results, meat should remain quite rare.

4. Remove meat from pan and keep warm. Pour off fat in skillet. Pour red wine and shallots into the skillet and bring to a boil. Boil until the wine is thick and syrupy and reduced by almost half. As it boils, scrape up the browned particles in the skillet with a wooden spoon.

5. Add tarragon. Remove from heat. Gently swirl in butter so that it slowly incorporates into the wine. Stir in the meat juices that have accumulated under the flank steak.

6. Quickly slice meat into thin slices, against the grain. Arrange slices on the platter, pour sauce down the center of them, and serve at once.

Variation: *Beefsteak with Pepper*

Scatter a generous amount of cracked peppercorns on a sheet of wax paper. Press the peppercorns into the flank steak on both sides. Follow above recipe, but omit the tarragon. Serve with potato-cheese gratin (see index).

Thai Beef Salad *(Yum Yai)*
Serves 4

1 pound flank steak
juice of 1 lime
1 fresh green chili pepper,
  shredded into fine strips
1½ teaspoons Nam prik pla (Thai
  fish sauce, available in Oriental
  markets)

1 cucumber, peeled and sliced thin
6 cherry tomatoes, halved
chopped fresh coriander leaves

1. Grill or broil flank steak, but keep it rare. Let it sit for 5 minutes, then slice thinly, against the grain. Cut each slice in half.

2. Toss the warm slices with lime juice, chili pepper, and fish sauce.

3. Arrange on a platter with the cucumbers and tomatoes. Sprinkle with coriander, and serve.

Beef with Mushrooms, Chinese style
Serves 6

2 cups dried black Chinese or
  Japanese mushrooms
4 cups hot water
2 pounds flank steak, sliced
  thinly, against the grain
½ cup soy sauce

2 tablespoons cornstarch
2 tablespoons dry sherry
2 teaspoons sugar
2 tablespoons peanut oil
1 thin slice ginger root, minced
4 tablespoons peanut oil

1. Place dried mushrooms in a bowl. Pour the hot water over them and let them soak for 30 minutes. Drain, squeeze dry, cut off the stems and cut each mushroom in half.

2. Place the beef in a bowl with the soy sauce, cornstarch, sherry, and sugar. Let marinate at room temperature for 1 hour.

3. Heat 2 tablespoons of oil in a wide skillet. Add the ginger and then the mushrooms and stir-fry over high heat for about 2 minutes. Remove them to a bowl with a slotted spoon.

4. Wipe out the skillet and then heat the remaining 4 tablespoons oil. Stir fry the beef slices in the oil for about 1 minute. They should be browned, but rare.

5. Add the mushrooms to the beef and stir to combine. Serve at once.

Beef with Broccoli, Chinese Style
Serves 4

1 pound flank steak, sliced thinly
  against the grain, as thinly as
  possible
3 tablespoons soy sauce
1 tablespoon corn starch
1 tablespoon dry sherry
1 teaspoon sugar

1 bunch broccoli
2 tablespoons peanut oil
2 thin slices peeled ginger root,
  minced
4 tablespoons peanut oil
1/2 teaspooon salt
1/2 cup beef stock

1. Place the sliced beef in a bowl. Stir together the soy sauce, cornstarch, sherry, and sugar, and add to the beef. Let marinate at room temperature for 1 hour.

2. Trim the broccoli of its tough stems. Peel the stalks and cut them in half. Slice into 2-inch lengths. Cut the tops into single flowerets about 2 inches long.

3. Heat the first 2 tablespoons of oil in a heavy wide skillet or wok. Add the ginger root and then the beef and stir and turn them in the hot oil for less than 2 minutes. The meat should be rare. Remove the meat to a plate.

4. Heat remaining 4 tablespoons of oil in the same skillet. Add the salt, then the broccoli, stir, and toss the broccoli in the oil for about 2 minutes. (Do this in two batches if necessary).

5. Return all broccoli to the skillet and add the stock. Quickly bring to a boil. Cook rapidly, uncovered, for 2 minutes more.

6. Add beef to the broccoli, stir once or twice, and serve immediately.

Franks Ma's Barbecued Ribs
Serves 6

3 pounds beef short ribs, cut 1 1/2
  inches wide and 7 inches long
1 1/2 tablespoons chopped ginger
1 head of garlic, cloves separated,
  peeled and chopped

1 bunch scallions, sliced—green
  and white parts
1 cup sugar
2 cups water
1 cup soy sauce

1. Slice each rib lengthwise, parallel to the bone, into 3 or 4 thin slices. Strip the fat and connective tissue from the back of the bones on each rib, and cut the bones into their natural sections.

2. With a meat mallet, pound each slice of meat with vigor, until it is about 1/8 of an inch thick. Place the slices in a shallow baking dish.

3. Slice the meat remaining on the ends of the bone, so that it is partially separated from the bone. Hit the meat with a knife blade to tenderize it, but do not separate it completely from the bone. Add the bones to the meat in the baking dish.

4. Add ginger, garlic, and scallions to meat. Combine sugar, water, and soy sauce and pour over meat. Let marinate at room temperature for about ½ hour. Preheat broiler or grill.

5. Drain meat. (The marinade may be refrigerated and used on another day). Grill or broil meat strips for a few minutes on each side until juicy, and still a bit rare inside. Grill the bones as well. Pile meat and bones on a platter and serve. (These are delicious when grilled on charcoal).

Beef Stews

Every cuisine produces characteristic versions of beef stew. They are wonderfully sustaining during the cooler months and freeze well, so it is possible to make them in huge batches and then squirrel them away. Beef stew, although it sounds impossibly stodgy, is wonderful food. Follow the rules and your stews will be worthy of both dinner parties and family meals. I have spent years searching out the perfect meats, the perfect methods, and the most interesting versions of stew. The stewing process, when applied to the proper chunks of meat, produces a succulent and intensely enjoyable dish.

Many cookbooks begin beef stew recipes by listing "three pounds of lean beef" as the first ingredient. This directive immediately produces utter confusion; there are many types of lean beef, many of them totally unfit for braising. Lean beef *should* mean beef well trimmed of surrounding fat. It must have a good marbling of fat *within* the meat or it will produce a hopelessly dry and stringy finished dish. The secret of nutritious and delicious beef stews is to use this fat marbling to advantage during the cooking process, and then to rid the finished dish of as much as possible. Here is how to do it:

1. Avoid lean cuts of meat, such as top and bottom round. The best stew meats are the flat pieces of meat above and below the ribs, sometimes called deckle; center cut brisket; shoulder or blade roast; and center cut chuck. For each of these meats, trim off all surrounding fat, gristle and connective tissue. Although tedious, this step is vital to the success of the finished dish. When the meat has been meticulously trimmed, cut it into cubes of the proper size. (Always buy more meat than you need to allow for trimming waste.).

2. Most recipes tell the cook, in no uncertain terms, to sear the meat well before braising. At the risk of arousing the ire of traditionalists, I am going to advise you to forget this step; it simply is not necessary. Let the meat stew slowly without preliminary browning. It will be tender and flavorful, the sauce will be very rich and you will have saved time and calories.

3. Never use water in a stew. Use stock, wine, tomato puree, beer, or whatever else seems interesting. The liquid should just barely cover the contents of the pot. Simmer it gently; never boil it. The finished meat should be meltingly tender, not shredded. The length of cooking time will depend on the type and quality of meat.

4. Choose your stewing pot very carefully. If it is too big, a good deal of evaporation will occur and the stew will not have a wonderfully abundant sauce. Too small and the liquid will overflow as the stew simmers. The pot must be of a non-reactive material (aluminum or cast iron will react with acid ingredients such as wine or tomatoes) and it must have a tight fitting cover, although, if necessary, the pot may be sealed with foil. Large earthenware or enameled paella pans make excellent braising vessels.

5. Simmer the stews in the oven, so that the heat passes evenly all around the pot. Keep the oven temperature adjusted during the cooking time; the contents of the pot must remain at a gentle simmer. You will be able to judge the simmering by the intensity of the bubbling sounds issuing from the pot.

6. When the stew is finished, cool it to room temperature, and then refrigerate it overnight. When chilled, the fat will have accumulated on the top of the stew, and congealed. Scrape off the fat and discard it. In this way, unnecessary fat and calories are eliminated, and the flavor of the dish is improved. Stews get better with age; they taste best a day or so after they have been prepared.

7. Some stews come out of the oven with sauces already thickened, others are very thin—it depends on the ingredients called for in the recipe. Thin sauces can be given more body by rapidly boiling and at the same time the flavor is intensified; simply strain the liquid into a saucepan and boil it until it is reduced by about one third. To thicken it more substantially, add bits of beurre manie to the boiling sauce in the following manner: mash together equal parts of softened, unsalted butter and flour; drop little balls of this mixture, 1 or 2 at a time, into the boiling liquid and whisk them in well. Be frugal with the little beurre manie balls—the stew should not be too thick and floury. I think that the best

braised beef dishes have unfloured sauces, but this is a matter of personal taste.

8. Serve the piping hot, fragrant stew right out of the stewing vessel or in a deep platter, garnished with bunches of watercress or parsley. With it, serve a starchy accompaniment that can be used to soak up some of the glorious sauce. Noodles, rice, wild rice, and boiled potatoes are all good, but as far as I am concerned, the best accompaniment is a big, rich, fluffy mountain of old fashioned mashed potatoes.

California Zinfandel Stew *(American)*
Serves 6

½ *pound bacon, coarsely diced*
2 *carrots, peeled and coarsely diced*
2 *onions, coarsely chopped*
3 *pounds well trimmed stew beef, cut into 1½-inch cubes*
1 *cup salad olives with pimientos*
1 *Turkish bay leaf or ½ California bay leaf*

1 *3-inch piece orange peel*
3 *cloves garlic, peeled but left whole*
½ *teaspoon dried thyme*
½ *cup raisins*
salt and pepper to taste
½ *tablespoon sugar*
1 *cup zinfandel*
beef stock

1. Preheat oven to 300 degrees.

2. In a heavy pot that can be covered, cook bacon, carrots and onions until the bacon is cooked but not crisp.

3. Add all remaining ingredients except stock and stir well to combine. Add enough stock to just barely cover the contents of the casserole. Cover tightly and simmer in the preheated oven until the meat is fork-tender, two hours or more. Adjust oven temperature down, if necessary, during this time to maintain a gentle simmer, not a boil.

4. When the meat is tender, cool and refrigerate. Next day, scrape off and discard congealed fat. Reheat stew, then drain liquid into a saucepan. Boil down until reduced by ⅓. Recombine sauce and meat, adjust temperature and seasonings, and serve.

Chili Con Carne *(American—Southwest)*
Serves 6

2 tablespoons corn oil
3 large onions, coarsely chopped
2 cloves garlic, minced
4 tablespoons chili powder
1 teaspoon ground cumin
1 teaspoon oregano

1 teaspoon red pepper flakes,
  or to taste
3 pounds well trimmed stewing
  beef, cut into ½-inch cubes
1 six ounce can tomato paste
salt and pepper to taste
beef stock to cover

1. Preheat oven to 300 degrees.

2. Heat oil in stew pot. Saute onions and garlic until tender. Stir in chili powder, cumin, oregano and pepper flakes. Stir over very low heat until the onions are coated with the spices, and the spices have lost their raw taste.

3. Stir in the remaining ingredients. The liquid should just barely cover the contents of the pot. Simmer in the preheated oven for 2 hours or more, until the beef is very tender. Make sure the chili simmers slowly during this time; it must not boil.

4. When the meat is tender, cool and then refrigerate. Next day, scrape off and discard congealed fat. Reheat and serve. Pass bowls of sour cream, cooked kidney beans, grated Cheddar cheese, chopped onion, diced, lemon-juice-tossed avocado, and chopped fresh coriander leaves, if available.

Stufatino *(Italian)*
Serves 6

3 tablespoons olive oil
2 onions, cut in half and sliced
  into thin half moons
3 pounds well trimmed stewing
  beef, cut into 1½-inch cubes
4 cloves garlic, peeled but left
  whole
½ teaspoon dried rosemary

½ teaspoon dried marjoram
salt and pepper to taste
½ small can tomato paste
1 cup Italian dry red wine (Barolo
  is best for this. Drink the
  remainder when the stew is
  eaten)
beef stock

1. Preheat oven to 300 degrees.

2. Heat oil in a pot that can be covered. Saute onions until limp and golden.

3. Stir in beef, garlic, seasonings, tomato paste, and wine. Add stock, if necessary, to just barely cover the contents of pot. Cover tightly and cook in the oven for two hours or more, until the meat

is fork tender. Adjust the oven temperature down during this time so that the contents of the pot remain at a gentle simmer. Cool and refrigerate.

4. Next day, scrape off congealed fat and discard. Reheat gently.

Daube de Boeuf (French)
Serves 8

4 pounds well trimmed stewing
   beef, cut into 2-inch cubes
½ teaspoon dried thyme
2 Turkish bay leaves or 1
   California bay leaf, crumbled
10 peppercorns
½ cup brandy
3 cups dry red wine
¼ cup olive oil
2 cloves garlic, peeled but left
   whole

6 carrots, peeled and sliced
6 onions, sliced
2 cups beef stock
1 cup flour, approximately
½ pound bacon, blanched for 5
   minutes in water to cover and
   diced coarsely
salt and pepper to taste

1. Place the beef in a large glass or ceramic container. Mix in the seasonings, brandy, wine, olive oil, garlic, carrots, and onion. Cover and marinate for at least 12 hours in the refrigerator, stirring every once in a while.

2. Remove meat from marinade. Strain marinade into a non-reactive saucepan. Reserve the vegetables. Add beef stock to marinade liquid, bring to a boil, reduce heat and simmer briskly, uncovered, until the liquid is reduced by about ⅓. Skim off scum.

3. Preheat oven to 300 degrees. Dry the beef cubes on paper towels. Dredge them in flour, shaking off the excess. (You may dredge them in a paper bag). Choose a casserole that can be covered. Spread some bacon on the bottom of the casserole. Top with a layer of reserved vegetables, then a layer of meat. Repeat, ending with a layer of vegetable and some bacon. Strain the simmered marinade-stock mixture over all. The liquid should just barely cover the contents of the casserole. Add some salt and pepper.

4. Cover the casserole tightly, with foil if necessary. Place in the oven and let it simmer until the meat is meltingly tender, 2 hours or more, depending on the meat. Adjust the oven temperature down during this time if necessary; the daube must simmer very gently—never boil.

5. When done, adjust seasonings, cool and refrigerate. Next day, scrape off and discard congealed fat, reheat gently and serve.

Kettle Goulash *(Hungarian)*
Serves 6

4 tablespoons bacon fat
5 large onions, coarsely chopped
2 large green peppers, coarsely
  chopped
3 cloves garlic, minced
1½ tablespoons Hungarian
  paprika

3 pounds well trimmed stewing
  beef, cut into 1½-inch cubes
salt and pepper to taste
1 six ounce can tomato paste
sour cream at room temperature

1. Preheat oven to 300 degrees.

2. Heat fat in a deep heavy pot. Cook the onions, peppers, and garlic until the onions are limp and transparent.

3. Add paprika. Stir over very low heat until the vegetables are well coated and the paprika has lost its raw taste.

4. Add beef and remaining ingredients, except sour cream. Stir well to combine.

5. Simmer in preheated oven for 2 hours or until the meat is very tender. Adjust oven temperature during cooking time so contents of pot remain at a simmer. Cool and refrigerate.

6. Next day, discard congealed fat and reheat the goulash. Serve in shallow bowls with a dollop of sour cream atop each serving.

Stefado of Beef *(Greek)*
Serves 6

3 pounds well trimmed stewing
  beef, cut into 1-inch cubes
1 6-ounce can tomato paste
½ cup fresh chopped parsley
salt and pepper to taste
1 Turkish bay leaf or ½ California
  bay leaf
1 teaspoon oregano, crumbled
1 teaspoon ground cinnamon

1 teaspoon ground cumin
½ teaspoon sugar
½ cup dry white wine
¼ cup red wine vinegar
24 tiny boiling onions, peeled
½ pound Feta cheese, crumbled
1 cup walnuts, coarsely choppped
½ cup additional fresh chopped
  parsley

1. Preheat oven to 300 degrees.

2. Combine all ingredients, except Feta cheese, walnuts, and additional parsley. Mix very well.

3. Place in a heavy pot that can be covered. Cover tightly and simmer for 2 hours or until the meat is very tender, and the onions have almost disintegrated. Adjust oven temperature during cooking time so contents of pot remain at a simmer. Do not let it boil.

4. When tender, cool and refrigerate. Next day, discard congealed fat and reheat gently. Serve in a deep platter, garnished with Feta cheese, walnuts, and parsley.

Pot Roasted Brisket, Jewish Style
Serves 6

Onions and garlic are important flavoring components of traditional Jewish dishes, but at one time their significance went far beyond their taste. Wise men of the Torah believed both onions and garlic to have aphrodisiac properties. It was correct to eat dishes laden with these powerful vegetables at the sabbath meal, and then to perform one's conjugal duties with vigor, later in the evening. This garlic and onion laden pot roast is my version of the traditional Jewish dish.

1 large first-cut beef brisket,
trimmed of almost all fat (leave
some on top)
8 to 10 onions, coarsely chopped
6 large cloves garlic, peeled

1 cup dry white wine
salt and pepper
1 teaspoon thyme
3 tablespoons brandy

1. Preheat oven to 325 degrees.

2. In a heavy shallow baking dish that can be closed tighly, place half of the onions, the brisket (fat side up), the remaining onions, and the garlic. Add the wine, salt, pepper, and thyme.

3. Close the pot tightly, with foil if necessary, and simmer in preheated oven for 3 to 4 hours, until meat is very tender. Adjust temperature down to keep the liquid at a slow simmer.

4. Allow the meat and liquid to cool at room temperature, in covered baking dish. Refrigerate covered dish overnight.

5. Next day, the fat will have congealed. Discard it. Remove the meat from the liquid and trim off all fat. Slice it thinly, against the grain. Set aside.

6. Stir the brandy into the liquid in the dish.

7. Pour liquid and onions into blender. (You may need to do this in two batches). Quickly turn blender on and off several times to achieve a rough puree. The onion puree should not be too smooth. Taste, and adjust seasonings.

8. You may now reheat the slices in the sauce or refrigerate them in the sauce to serve at a later time. The pot roast will keep several days in the refrigerator. Plan to have leftovers; there is no limit to the versatility of leftover pot roast. Two examples follow.

Beef Mushroom Cheese Salad
Serves 6

1½ pounds cold leftover pot
   roast, sliced thinly
3 tablespoons olive oil
1 pound mushrooms, trimmed
   and sliced
juice of 1 lemon
½ cup mustard vinaigrette (see
   index) seasoned with tarragon
   and thyme to taste

½ cup fresh chopped parsley
½ pound Swiss cheese, cut into
   ½-inch cubes
leftover onion puree, from pot
   roast

1. Cut the meat slices into strips, set aside.

2. Heat oil in a skillet. Saute the mushrooms in the oil with the lemon juice until just cooked. Set aside in the skillet to cool.

3. Add any mushroom liquid that collects in the skillet to ½ cup of mustard vinaigrette.

4. Combine meat, mushrooms, parsley and cheese. Pour the dressing over the salad and toss gently. Stir in a few spoonfuls of onion puree. Let the salad marinate at least 2 hours to blend flavors. Serve at room temperature.

Picadillo Crepes
Serves 8-9

3 tablespoons olive oil
1 large onion, coarsely chopped
1 clove garlic, minced
1 large green pepper, coarsely
   chopped
4 cups leftover brisket, coarsely
   chopped
1 can (1 pound 12 ounces)
   tomatoes, drained and mashed
   with the hands
1 can (3 ounces) chopped green
   chilies, drained

1 cup raisins, soaked in 1 cup dry
   sherry for 10 minutes
1 cup onion puree from brisket
¼ teaspoon ground cinnamon
salt and pepper to taste
½ cup blanched, slivered almonds
16 to 18 crepes (see index)
2 tablespoons butter
2 cups grated mild white Cheddar
   cheese
2 cups sour cream, at room
   temperature

1. Heat oil. Saute the onion, garlic, and green pepper until tender but not browned. Stir in the meat, and cook, stirring, over moderate heat for 2 to 3 minutes.

2. Stir in tomatoes, chilies, raisins, and sherry, onion puree, cinnamon, salt, and pepper. Bring the mixture to a boil, reduce heat and simmer, uncovered, for a half hour, or until the mixture is

very thick, but not scorched or completely dry.

3. Stir in almonds. Taste, adjust seasoning and set aside.

4. Preheat oven to 350 degrees. Oil or butter a shallow large baking dish.

5. Fill each crepe with an equal amount of the picadillo mixture. Roll and place, seam side down, in a single layer in the baking dish. Dot with butter and cover with grated cheese. Place in the oven. When cheese is melted and the crepes are heated through, about one half hour, top each crepe with a dollop of sour cream and serve. [As an alternate, omit butter and sour cream. Cover the crepes with a layer of mornay sauce (see index) and grated cheese and cook in the oven until browned and bubbly.]

Hamburgers

The secret of the original hamburger has been lost in the mists of time; it has been credited to the Germans, the Russians, the St. Louis World's Fair of 1904, a New York delicatessen, and a joint in New Haven. Whatever its origins, there is no doubt that the hamburger sandwich and its accompanying fried potatoes have become the quintessential American meal. Unfortunately, in recent years, we have been buried under an avalanche of fast food hamburgers and fries ranging from the mediocre to the downright wretched—it is easy, under such an onslaught, to lose sight of the excellence of that most typical of American meals.

At its best, a hamburger is a thick patty of red, juicy, flavorful meat, encompassed by a crunchy, blackened crust and resting between the halves of a slightly sweetened, tender bun. When the fragrant, beefy burger is festooned with deeply browned onions and paired with a heap of freshly made, golden brown fried potatoes, it becomes something very special indeed.

Use lean ground chuck or ground round for a digestible and tender hamburger. Handle the meat as little as possible when adding seasonings and shaping into patties. If the hamburgers are to be grilled outdoors over charcoal, make sure that you have a good bed of glowing coals and ash, with no flame. Charcoal briquets will form a perfect bed for cooking about 30 minutes after light up. Do *not* use a chemical starter on the coals; it will impart a revolting flavor to the cooked meat. Keep a water pistol around for quenching flareups that may occur as fat from the cooking hamburgers drips onto the coals. For a really special taste, throw a clove of garlic or a few sprigs of a fresh herb on the coals as the burgers cook. When cooking indoors, hamburgers are best pan sauteed, although this method creates a lot of smoke. In either case, indoors or out, cook them to rare or medium rare.

Hamburgers

1½ pounds ground chuck or   *salt and pepper to taste*
    ground round—use the freshest
    meat possible

1. Divide the ground meat into four portions. Handle the meat as gently as possible. Shape each portion into a rough patty. Do not press them down. Each patty will look something like a lumpy meatball. Sprinkle these objects with salt and pepper.

2. If the hamburgers are to be grilled over charcoal, rub the grill with a bit of cooking oil. Grill the burgers close to the coals for a minute on each side to sear them (use tongs and a pancake turner to turn them gently), then raise the grill a few inches and cook, until the meat is done to your liking. Avoid cooking them to the well-done stage, when they become dry, grey, crumbly, and thoroughly unappetizing.

3. If the hamburgers are to be cooked indoors, use a heavy skillet. Film the bottom with a very small amount of oil and heat. Sear the hamburger over high heat for a minute on each side, then reduce heat and cook until the meat is done the way you like it. You must have a powerful exhaust fan or an open kitchen window for this method; it makes a lot of smoke.

Cheeseburgers

1½ pounds ground chuck or   *1½ teaspoons chopped fresh basil*
    ground round   *(optional)*
salt and pepper to taste
2 cups grated Swiss Gruyere
    cheese

Gently combine ingredients with your hands. Shape gently into 6 fat patties. Broil according to directions in previous recipe.

Serve both hamburgers and cheeseburgers with homemade hamburger buns, fried potatoes, and browned onions (see index for recipes).

Niko's Greek Stuffed Eggplants
Serves 8

8 eggplants, about 12 ounces each
½ cup vegetable oil
2 large onions, coarsely chopped
2 cloves garlic, minced
2 pounds ground beef chuck
½ cup raw rice
½ pound potatoes, peeled and
   diced
1 cup fresh mint, chopped
½ cup fresh parsley, chopped

1 teaspoon sugar
salt and pepper to taste
4 ounces tomato paste
2 cups canned crushed tomatoes
1 teaspoon ground cinnamon
½ cup vegetable oil
1 additional cup crushed tomatoes
2 additional ounces tomato paste
4 cups water
8 half slices ripe tomato

1. Preheat oven to 375 degrees.

2. Trim stem end of each eggplant. Cut a slice off the top of each eggplant lengthwise, starting and ending ½ inch from each end of the eggplant. Scoop out pulp from the eggplants and dice ⅓ of it. Save excess eggplant for another use. You will have eight boat-shaped eggplant shells.

3. In a large saucepan, heat ½ cup oil. Saute onions and garlic until limp. Add meat and cook until brown, breaking it up with a wooden spoon as it cooks. Add rice, diced potatoes, mint, parsley, sugar, salt and pepper, 4 ounces tomato paste, 2 cups crushed tomatoes, cinnamon and the diced eggplant pulp. Stir well and simmer for 3 minutes.

4. Fill eggplant shells with the mixture. Place eggplant in a large baking pan that will hold them all snugly in one layer.

5. In a mixing bowl, pour the remaining ½ cup oil, the additional 1 cup crushed tomatoes, the additional 2 ounces tomato paste, and 4 cups water. Mix well and pour around eggplants in pan. Cover the pan with aluminum foil. Bake for 1 hour and 30 minutes.

6. Take aluminum foil off. Place ½ slice of tomato of top of each eggplant. Bake uncovered for another 35 mintues. Serve at once, or cool and refrigerate. Reheat gently at serving time.

Corned Beef Hash Mornay
Serves 6

Hash—I love it. The canned substance perpetrated on an unwary public under the name of hash has made a bad name for the heavenly stuff, but properly made at home, it can be utterly delicious. To a hash lover, Thanksgiving turkey and Sunday roast beef are mere stopovers on the way to tomorrow's glorious hash. If my nine year old keeps his promise, and takes his aged mother all over the galaxy when he becomes an astronaut, my first question of the strange creatures at each planetary stop will be "Do you make hash here?" An affirmative answer and we will know that we have uncovered a civilization of extreme intelligence and refinement. A negative answer? Fly on . . . fly on. Think of the recipe collecting. Can Venusian swamp turtle hash fail to be delicious?

In the meantime, this terrestial hash recipe keeps me very well satisfied.

6 slices bacon, coarsely diced	freshly ground pepper to taste
6 onions, coarsely chopped	⅓ cup half and half
2 tablespoons butter	2 cups mornay sauce (see index)
4 cups diced or shredded cooked corned beef (see below)	1 cup grated Swiss cheese

1. Preheat oven to 400 degrees.

2. Saute the bacon slowly with the onions in a wide heavy skillet until the onions are tender and deeply browned.

3. Stir in the butter. When melted, stir in the diced corned beef and lots of freshly ground pepper. Do not add salt—corned beef is salty. Stir over moderate heat for 2 to 3 minutes.

4. Pour in half and half. Simmer until it is absorbed. Stir and cook mixture until it begins to brown very slightly.

5. Put the hash into a shallow casserole. Cover with mornay sauce. Sprinkle with cheese. Place in oven until browned and bubbly, about ½ hour.

Corned Beef

In the meat department of the supermarket, you will find cryovac wrapped corned beef briskets. Choose a large, nicely shaped one. The fat should be on top and bottom only, not running through the muscle. I prefer the mild cure for this dish, but the spicy cure will work also. Preheat the oven to 300 degrees. Remove the corned beef from its cryovac wrapping and place it on a large piece of heavy duty foil, pour any juices from the package around it, bring the foil up around the beef and crimp it well so that no juices or steam can escape. Place the foil package in a baking pan and put it in the oven for 3 hours, or until the corned beef is very tender. Test it by opening the package and inserting a skewer into the meat. Rewrap and let the beef cool in its foil package. When cool, remove from foil, wrap well in plastic wrap and refrigerate until needed. When you are about to make the hash, trim the meat of all fat. Slice thinly against the grain. With a chef's knife, shred or chop the slices—do not use a grinder. This meat is also wonderful in sandwiches. Try it with hot mustard on homemade corn-rye (see index).

Veal

Veal Antonio
Serves 1

This is a speciality of Antonio Pecondon, chef at Atlanta's La Grotta restaurant. Make it when fresh herbs are available—do not substitute dried herbs.

2 pieces of milk-fed veal
   scallopini, 2½ ounces each
4 tablespoons butter
2 tablespoons chopped shallots
¼ cup white wine

generous pinch each of chopped
   thyme, basil, and Italian
   parsley
pinch each of rosemary and sage

1. Flatten out the scallopini as thinly as possible with a meat mallet or the side of a wide knife. Remove any skin or sinews.

2. Heat half of the butter in a wide pan and lightly saute the scallopini on both sides. As soon as the scallopini are done, remove to a heated serving dish and keep hot.

3. Add the chopped shallots and let cook until lightly browned. Add the white wine.

4. When the wine has been slightly reduced, add the herbs and turn off the heat. Swirl in the remaining butter. Pour sauce over the scallopini and serve immediately.

Veal alla Valdostana
Serves 4

"Valdostana" refers to the Valley of Aosta in Northern Italy; an area that has been producing that noblest of cheeses—Fontina—for hundreds of years. A dish designated "Valdostana" by definition usually contains Fontina d'Aosta. Unfortunately, many American restaurants present so-called Valdostana dishes made with Danish or Swedish Fontina, or even, I shudder to report, Mozzarella or Swiss. Of course, these substitution cheeses are pleasant enough, but their melting qualities and taste are quite different from real Italian Fontina; the resulting dishes do not reach the magnificence of an authentic Valdostana preparation. The real Fontina is excellent eaten at room temperature with wine, crusty bread and sweet butter, or with fruit, but it reaches its ultimate potential when used in cooking. The buttery pungent cheese melts down and melds with other ingredients in the dish to form a wonderful, creamy, distinctive sauce. True Fontina d'Aosta is ivory colored with an orangy-brown rind (never bright red), and a distinctive pungent odor. In addition to classic Valdostana preparations, it can be used in any dish that calls for Mozzarella. Lasagna or canneloni (see index) for instance, made with Fontina, are dishes to be cherished.

2 tablespoons butter
1/4 pound mushrooms, trimmed, cleaned, and sliced
salt and pepper to taste
4 tablespoons butter

4 veal loin chops, 1/2-inch thick, with tails trimmed off
1/2 cup dry vermouth
1/2 cup Madeira
1 cup grated Fontina cheese (about 1/4 pound)

1. Heat butter in a skillet; saute mushrooms until cooked through. Season to taste. Set aside.

2. Heat remaining butter in a wide heavy skillet. Sprinkle the veal chops with salt and pepper. Saute the chops over medium heat, turning frequently with tongs, until the chops are just cooked through, 5 to 7 minutes in all. Do not let them overcook. Place the chops in a shallow baking dish, and cover each one with some sauteed mushrooms. Preheat broiler.

3. Pour the vermouth and Madeira into the skillet and boil rapidly, scraping up the browned bits in the skillet with a wooden spoon. When the liquid has reduced by about half, pour it over the veal.

4. Sprinkle the grated Fontina evenly over the veal and mushrooms and place the dish under the broiler for a few moments, just long enough to melt the cheese. Do not let it brown.

Grillades and Grits
Serves 6

This marvelous combination makes a traditional New Orleans breakfast. For the grits, use regular, not quick cooking, and stir in the butter lavishly.

¼ cup flour
1½ teaspoons salt
¼ teaspoon cayenne pepper
a generous grinding of black
    pepper
1½ pounds of veal round
3 tablespoons butter
1 tablespoon olive oil
1 tablespoon butter
2 stalks celery, chopped
2 green peppers, chopped

2 onions, chopped
2 cloves garlic, chopped
1 can (1 pound 16 ounces)
    tomatoes, drained and chopped
2 tablespoons tomato paste
1½ cups water or stock
1 bay leaf
½ teaspoon thyme
½ teaspoon Tabasco sauce
salt and pepper to taste.

1. Combine the flour, salt, cayenne, and black pepper in a shallow bowl. Set aside.

2. Cut the veal round into slices about ½ inch thick. Trim off all fat and gristle and cut the slices into squares that are two inches on each side.

3. Dip each piece of meat into the flour-spice mixture. Make sure both sides are coated. Pound the slices with a meat mallet until they are ¼ inch thick. Dip both sides into the flour mixture again, shaking off the excess.

4. Heat three tablespoons butter and one tablespoon oil in a heavy skillet. Saute meat, a few pieces at a time, until nicely browned. Set aside on a plate.

5. When all the meat is browned and on the plate, add an additional tablespoon of butter to the skillet. Add celery, peppers, onions, and garlic, and saute, stirring and scraping the bottom of the pan, until the vegetables are tender. Stir in the tomatoes, tomato paste, stock, and seasonings. Bring to a simmer. Add sauteed meat slices.

6. Simmer, covered, for about one hour, stirring occasionally. When the meat is fork tender and the liquid has cooked down to a thick, reddish-brown gravy, the grillades are done. Serve with buttered grits. The grillades are best when reheated, so make them a day or so in advance.

Stuffed Breast of Veal
Serves 6

2½ cups beef stock
1½ cups cream sherry
2 tablespoons butter
1 medium onion, chopped
2 cloves garlic, chopped
½ pound ground pork
½ pound ground veal
½ cup bread crumbs
2 eggs, lightly beaten
2 tablespoons chopped parsley
salt and pepper to taste

grated zest of 1 lemon
1 boned veal breast, about 3
  pounds
2 tablespoons butter
1 tablespoon vegetable oil
1 onion, chopped
1 carrot, peeled and chopped
1 stalk celery, chopped
1 clove garlic, chopped
bones from veal breast

1. Preheat oven to 350 degrees.

2. Combine stock and sherry in a saucepan. Broil rapidly until reduced by ½. Set aside.

3. Heat butter, saute onion and garlic until tender. Scrape into a bowl. Add ground pork, ground veal, bread crumbs, eggs, parsley, salt, pepper, and lemon zest. Use your hands to combine it.

4. Lay out the veal breast, boned side up. Trim away some of the fat and connective tissue but be careful not to cut through the meat. Sprinkle on some salt and pepper.

5. Spread the ground meat mixture over the veal breast, leaving a one inch margin all around. Roll the veal neatly and tie securely.

6. In a deep heavy pot, of a size to accomodate the veal roll, heat the remaining butter and oil. Saute the veal roll on all sides until deeply browned. Remove from pot and set aside.

7. In the fat remaining in the pot, saute the onion, carrot, celery and garlic until tender. Stir and scrape the bottom of the pan to loosen browned particles. Place veal bones in pot.

8. Place veal roll on top of the bones and pour in wine-stock mixture. Cover pot, and cook for about 2½ hours, until the veal is very tender. Adjust heat during cooking time to maintain a simmer.

9. When tender, remove veal and let rest. Discard bones. Pour pan juices into a container and place in freezer for a few minutes so that the fat rises quickly to the top. Skim fat, and puree sauce by rubbing through a fine sieve into a saucepan. Boil rapidly for a few minutes to reduce, thicken, and intensify flavors. Taste and adjust seasonings.

10. Slice veal and arrange on a platter. Spoon some hot sauce over each slice and pass the rest separately.

Veal Marengo
Serves 6

¼ cup corn oil
4 pounds well trimmed veal
   shoulder, cut into 1-inch cubes;
   or veal shank cut off the bone,
   trimmed well, and cut into 1-
   inch cubes
salt and pepper to taste
4 tablespoons butter
3 tablespoons flour
2 tablespoons butter
3 onions, cut in half, and sliced
   into half moons

3 cups dry white wine
1 cup tomato puree
1 teaspoon tarragon
½ teaspoon thyme
3 cloves garlic, minced
2 tablespoons brandy
1 3-inch piece orange rind
2 tablespoons butter
1 pound fresh mushrooms,
   quartered

1. Heat oil in a wide, heavy skillet. When hot, brown the veal on all sides. Do not crowd; do it in several batches if necessary. With a slotted spoon, transfer the browned veal to a deep heavy pot. Discard oil and any liquid from skillet.

2. Season the veal with salt and pepper. Add the 4 tablespoons butter and let it melt over low heat. Sprinkle the flour over the meat and stir it over moderate heat for about 5 mintues.

3. Melt 2 tablespoons butter in the skillet; brown the onions.

4. When the onions are browned, add the wine to the skillet. Boil rapidly for 2 to 3 minutes. Scrape up all the browned particles with a wooden spoon or spatula. Add the wine and onions to the veal.

5. Add tomato puree, tarragon, thyme, garlic, brandy, and orange rind. Stir to combine everything well. If you are using veal shanks, wrap 2 of the bones in cheesecloth and add them to the pot.

6. Cover the pot and simmer over very low heat for 1 to 1½ hours, or until the veal is very tender but not falling apart.

7. Meanwhile, saute the mushrooms in 2 tablespoons butter until they are tender and beginning to render their juices. Add the mushrooms and their juices to the tender veal. Remove shank bones. (The cooked marrow from the bones makes a delicious snack on toast).

8. Drain all the sauce from the veal into a saucepan. Cover the veal well to prevent drying out. Simmer the sauce rapidly until reduced to 2 cups and thickened.

9. Combine the sauce with the veal and serve at once, or cool, and then refrigerate. The next day, bring to room temperature before gently reheating. Serve with white rice or wild rice.

Lamb

Crown Roast of Lamb
Serves 8

A crown roast of lamb is for state occasions. Don't ruin it by cooking it to the well done stage.

*1 16-bone crown roast of lamb,
    oven-ready
juice of 1 lemon
pepper
3 cloves garlic
2 cups stock
1 cup white wine
1 pound ground lamb trimmings
    (the butcher will give you
    these)*

*1 onion, choppped
½ cup dry white wine
¼ cup tomato puree
1 egg, lightly beaten
2 tablespoons Parmesan cheese
1 tablespoon bread crumbs
salt and pepper to taste
1½ pounds mushrooms
olive oil
watercress or fresh mint*

Stuffing Choices:

*Ratatouille
Kasha
Rice Pulao*

*Wild Rice
(See index for recipes)*

Paloise sauce (bearnaise with mint substituted for tarragon, see index)

1. Preheat oven to 400 degrees.

2. Rub the lamb crown with lemon juice, pepper, and garlic. Place on a rack in a roasting pan. Roast for 1 to 1½ hours or until medium rare. (Internal temperature 145 to 150 degrees; use a Bi-therm thermometer and stick it between the ribs, at the bottom).

3. Meanwhile, cook ground lamb and onion in a heavy skillet, breaking up lamb as it cooks. (Add some butter if the lamb does not render sufficient fat). Drain off all fat.

4. Stir in wine and tomato puree, simmer until the mixture is almost dry. Cool slightly. Stir in egg, Parmesan cheese, bread crumbs, salt and pepper.

5. Remove stems from mushrooms, save stems for another use. Stuff caps with ground lamb mixture, mounding the stuffing over the top. Oil a baking dish and place filled caps in it.

6. Bake mushrooms in the oven with the lamb during the last 20 to 30 minutes of roasting.

7. When lamb registers 145 to 150 degrees, (medium rare), remove to a warm platter and let sit for 10 minutes. Fill crown with stuffing of your choice. Garnish the platter with the mushroom caps and with bunches of mint or watercress. Carve into chops at the table. Pass sauce paloise separately.

Mushroom-Stuffed Lamb Leg
Serves 8

My friend, John Thompson, builds houses for a living, but he cooks for fun and relaxation. This lamb leg is his creation.

1 whole leg of lamb, boned   *1 tablespoon coarse ground pepper*
1 tablespoon dried rosemary   *rock salt*
2 tablespoons coarse salt (Kosher)

1. Preheat oven to 250 degrees.

2. If possible, have lamb boned by cutting out bone without piercing through the skin so that a pocket is formed for stuffing. If the butcher will not do this, it may be boned in the usual manner and then rolled and tied after stuffing if necessary. Trim excess fat from lamb. Stuff cavity with prepared dressing (see below). Roll and tie securely if necessary. Rub leg with mixture of dried rosemary, coarse salt, and pepper. Set on a roasting pan approximately the same size as roast, containing ¼ inch bed of rock salt.

3. Place in the oven for approximately 35 minutes to the pound or until 145 degrees is reached on a meat thermometer for medium rare. The meat will still be quite pink when sliced but the texture will be firm. Let the roast stand for 20 minutes or so before carving and serving.

Dressing
1 pound fresh mushrooms, sliced   *2 tablespoons butter*
1 tablespoon fresh rosemary,   *½ cup plain bread crumbs*
  chopped (½ teaspoon dried)   *salt and pepper to taste*

Saute the mushrooms and the rosemary in butter until tender (but not dry). Add the bread crumbs, salt and pepper, and lightly toss.

Moussaka *(Greek Layered Lamb Casserole)*
Serves 12

3 medium eggplants
salt
2½ pounds lean ground lamb,
  shoulder or leg
3 onions, chopped
1 small can (6 ounces) tomato
  paste
½ cup parsley, chopped
salt and pepper to taste
1 cup dry red wine
3 eggs
1 cup grated Parmesan cheese

½ cup bread crumbs
1 teaspoon cinnamon
approximately 6 tablespoons olive
  oil
8 tablespoons butter
8 tablespoons flour
5 cups milk, scalded
¼ cup freshly grated Parmesan
  cheese
4 egg yolks
½ cup additional freshly grated
  Parmesan cheese

1. Do not peel eggplant. Slice about ½ inch thick. Sprinkle with salt and let stand ½ hour then rinse, drain, and dry well.

2. Preheat oven to 400 degrees. Meanwhile brown meat and onions in a heavy skillet. Do not add fat. The meat should render enough fat for cooking. Break up the meat with a wooden spoon as it cooks. When browned, drain off all fat.

3. Add the tomato paste, parsley, salt, pepper, and wine. Simmer until liquid is absorbed, ½ hour or more. Cool slightly. Stir in eggs, cheese, bread crumbs, and cinnamon. Set aside.

4. Lightly oil two baking sheets with olive oil. Place eggplant slices in one layer on the sheets. Brush tops of slices with remaining oil. Use more oil if necessary. Place in 400 degree oven for 30 minutes or so, until the slices are soft and browned. Turn once during this time. Remove browned slices to paper towels to drain. Reduce oven temperature to 350 degrees.

5. Line bottom and sides of a large, fairly shallow baking dish with eggplant. Spread the meat mixture over the eggplant. Set baking dish aside.

6. Heat butter in a heavy, deep saucepan. Stir in flour with a wire whisk. Cook gently, whisking constantly for 3 to 4 minutes. Whisk in scalded milk. Simmer gently for about 10 minutes, stirring frequently until thick. Remove from heat. Fold in Parmesan cheese. Add salt and pepper to taste. Beat a few spoonfuls of sauce into the egg yolks. Then, stirring constantly, pour the yolk mixture into the sauce. Heat, stirring gently for a few moments. Let one or two bubbles form on the surface of the sauce, then remove from the heat. (The flour in the sauce will prevent the yolks from curdling). Taste and adjust seasoning.

7. Pour sauce evenly over meat and eggplant in baking dish. Sprinkle with remaining cheese. Bake for 1 hour until puffed and golden (the topping will puff up almost like a souffle). Let sit for at least 10 minutes before cutting into squares and serving. This reheats well. It may be prepared a day or so in advance.

Stuffed Squash, Middle Eastern Style
24 squash

24 yellow squash
1 cup raw rice, rinsed in cold
*   water*
3 pounds ground lamb
salt and pepper to taste
¼ teaspoon cinnamon

2 cans tomato puree
water
2 cloves garlic
juice of ½ lemon
pinch of sugar
1 teaspoon dried mint crumbled

1. Wash squash thoroughly, and trim. Cut off necks and reserve. Core squash, using an apple corer or the handle of an iced teaspoon to remove pulp.

2. Combine rice, lamb, salt, pepper, and cinnamon. Use this mixture to stuff squash cylinders. Fill only ¾ of capacity to allow for expansion of stuffing. Form any extra stuffing into small meat balls.

3. Pack stuffed squash neatly in layers in a deep, heavy pot. Pour tomato puree around squash. Pour in enough water to cover squash. Bury garlic and squash necks in liquid. Arrange any meatballs over squash. Bring to a boil. Reduce heat and simmer, covered, until squash are tender but not disintegrating and rice is cooked, 45 minutes to 1 hour.

4. Remove squash and meatballs to a platter. Stir lemon juice, sugar and mint into sauce. Boil for a few mintues until slightly reduced and thickened. Pour over squash and serve.

Middle Eastern Green Bean, Lamb Stew
Serves 8

Every fall, the St. Elias Orthodox Church in Atlanta puts on an extravaganza of Middle Eastern food and culture. The food is always staggeringly good. This stew is from the women of the church.

2 tablespoons olive oil
1 large onion, chopped
1½ pounds well trimmed lamb
*   shoulder, cut into small cubes*
water
2 pounds trimmed green beans or
*   pole beans*

1 can (1 pound, 12 ounces)
*   tomatoes, undrained and*
*   chopped*
1 can (8 ounces) tomato puree
1 tomato puree can of water
salt and pepper to taste
½ teaspoon cinnamon

1. Heat oil in in a heavy pot. Saute onion in oil until limp and transparent. Add lamb cubes and saute until meat is brown.

2. Add water to just barely cover meat. Bring to a boil, reduce heat, and simmer, covered, until meat is tender, about 1 hour.

3. Stir in beans, tomatoes and their juice, tomato puree, water, and seasonings. Mix together very well. Bring to a boil, reduce heat, and simmer, covered, until the beans are tender and the sauce is very thick.

Pork

Five-Fragrance Pork
Serves 6

2 pounds well trimmed pork
*   tenderloin*
1 tablespoon cornstarch
1 teaspoon Chinese five-spice
*   powder*
salt
4 tablespoons pale dry sherry
2 tablespoons peanut oil

1 cup raw peanuts
3 tablespoons peanut oil
1 pound mushrooms, trimmed
*   and sliced*
½ cup scallions, sliced, green and
*   white parts*
½ cup chicken stock
salt

1. Cut pork into very thin slices. Then cut each slice into julienne strips. Mix the next four ingredients and add them to the pork. Let marinate for 1 hour, stirring occasionally.

2. Heat oil in a heavy skillet or wok; when hot but not smoking, add the peanuts and toss and stir in the hot oil. When they just begin to brown (only a minutes or so), remove them and drain well on paper towels. Wipe out the skillet.

3. Heat remaining oil. Add pork and toss in the pan, over high heat for 1 minute. Remove to a bowl with a slotted spoon.

4. In the same skillet, cook mushrooms and scallions, stirring constantly for 2 minutes, adding a bit more oil if necessary. Return pork and peanuts to the skillet.

5. Stir stock into the pork and mushrooms. Bring mixture to a boil, reduce heat, and simmer for 2 minutes. Taste and add salt if necessary. Serve immediately.

Pork Paprikash
Serves 6

1 tablespoon butter
1 tablespoon corn oil
1 pound mushrooms, trimmed
 and sliced
1 tablespoon butter
2 tablespoons corn oil
2 pounds well trimmed pork
 tenderloins, sliced ¼ inch
 thick
salt and pepper
1 large onion, chopped

1 small clove garlic, minced
1 teaspoon sweet Hungarian
 paprika
½ cup dry white wine
½ cup chicken stock
1 teaspoon Dijon mustard
¼ cup half and half, at room
 temperature
¼ cup sour cream, at room
 temperature
½ cup fresh, chopped parsley

1. Heat butter and oil. Saute the mushrooms in a heavy skillet until just limp. Scrape into a bowl and set aside.

2. Heat remaining butter and oil in the skillet. Sprinkle the pork slices with salt and pepper and add to the skillet. Cook over high heat, turning the slices in the hot oil until browned, about 2 minutes. Add the pork slices to the mushrooms.

3. Add the onion and garlic to the fat remaining in the skillet. Saute them until the onions are limp and transparent.

4. Add the paprika and stir over low heat until the onions are well coated. Transfer the onions to the bowl with the pork.

5. Add the wine and stock to the skillet and cook over high heat for 3 minutes. Use a wooden spatula or spoon to scrape up any brown bits adhering to the pan. Stir in the mustard.

6. Return the onions, mushrooms, and pork to the skillet. Simmer for 5 minutes.

7. Combine the half and half and sour cream. Blend some of the liquid in the pan into the cream. Then stir the mixture back into the pork and mushrooms. Simmer over very low heat for 3 to 5 mintues, or until the pork is just cooked through. Do not boil. Sprinkle with parsley and serve at once.

Pork Tenderloin Dijon
Serves 6

2 pork tenderloins, very well
   trimmed (about 1 pound each)
3 tablespoons dry vermouth
9 tablespoons Dijon mustard
1½ cups breadcrumbs
salt and pepper to taste
4 tablespoons butter

4 tablespoons corn oil
2 tablespoons butter
2 tablespoons minced shallots
½ cup dry vermouth
⅔ cup whipping cream
½ tablespoon Dijon mustard

1. Preheat oven to 200 degree.

2. Slice pork tenderloins into 1-inch thick medallions.

3. Whisk vermouth into mustard in a soup plate and set aside.

4. Spread crumbs out on a platter and season with salt and pepper. Set next to mustard.

5. Coat pork medallions on all sides with mustard. Roll in crumbs, pressing with your hand to help crumbs adhere. Place coated pork on a rack and refrigerate for an hour or more to help the coating firm up.

6. Heat 4 tablespoons butter and 4 tablespoons oil in a heavy, wide skillet. Cook pork medallions over moderate heat, turning carefully with tongs until golden brown and crusty, and *just* done through, about 15 to 20 minutes. Blot gently on paper towels, and place on a serving platter in the oven to keep warm.

7. Pour out cooking fat and wipe out skillet. Heat remaining 2 tablespoons butter in skillet, and saute shallots until tender.

8. Pour vermouth and cream into the skillet. Whisk in mustard. Boil rapidly, stirring, until liquid is reduced to a little less than half and thickened. Spoon some sauce over each pork medallion and serve.

Garlic Stuffed Pork Roast
Serves 6

1 pork shoulder roast (Boston butt) boned, trimmed of top fat and butterflied, about 4 pounds
salt and pepper to taste
5 cloves garlic, coarsely chopped
3 heaping tablespoons freshly grated Romano cheese

20 sprigs of parsley, trimmed of stems (save stems for a future stock)
2 tablespoons pine nuts
stock
dry white port or dry white vermouth

1. Preheat oven to 325 degrees.

2. Spread butterflied pork roast flat on your work surface, boned side up. With a sharp knife, score the top surface in several places. sprinkle with salt and a generous amount of freshly ground pepper.

3. Sprinkle garlic, cheese, parsley and pine nuts over meat. Roll roast and tie securely in several places.

4. Place on a rack in a shallow roasting pan. Pour in ½ cup stock and ½ cup port. Roast in the preheated oven.

5. When the liquid in the pan is about gone (after about 1 hour), and beginning to leave an encrustation on the bottom of the pan, replenish with more stock and a splash of port. Continue roasting until roast is done, 1 to 1½ hours more, replenishing stock and wine as needed. (A meat thermometer will register a temperature of 170 to 175 degrees).

6. Remove roast to a cutting board and let rest for 10 minutes. Meanwhile pour pan juices into a container, and place in the freezer for a few minutes, so that fat will rise to the top rapidly. Spoon off fat and discard. Measure juices; add enough stock and a bit of wine to measure 1 cup.

7. Strain the liquid into the roasting pan and bring to a boil on top of the stove. Boil rapidly for 2 or 3 minutes, scraping up the browned bits and encrustations on the pan as the liquid boils.

8. Remove strings from roast and slice. Arrange on a platter and serve. Pass pan juices separately.

Pork Chops Stuffed with Piperade
Serves 6

1 tablespoon olive oil
1 small green pepper, chopped
1 small onion, chopped
1 small clove garlic, minced
2 plum tomatoes, drained and
    chopped
¼ cup fresh chopped parsley
salt and pepper to taste
⅛ teaspoon oregano
⅛ teaspoon basil
6 rib pork chops, about ½ inch
    thick

6 ¼-inch thick slices Gruyere
    cheese, cut slightly smaller than
    the pork chops
½ cup flour
salt and pepper
1 egg
2 tablespoons water
1½ cups bread crumbs
6 tablespoons butter
4 tablespoons olive oil

1. Heat the oil in a skillet. Saute the onions, peppers, and garlic until soft but not browned. Add the tomatoes, increase heat, and cook until the liquid is almost gone. Stir in the parsley, salt, pepper, oregano, and basil. Set aside.

2. Trim the chops of all fat. Split them horizontally to the bone, forming a pocket for stuffing. (Have the butcher do this, if possible).

3. Stuff each chop with an equal amount of the tomato mixture. Insert a slice of cheese. Sew up the opening with a tapestry or darning needle and string.

4. Place the flour mixed with the salt and pepper on a sheet of wax paper on your work surface. Lightly beat the egg and water in a shallow bowl or pie plate. Place it next to the flour. Spread the bread crumbs on another sheet of wax paper. Place it next to the egg.

5. Dredge each chop in flour. Shake off excess. Dip the floured chops in egg and then in bread crumbs. Press the crumbs in with your hand. As the chops are breaded, place then on a rack.

6. Heat oil and butter in two heavy, wide skillets. Slowly cook the chops until golden brown and cooked through, about 15 minutes on each side. Drain on paper towels and serve at once.

Note: Leftover ratatouille (see index) can be used in place of the onion-pepper mixture.

Consuelo's Penakbit *(Philippine Pork and Vegetable Stew)*
Serves 8

Save this dish for spring and summer, when bitter melons, (they look like bumpy cucumbers), are in season and available in the Oriental markets. They are available in cans, but—as with many vegetables—are best fresh. This dish exhibits the slightly tart taste so typical of Philippine cookery. It is excellent with rice.

2 tablespoons corn oil
2 pounds well trimmed pork
    shoulder, cut into ½-inch cubes
5 cloves garlic, peeled and mashed
3 large onions, sliced
6 large tomatoes, peeled, seeded,
    and diced
2 cups water
salt and pepper to taste
½ teaspoon MSG (optional)
4 to 5 baby Chinese eggplant,
    unpeeled, trimmed and
    quartered or 2 small eggplants,
    unpeeled, trimmed and cut into
    halves crosswise, then each half
    cut into eighths lengthwise

6 bitter melons; if mature (the
    center will be reddish), cut in
    half and scoop out seeds and
    discard. Slice the melon like a
    cucumber. If young, just
    quarter them.

1. Film a large heavy skillet with oil. Heat. When hot, add pork and fry until some of its fat is rendered.

2. Add the garlic and onions and fry until everything is well browned.

3. Add tomatoes and stir them in. Cook until tomatoes are saucy.

4. Pour in water and add salt, pepper, and M.S.G. Bring to a boil and simmer briskly, uncovered, for 10 minutes. Cover and simmer for 45 minutes.

5. Transfer contents of skillet to a large Dutch oven. Place eggplant and bitter melon on top of tomato mixture. Cover and cook for ½ hour or until eggplant and melon are tender.

6. Grasp pot and cover and shake vigorously to mix contents. (This takes muscles and coordination). Serve with lots of white rice.

Szekely Goulash
Serves 6

One of my earliest food memories is of a sizzling hot, bursting-with-juice frankfurter, a disintegrating, mustard-smeared bun, and a tangle of sauerkraut. Almost 40 years later, the first bite of that sandwich with its garnish of crisp, pungent sour cabbage, is still vivid and unforgettable. The sauerkraut came from the barrel of a pickle vendor on the Lower East Side of New York; it was fresh, crunchy, and indescribably delicious.

Good, fresh sauerkraut still sends me into paroxysms of delight. In adulthood, however, I have learned that it can be much more than a crunchy, tangled heap on a frankfurter. Europeans, particularly Hungarians, treat it with respect and affection; the savory sauerkraut casseroles and stews that are typical of Hungarian cookery always come as a wonderful surprise to those who equate the fermented cabbage with limp, horrid, smelly stuff that comes in cans.

Fortunately, Atlanta has a true sauerkraut master—Harry Zaidel—affectionately called Harry-the-Pickle by his devoted customers. Polish born and New Jersey trained, Harry turns out the best sauerkraut I have tasted since my early hot dog days on New York's Lower East Side. At his plant, the Premier Pickle Company in Norcross, he layers shredded cabbage in big barrels with salt and water, and lets it ferment naturally. If you have never tasted fresh sauerkraut, I urge you to try some first on a grilled hot dog, or better yet, right out of the jar. After you have suppressed the uncontrollable urge to polish off most of a jar by yourself, plan to try some in Szekely goulash, or choucroute garnie (see index).

1½ quarts fresh sauerkraut	2 tablespoons caraway seeds
6 slices bacon, diced	1 large can (1 pound 12 ounces)
3 onions, coarsely chopped	tomatoes, drained and chopped
4 cloves garlic, minced	salt and pepper
4 tablespoons sweet Hungarian	3 pounds well-trimmed pork
paprika	shoulder, cut into 1-inch cubes
1 tablespoon hot Hungarian	1½ to 2 cups chicken stock
paprika (or use 5 tablespoons	2 tablespoons flour
sweet paprika and cayenne	1 cup sour cream, at room
pepper to taste)	temperature

1. Drain sauerkraut in a colander. Rinse it well in cold water, then drain and squeeze as dry as possible. (Save the juice for drinking. It's reputed to be just the thing for battling particularly virulent hangovers). Set aside.

2. Slowly cook diced bacon in a deep, heavy pot that can be covered. When the bacon is not quite crisp, remove it with a slotted spoon and set aside.

3. Add onions and garlic to bacon fat. Cook slowly until limp, but not brown.

4. Add the paprika and stir over very low heat until the onions are well coated. Stir in the caraway seeds and reserved bacon.

5. Add tomatoes, salt, pepper, pork, and sauerkraut. Toss gently to combine.

6. Pour in enough stock to barely cover contents of pot. Bring to a simmer, cover, and simmer over very low heat about 1½ hours, or until pork is tender.

7. With a wire whisk, stir flour into sour cream. Stir a bit of the hot liquid from the pot into the sour cream, then pour the sour cream mixture back into the goulash, stirring constantly. Simmer an additional 10 minutes, stirring occasionally. Prepare this dish a few days in advance for maximum flavor.

Meatballs

Meatballs, although they sound so dull, have an almost universal appeal. Every cuisine has several versions of the little juicy brown objects, bathed in sauce or not, spicy or bland, but always satisfying. My mother was an enthusiastic meatball maker when I was a child. Those round, meaty things seemed to have lots of potential, but their textural resemblance to cannon balls always put me off.

When I married and became mistress of my own kitchen, one of the first things I tried to make was meatballs. My mother always applied a liberal amount of dry oatmeal to her meatball mix to keep it all stuck together; instinctively, I knew this to be wrong, but hadn't the faintest idea of what to substitute in its place. I just left it out and hoped for the best. The meatball mixture was very wet and loose; I was desperately trying to avoid the cannonball effect. At the end of the cooking time they had completely disintegrated—I was the proud, yet disgruntled inventor of meat sauce.

The following recipes are an international sampling of meatball cookery. You will not find one cannonball in the lot. What they lack in elegance and snob appeal they more than make up for in taste.

Lion's Head *(Chinese Pork Balls)*
Serves 6-8

10 *water chestnuts, finely minced*
2 *thin slices fresh peeled ginger*
  root
2 *scallions minced, green and*
  white parts
2 *pounds ground pork*
⅓ *cup soy sauce*
1 *tablespoon pale dry sherry*
1 *tablespoon corn starch*
½ *cup chicken stock*

1 *teapsoon brown sugar*
6 *tablespoons additional corn*
  starch
¼ *cup chicken stock*
1 *cup chicken stock*
2 *teaspoons white sugar*
4 *tablespoons soy sauce*
1 *large head Chinese cabbage*
3 *tablespoons peanut oil*

1. Combine water chestnuts, ginger root, scallions and pork in a bowl.

2. Mix together the soy sauce, sherry, corn starch, stock and brown sugar, and stir well to dissolve the starch and sugar. Add to the pork mixture.

3. Use your hands to mix thoroughly and gently. Shape the mixture into eight equal meatballs.

4. Heat the oven to 400 degrees.

5. While it is heating, mix the additional corn starch with ¼ cup chicken stock in a bowl. Stir well to dissolve the starch. (It will form a paste.) Dip the pork balls, one at a time, in this paste and coat them well.

6. As each meatball is coated, place it on a baking sheet. Place the baking sheet in the oven for 15 to 20 minutes or until the meatballs are browned. Turn once during this time, using a pancake turner. Place the browned meatballs in a deep wide pot.

7. When all the meatballs are browned and in the pot, stir together 1 cup chicken stock, 2 teaspoons white sugar, and 4 tablespoons soy sauce and add the mixture to the pot. Bring to a boil, reduce heat and simmer, covered, for 1½ hours. Turn once, after they have been cooking 45 minutes.

8. While the pork is cooking, wash the cabbage well. Cut off the root end and discard. Cut the stalks and leaves into two inch sections.

9. Heat the remaining oil in a large skillet. Add the cabbage and toss and turn over high heat for 2 minutes. Do this in batches if necessary. With a slotted spoon, arrange the cabbage on the bottom of an attractive baking dish.

10. When the meatballs have completed 1½ hours of simmering,

144

remove them from the pot and arrange on the cabbage. Skim as much fat as possible from the pan liquid, and then pour skimmed liquid over the pork balls. Cover the baking dish (with foil if necessary) and place in a 300 degree oven for 20 minutes.

Serve hot. This is delicious reheated, so it may be made in advance.

Koftah Curry
Serves 6

Meatballs

1 egg
dash ground cloves
½ teaspoon ground cumin
½ teaspoon ground coriander
½ teaspoon ground cinnamon

1 thin slice ginger root, finely
* minced*
salt and pepper to taste
2 pounds ground lamb, shoulder
* or leg*

Sauce

2 tablespoons clarified butter
2 onions, slivered (cut onion into
* fourths, then eighths, and*
* separate petals)*
2 thin slices ginger root, minced
2 cloves garlic, minced
1½ teaspoons ground turmeric
1½ cups clear chicken or lamb
* stock*

3 tablespoons tomato paste
½ teaspoon cinnamon
2 teaspoons coriander
¼ teaspoon ground cumin
salt to taste
dash red pepper flakes

1. Beat egg and spices together. Add to lamb. With hands, combine and shape into small balls, about 25. Fry a tiny piece in a skillet. Taste and adjust seasonings to your liking.

2. Heat butter in a large heavy skillet. Saute onion slivers, ginger, and garlic until limp and transparent.

3. Add turmeric to onions and toss until onions are coated.

4. With a slotted spoon, transfer onions into a casserole and set aside.

5. Brown meatballs on all sides in the same skillet. Do not add fat. When browned, drain off all fat and blot meatballs on paper towels. Add meatballs to casserole.

6. Combine remaining ingredients. Add to meatballs.

7. Bring to a boil. Reduce heat and simmer, covered, for about ½ hour. This is best when prepared a day or so before serving and reheated. Skim off any fat before reheating.

Meatballs, Russian Style
Serves 6

Meatballs

½ *pound beef chuck, ground*
 twice
½ *pound veal, ground twice*
½ *pound pork shoulder, ground*
 twice
2 *slices good white bread, soaked*
 in water and squeezed dry

2 *eggs, lightly beaten*
1 *tablespoon fresh chopped dill or*
 1 *teaspoon dried dill weed*
salt and pepper to taste

Sauce

4 *tablespoons butter*
1 *pound button mushrooms, left*
 whole (if only large mushrooms
 are available, quarter them)
1 *bunch scallions, sliced, green*
 and white parts
1 *teaspoon Hungarian paprika*
2 *teaspoons Dijon mustard*
2 *teaspoons chili powder*

several drops Tabasco sauce
salt and pepper to taste
1 *teaspoon flour*
3 *tablespoons tomato paste*
2 *cups sour cream, at room*
 temperature
1 *tablespoon fresh chopped dill, if*
 available

1. Preheat oven to 400 degrees.

2. Combine all meatball ingredients and knead well with the hands until thoroughly combined. Fry a tiny piece in a skillet. Taste and adjust seasoning to your taste. Shape into small balls, about 25. Place the meatballs on a baking sheet in one layer.

3. Place baking sheet in the preheated oven. Bake the meatballs for 20 to 25 minutes or until cooked through. Shake the pan occasionally during this time to insure browning on all sides.

4. With tongs, lift the finished meatballs onto paper towels to drain. Discard all fat.

5. While the meatballs are browning, make sauce: Heat butter in a wide heavy skillet. Cook mushrooms and scallions in the skillet until the mushrooms are tender and their juices have almost evaporated.

6. Stir in the paprika, mustard, chili powder, Tabasco sauce, salt, pepper, and flour. Stir well until the mushrooms are completely covered with the spice-flour mixture. Add the tomato paste and stir it in very well.

7. Stir in the sour cream. Everything must be well combined. Bring the sauce to a simmer, and simmer for 5 to 10 minutes, stirring occasionally.

8. Add meatballs to sauce. Cover pan and simmer gently for 15-20 minutes, or until they are thoroughly hot. Taste and adjust seasoning. Sprinkle with dill. Serve piping hot. This dish can be made several days in advance. Just reheat gently at serving time.

Sausages

Paul Masselli is a Picasso of pork butts and pig intestines; a flamboyant, likeable, hard living individual whose devotion to sausage perfection borders on the fanatical. At Sausage World, his plant and store in Lilburn, Georgia, he turns out a staggering array of interesting and delicious fresh pork links, from the traditional Italian, German and Polish varieties to more exotic concoctions involving orange peel and liver, tomatoes and basil, and once, in a fit of madness, mushrooms and Cheddar cheese.

When Paul, his wife Ann, (a wonderful cook), and I get together, the conversation invariably turns to food. Nothing makes Paul happier than a new idea for a sausage, or a new way to cook the old ones; he has an insatiable capacity for sausage lore. The next three recipes are Masselli family specialties.

Baked Sausage
Serves 6

olive oil
1½ pounds Italian Sausage (mild or hot or combination of both), pricked with a fork
2 large baking potatoes, peeled and quartered
2 large sweet potatoes, peeled and quartered

2 large onions, peeled and very thinly sliced
2 large green peppers sliced
½ cup water or ¼ cup water and ¼ cup dry white wine
salt and pepper to taste

1. Preheat oven to 350 degrees.

2. Lightly oil a shallow baking dish with olive oil. Place sausage, potatoes, onions and peppers in the dish. Pour water, or wine and water over all, and add salt and pepper to taste.

3. Bake uncovered in the preheated oven for 1 to 1½ hours, or until the sausage and potatoes are browned and cooked and the onions have almost cooked down to a puree. If the baking pan becomes too dry at any time, add a bit more water.

Sausage Carbonara
Serves 8

2 pounds Italian Sausage (hot,
  mild or a combination of both)
2 large onions, coarsely chopped
2 to 3 tablespoons chopped fresh
  parsley
2 to 3 tablespoons chopped fresh
  basil

salt and pepper to taste
1½ cups chicken stock
2 eggs
1 pound ziti or rigatoni
½ cup freshly grated Romano
  cheese

1. Remove sausage meat from its casing and crumble. In a wide heavy skillet, cook sausage meat with onions until the sausage is cooked and the onions are limp. Break up meat with a wooden spoon as it cooks.

2. Add herbs, seasonings and stock. Bring to a simmer, cover pan and simmer for 15 minutes.

3. Meanwhile, beat the eggs in a large shallow bowl. Set aside.

4. Cook the ziti or rigatoni in boiling salted water until al dente, that is it should be cooked but still slightly resistant to the bite.

5. Drain well and stir the hot macaroni and the grated cheese into the beaten eggs in the big bowl. Cover the bowl at once and let it stand for two minutes or so. The heat of the macaroni will cause the eggs to become thickened and the cheese to melt.

Uncover and toss in the hot sausage-onion mixture. Serve at once. Pass additional grated cheese at the table.

Sausage Bolognese

1. Make sausage into desired size links by pinching meat through casing until fingers meet. Twist entire sausage three to four times. Take a sharp knife and cut on twist.

2. Grill links on charcoal grill. Puncture casing while cooking. The sausage is cooked when it is a rich brown all over. Remove from grill. Cut links lengthwise (split), and squeeze fresh lemon over each link. Serve at once.

Sausages and Peppers with Pesto
Serves 6

2 tablespoons olive oil
12 Italian sausage links, hot,
   sweet or combination
2 large onions, cut in half and
   sliced into thin halfmoons
4 green peppers, sliced into strips
   (use half red peppers if
   available)
2 garlic cloves minced

½ cup red wine
1 can (1 pound, 12 ounces) plum
   tomatoes, drained and chopped
3 tablespoons butter
1 pound mushrooms, quartered
1 cup pesto sauce (see index)
½ cup chopped fresh parsley
2 tablespoons pine nuts

1. Heat oil in a wide, heavy skillet. Prick sausages all over with a fork. Brown over high heat for 5 minutes.

2. Reduce heat somewhat, add onions and cook, stirring, for 5 minutes more.

3. Add peppers and garlic and cook, stirring occasionally, for 5 minutes.

4. Dump contents of skillet into a large colander to drain away fat. Return to skillet and pour in wine.

5. Cook over high heat until wine has cooked away.

6. Toss in tomatoes, reduce heat and simmer until sausages are cooked through and the tomatoes are no longer saucy.

7. Meanwhile, melt butter in a skillet, toss in mushrooms and saute until tender and the mushroom juices have evaporated.

8. Cut the sausages into one inch pieces. Toss in the mushrooms. At the very last minute, stir in the pesto. Mound in a deep platter, sprinkle with parsley and pine nuts and serve at once.

Lasagna
Serves 10

This is a very special lasagna, it uses Fontina cheese in place of Mozzarella, as well as a few other special things; mushrooms sauteed in butter and stirred into the meat sauce at the last minute for smoothness, and eggs beaten into the Ricotta cheese for creaminess. This lasagna is best on the first day, immediately after baking. It is messy to cut and serve because of its extreme creaminess, but the flavor and texture are incomparable. If you wait and reheat it the next day, you will be able to cut and serve your lasagna in neat squares, and it will be quite good, but the flavor and texture will be different from what it was in its glory, the day before. For this recipe, please do not substitute ingredients. Do not use cottage cheese in place of Ricotta, margarine for butter or Mozzarella for Italian Fontina. Use the best quality of everything called for, and serve the lasagna as soon as it is ready.

3 *pounds best quality Italian sausage, removed from casing (half hot, half sweet)*
4 *onions, chopped*
4 *cloves garlic, minced*
2 *large cans Italian plum tomatoes, (1 pound 12 ounces each) drained and chopped*
1 *small can tomato paste*
½ *cup dry vermouth*
1 *teaspoon basil*
1 *teaspoon oregano*

½ *cup fresh chopped parsley*
Pinch of sugar
salt and pepper to taste
½ *cup freshly grated Parmesan cheese*
½ *stick butter*
1 *pound mushrooms, sliced*
1½ *pounds Ricotta cheese*
2 *eggs beaten*
¾ *package lasagna noodles*
2 *cups grated Italian Fontina cheese*

1. Preheat oven to 375 degrees.

2. Saute sausage, onions and garlic in a wide deep dutch oven. Break up the sausage meat with a wooden spoon as it cooks. Drain well in a colander, then return to pot.

3. Add the tomatoes, tomato paste, vermouth, basil, oregano, parsley, sugar, salt and pepper and Parmesan cheese. Bring to a boil, then reduce heat and simmer for about ½ hour. The sauce should be thick.

4. Meanwhile, melt butter, saute mushrooms in the melted butter until soft. Stir the mushrooms into the sauce.

5. Combine the Ricotta cheese and the eggs.

6. Prepare lasagna noodles. Taste to make sure they are al dente—do not let them overcook. Rinse well in cold water and drain.

7. In a shallow rectangular baking dish, spread a very thin layer of sauce. Top with a layer of noodles, then a layer of sauce, Ricotta cheese, and Fontina cheese. Keep repeating ending with noodles, sauce and Fontina cheese.

8. Bake for ½ hour in the preheated oven. Let set for 5 minutes, then serve at once.

Canneloni
12 filled crepes

Italian sausage sauce (see previous recipe, steps 2 through 4)
½ pound Ricotta cheese, pushed through a fine sieve
½ pound Fontina cheese, cut into ½-inch cubes

¼ teaspoon nutmeg
salt and pepper
2 eggs, beaten
½ cup freshly grated Parmesan cheese
12 crepes (see index)

1. Prepare Italian sausage sauce according to directions in lasagna recipe.

2. Preheat oven to 350 degrees.

3. Combine the Ricotta and Fontina cheese in a bowl. Add the nutmeg, salt, pepper, and beaten eggs. Mix it all together very well. Set aside.

4. In a wide, shallow baking dish spread a layer of meat sauce. Sprinkle with half the Parmesan cheese.

5. Place an equal amount (about 1½ tablespoons) of the cheese-egg mixture on each crepe and roll up. Place the filled crepes, seam side down, in a single layer in the baking dish. Cover with the remaining sauce and sprinkle the remaining Parmesan cheese over the top.

6. Bake in the preheated oven for 30 to 40 minutes, or until hot and bubbly.

Choucroute Garnie
Serves 8

This is a wonderful party dish. Corned beef takes the place of the corned pork that is often served with this dish, and is hard to find. Although the sauerkraut must cook for hours, most of that time it is unattended.

1½ quarts fresh sauerkraut
4 tablespoons butter
½ pound sliced bacon, diced coarsely
1 large onion, cut in half and sliced into thin half moons
2 large carrots, scrubbed and sliced
1 Turkish bay leaf or ½ California bay leaf
salt and pepper to taste

¼ cup gin
1 cup dry vermouth
2½ cups chicken stock, approximately
3 pounds fresh bratwurst
3 pounds good quality knockwurst, skinned if necessary
1 freshly cooked corned beef (see index)

1. Preheat oven to 350 degrees.

2. Drain sauerkraut in a colander. Wash thoroughly under cold running water. Squeeze very dry.

3. Melt the butter in a deep, heavy pot that can be covered. Cook the bacon, onions and carrots slowly, covered, in the butter.

4. When the vegetables are tender but not browned (after about 10 minutes), toss in the sauerkraut. Cook, covered, for another 10 minutes.

5. Stir in seasonings, gin and vermouth. Add enough stock to just barely cover the sauerkraut. Cover pot. Simmer in preheated oven for 4 hours, until almost all liquid is absorbed and the sauerkraut mixture is a beautiful, deep amber. Adjust oven temperature down during this time, if necessary, so contents of pot remain at a gentle simmer. It must not boil. Stir sauerkraut every once in a while during this time.

6. When sauerkraut is done, brown bratwurst in a skillet, but don't cook them through. Arrange browned bratwurst and knock-wurst in the bottom of a wide casserole. Top with sauerkraut. Cover casserole.

7. Cook in the 325 degree oven for an additional hour, until bratwurst is cooked through.

8. Arrange the sauerkraut, sausages and sliced corned beef on a platter. Serve with boiled potatoes and interesting mustards.

Rice with Chicken and Sausage, Spanish Style
Serves 6-8

1 chicken, 1½ pounds
1 eggplant, sliced ¼-inch thick
salt
olive oil
1 pound fresh garlic or Italian
*   sausages*
¼ cup olive oil
1 large onion, chopped
2 cloves, garlic, minced
1½ cups raw, long grained rice
2 large summer tomatoes, peeled,
*   seeded, juiced and chopped*
*   (substitute 1 can of drained,*
*   chopped canned tomatoes if*
*   necessary)*

2 green peppers, chopped
½ cup chopped fresh parsley
½ tablespoon fresh thyme (¼
*   teaspoon dried)*
salt and pepper to taste
½ cup sliced, pimiento stuffed,
*   green olives*
1 10 ounce package frozen
*   artichoke hearts, thawed*
2 large tomatoes, peeled and
*   sliced ¼ inch thick*
2 cups grated Gruyere cheese
1 cup whole pimiento stuffed
*   green olives*

1. Simmer chicken in water to cover for 45 minutes to one hour, until tender and succulent. Cool slightly, then pull meat off bones; discard skin. Reserve stock.

2. Meanwhile, preheat oven to 400 degrees. Salt eggplant slices liberally and let stand for ½ hour, then drain and dry. Place them on an oiled baking sheet, brush with more olive oil and place in the oven for 15 minutes or until browned. Set aside.

3. Cook sausages in a heavy skillet, pricking them with a fork as they cook so that they brown nicely in their own fat. Drain, and slice into 1-inch pieces. Set aside.

4. In a heavy skillet, heat olive oil. In it, saute onion and garlic until tender. Add rice and saute for a minute or so. Stir in tomatoes, sausage, green pepper, parsley, thyme, salt, pepper and three cups of stock. (Use reserved stock—add to it if necessary.) Bring to a boil, reduce to a simmer, cover and simmer for 20 mintues or until rice is tender, and liquid is absorbed.

  Stir in chicken, sliced olives and artichoke hearts. Taste and adjust seasonings. Put the mixture into a paella pan or other similarly shaped oven proof casserole. Place the tomato and eggplant slices overlapping around perimeter of dish. Sprinkle with grated cheese. Pile olives in the middle. Place in 400 degree oven for 10-15 minutes or until the cheese is melted and lightly browned, and the whole dish is thoroughly hot.

Red Beans and Sausage, New Orleans Style
Serves 6-8

1 pound red kidney beans
2 quarts cold water
1 large hambone, cracked, or 2
  ham hocks
1 thick slice ham, cubed
2 bunches scallions, sliced
2 onions, coarsely chopped
2 stalks celery, chopped
2 cloves garlic, chopped
several dashes Tabasco sauce
several dashes Lea & Perrins
  Worcestershire sauce

1 Turkish bay leaf, or ½
  California bay leaf
salt and pepper to taste
1 pound hot, smoked sausage,
  sliced
1 bunch scallions, sliced
¼ cup chopped fresh parsley
2 tablespoons olive oil
¾ tablespoon vinegar

1. Wash kidney beans under cold, running water and pick over. Place in a deep pot and cover with water.

2. Add hambone, ham, scallions, onions, celery, garlic, Tabasco sauce, Worcestershire sauce, and bay leaf. Bring to a simmer. Simmer, covered, for 1½ hours, stirring occasionally.

3. Add salt, pepper, and sliced sausage. Simmer for another two hours or more, until the beans are very tender. During the last half hour, as you stir, crush some of the beans against the side of the pot to form a thick, creamy sauce. Remove ham hock or hambone. Cut meat from bone and return to pot. Discard rind, fat, skin, and gristle. Taste and adjust seasonings.

4. Serve beans with fluffy white rice. (These beans taste best on the second day.) When serving, toss together scallions, parsley, oil and vinegar. Top each serving with a tablespoon of the mixture.

Knockwurst Salad
Serves 6

1 pound knockwurst, skinned if
  necessary
mustard vinaigrette (see index)
¼ teaspoon thyme
1 tablespoon capers

1 tablespoon chopped cornichons
½ cup sliced scallions, green and
  white parts
½ cup chopped fresh parsley

1. Slice knockwurst ¼ inch thick.

2. Toss in a bowl with mustard vinaigrette and thyme. Toss in remaining ingredients. Let marinate an hour or so before serving.

Sausage, Potato Ragout
Serves 6

3 tablespoons bacon fat
3 onions, coarsely chopped
2 cloves garlic, minced
2 large green peppers, coarsely
  chopped
2 tablespoons Hungarian paprika
1 teaspoon marjoram
salt and pepper to taste
pinch or 2 of cayenne pepper (to
  taste)

1 large can (1 pound, 12 ounces)
  tomatoes, drained and chopped
5 to 6 medium potatoes, peeled
  and cut into 1-inch cubes
1 to 1½ cups chicken stock
1 pound good quality
  frankfurters, sliced into ½-inch
  pieces
½ cup diced green pepper
½ cup chopped parsley

1. Heat fat in a deep heavy pot. Saute onions, garlic and green pepper until onions are limp and cooked.

2. Stir in paprika, marjoram, salt, pepper and cayenne pepper. Stir for a minute or two, until the vegetables are well coated with the spices. Stir in the tomatoes, potatoes and enough stock to barely cover the contents of the pot. Bring to a boil, reduce heat and simmer, covered until the potatoes are almost done.

3. Stir in the frankfurters and simmer, uncovered, until the potatoes are completely done. Garnish with the diced raw green pepper and parsley.

   This can be made in advance. Do not add diced green pepper and parsley garnish until the dish is ready to be served.

Chinese Sausage and Cabbage
Serves 6

1 pound Chinese pork sausage,
  sliced thinly (available in
  Oriental markets. Do **not** get
  the kind with liver in it)
2 tablespoons peanut oil

2 thin slices ginger root, minced
1 large head green cabbage, cored
  and sliced into strips
salt to taste
¼ cup chicken stock

1. Steam sausage in a colander over boiling water for 15 minutes or until translucent. Set aside.

2. Heat oil in a wok or wide heavy skillet. Add ginger and cabbage and stir-fry until cabbage begins to become tender and lessen in volume, about 4 minutes.

3. Add salt and then sausage. Stir fry a minute or so more.

4. Add stock, bring to a boil, then cover and simmer for 3 or 4 minutes until cabbage is crisp-tender. Serve at once.

Stuffed Cabbage

There are two magic words in my life, the very mention of which sets my mouth to watering, causes my heart to sing, and in general, puts into motion all the other cliches that occur when magic words are uttered. Those two exquisite words are . . . Stuffed Cabbage.

I have never met a stuffed cabbage I didn't like. In fact, I can hardly remember a stuffed cabbage I didn't love. What is it about a homely concoction of cabbage leaves, ground meat, and pinches of this and that, that causes me to lose my culinary cool? I don't know. Why don't you try one of the following recipes yourself and see if bells ring for you.

Stuffed Cabbage, Hungarian Style
15-18 rolls

1 large head cabbage
boiling water
1 jar (1 quart) fresh sauerkraut
8 slices bacon, diced
4 onions, chopped
2 cloves garlic, minced
1 tablespoon Hungarian paprika
salt and pepper to taste
¼ cup rice
1½ pounds lean pork, ground
*   twice*

2 eggs, lightly beaten
¼ teaspoon marjoram
salt and pepper
½ cup tomato puree
½ cup stock or more
2 tablespoons flour
2 cups sour cream, at room
*   temperature*

1. Cut the core out of the cabbage and pull off the tough outer leaves. Cook the cabbage, in enough boiling water to cover, for 5 minutes, until the cabbage leaves begin to separate and become flexible. As they separate pull them out carefully with two wooden spoons or tongs and drain. You should end up with 15 to 18 nice leaves. Spread the drained leaves on paper towels and cover with additional paper towels to drain well.

2. Drain sauerkraut into a colander. Rinse it very well under cold running water, then drain again and squeeze it as dry as possible. Set aside.

3. Cook the diced bacon in a wide, heavy skillet until it begins to render its fat. Add onions and garlic and saute until onions are limp and slightly browned. Stir in paprika, salt, and pepper. Stir over *very* low heat for about 1 minute, so paprika loses its raw taste. Set aside.

4. Parboil rice in water to generously cover, for 10 minutes. Drain and rinse under running hot water. Set aside.

5. Preheat oven to 350 degrees. Place ground pork in a large bowl. Scrape in half of the onion-paprika mixture. Add beaten eggs, marjoram, salt, pepper and rice. Use your hands or a wooden spoon to mix very well.

6. Add the drained, squeezed sauerkraut to the remaining onion-paprika mixture. Stir it around so the sauerkraut is coated with the paprika. Spread half the mixture on the bottom of a baking dish wide enough to hold the cabbage rolls snugly in one layer.

7. Lay a cabbage leaf, curly side down, on a flat surface. With a sharp knife, pare down the tough vein. Turn the leaf so that it is curly side up. Place some of the meat mixture on the leaf, tuck in the ends, and roll to make a neat parcel. Place seam side down on the sauerkraut in the baking dish. Repeat until all the leaves and stuffing are used. Cover the cabbage rolls with the remaining sauerkraut-onion mixture. Combine the tomato puree and stock and pour over the cabbage. Add more stock, if necessary, to just barely cover the cabbage rolls. Cover the baking dish with foil and put into the preheated oven for 2 hours.

8. When done, transfer cabbage rolls to a dish and set aside. Pour sauerkraut and sauce into a saucepan. Whisk the flour into the sour cream. Whisk some of the hot sauce into the sour cream, then whisk the sour cream back into the sauce in the saucepan. Bring to a simmer, stirring, and simmer for 5 minutes or so, until the sauce is thickened, and flour has lost its raw taste.

9. Spread half the sauerkraut and sauce onto the bottom of the baking dish. Place the cabbage rolls on it, seam side down, and cover with remaining sauerkraut and sauce. Cover the dish and refrigerate until it is time to reheat it. (It can stay in the refrigerator for several days—the flavor will only improve.)

10. To reheat, bring the dish to room temperature. Place covered, in 350 degree oven for 45 minutes to 1 hour, until hot and bubbling.

Sweet and Sour Stuffed Cabbage, Jewish Style
approximately 15-18 rolls

1 large head or 2 small heads
  cabbage
boiling water
3 tablespoons fat or oil
2 large onions, chopped
1 large can crushed plum
  tomatoes
1 6-ounce can tomato paste
salt and pepper to taste
3 tablespoons honey
¼ cup fresh lemon juice
½ cup raisins
½ cup dried apricots, diced
3 tablespoons fat or oil
4 onions, chopped
¾ pound veal, ground twice
¾ pound beef, ground twice
¼ teaspoon cinnamon
⅛ teaspoon nutmeg
salt and pepper to taste
2 eggs
⅓ cup matzoh meal or bread
  crumbs

1. Cut the core out of the cabbage and pull off the tough outer leaves. Cook the cabbage, in enough boiling water to cover, for 5 minutes, until the cabbage leaves begin to separate and become flexible. As they separate, pull them out carefully with two wooden spoons or tongs and drain. You should end up with 15 to 18 nice leaves. Spread the drained leaves on paper towels and cover with additional paper towels to drain well. Chop all remaining cabbage and reserve.

2. Make sauce: melt 3 tablespoons fat, cook onions in fat until tender but not browned. Add tomatoes, tomato paste, salt and pepper. Simmer until thick, about ½ hour. Stir in honey, lemon juice, raisins, apricots, and half the reserved chopped cabbage. Taste and adjust seasonings. The sauce should have a nice balance of sweet and sour. Set aside.

3. Make filling: heat 3 tablespoons fat or oil, cook onions in hot fat until tender and browned. Place remaining ingredients in a large bowl. Scrape in the onions and the remaining chopped cabbage. Use your hands to mix it all together very well. Fry a tiny piece and taste it. Adjust seasonings.

4. Preheat oven to 350 degrees.

5. Choose a baking dish wide enough to hold 16 cabbage rolls in one layer. Spread a thin layer of sauce on the bottom of the dish.

6. Lay a cabbage leaf, curly side down, on a flat surface. With a sharp knife, pare down the tough vein. Turn leaf so that it is curly side up. Place some of the meat mixture on the leaf, tuck in the ends and roll to make a neat parcel. Place seam side down on the sauce in the baking dish. Repeat until all the leaves and stuffing are used. (Form any extra stuffing into small meatballs. Brown on

all sides and bake with the cabbage rolls.) Cover the cabbage rolls with the remaining sauce. Cover the baking dish and put into the preheated oven for 2 hours.

To serve, arrange the cabbage rolls on an attractive platter. Serve the sauce, which will be thick and chunky, separately.

Note: this can be prepared several days in advance. The flavor will improve.

Stuffed Cabbage, Italian Style
16-18 rolls

Stuffed cabbage is usually hearty, cold weather fare; this particular version, however, is light, delicate, and summery. Serve it with linguine, cooked al dente, and tossed with olive oil and Parmesan; spoon some of the onion-tomato sauce over the pasta.

1 large head or 2 small heads
  cabbage
boiling water
¾ pound lean beef, ground twice
¾ pound lean veal, ground twice
2 eggs
3 tablespoons chopped fresh
  parsley
½ teaspoon grated nutmeg
¼ cup freshly grated Parmesan
  cheese

⅓ cup fresh bread crumbs
salt and pepper to taste
2 tablespoons olive oil
2 large Vidalia onions (or other
  sweet onions), cut in halves
  and sliced into thin half moons
2 cloves garlic, minced
4 large summer tomatoes, peeled,
  seeded, juiced, and chopped
1 tablespoon chopped fresh basil
salt and pepper to taste

1. Cut the core out of the cabbage and pull off the tough outer leaves. Cook the cabbage in enough boiling water to cover for 5 minutes or so, until the cabbage leaves begin to separate and become flexible. As they separate, pull them out carefully with two wooden spoons or tongs and drain. You should end up with about 18 nice leaves. Spread the drained leaves on paper towels and cover with additional paper towels to dry well.

2. Make stuffing: Combine beef, veal, eggs, parsley, nutmeg, cheese, crumbs, salt and pepper in a large bowl. Mix well with your hands, but do not overhandle it. Fry a tiny piece in a skillet, and taste for seasonings. Adjust seasonings to your liking.

3. Make sauce: Heat 2 tablespoons olive oil. Toss onion and garlic in oil. Cover skillet. Cook over low heat for 10 minutes. Uncover, raise heat a bit, and stir and cook for 5 to 10 minutes more. The onions should be tender but not browned.

4. Stir in tomatoes, basil, salt, and pepper. Simmer over moderate heat for 15 to 20 minutes.

5. Preheat oven to 350 degrees.

6. Choose a shallow baking dish wide enough to hold 18 cabbage rolls in one layer. Oil it lightly with olive oil.

7. Lay a cabbage leaf, curly side down, on a flat surface. With a sharp, small knife, pare down the tough vein. Turn the leaf curly side up. Place some of the meat mixture on the leaf, tuck in the ends, and roll to make a neat parcel. Place seam side down in the baking dish. Repeat until all the leaves and stuffing are used.

8. Cover the cabbage rolls with the tomato sauce. Spread it out over the rolls. Cover the baking dish (with foil if necessary) and bake in the preheated oven for 1 hour. Serve hot with pasta or at room temperature with lemon wedges. May be prepared a day in advance.

Vegetarian Main Dishes

Eggplant Gratin
Serves 6

This is an extraordinary dish, well worth the time and trouble it takes to make it. The garlic sauce is mild and delicious. Serve the gratin with a crisp, green salad or a lightly steamed green vegetable.

2 medium eggplants, sliced into
    ¼ inch thick rounds
salt
1 tablespoon olive oil
1 medium onion, chopped coarsely
2 large cans plum tomatoes,
    drained and crushed with the
    hands
1 teaspoon dried basil, or 1
    tablespoon chopped fresh basil
½ teaspoon dried thyme or 1½
    teaspoons fresh

1 Turkish bay leaf, or ½
    California bay leaf
salt and pepper to taste
60 cloves of garlic
boiling water to cover
chicken or vegetable stock
¼ cup olive oil
4 tablespoons butter
4 tablespoons flour
2½ cups scalded milk
1 egg at room temperature
½ cup grated Parmesan cheese

1. Place eggplant slices in a bowl. Salt liberally and mix with hands to distribute salt. Let stand to sweat for ½ hour.

2. Meanwhile, heat 1 tablespoon olive oil in a heavy pan. Saute onion until limp and golden. Add tomatoes, basil, thyme, bay leaf, salt and pepper. Bring to a boil, reduce heat and simmer, uncovered, for about ½ hour, until the sauce is thick and chunky.

3. Preheat the oven to 400 degrees.

4. Boil the unpeeled garlic cloves in water to cover for 2 minutes. Hit each garlic clove very lightly with a mallet or the flat side of a wide knife. Peel each clove. Place in a small saucepan with stock to cover. Simmer until the garlic becomes very tender and is falling apart, about 45 minutes. Replenish stock as needed. Whirl the garlic and stock in the blender until pureed.

5. Rinse and drain eggplant. Dry the pieces well.

6. Brush a large baking sheet with ¼ cup olive oil. Place in oven until oil is hot. Place eggplant slices on hot pan: Bake for 25 to 30 minutes. Check them frequently—they must not get burnt or crisp. Turn slices with tongs after 15 minutes. Add more oil if necessary. When soft, golden, and cooked, drain and blot on paper towels. Reduce oven temperature to 350 degrees.

7. Make sauce: Heat 4 tablespoons butter in a heavy saucepan. Whisk in flour. Let this roux cook over low heat, stirring constantly, for 3 to 4 minutes. Whisk in scalded milk. Cook gently, stirring frequently for 10-15 minutes. Add salt and pepper, and stir in garlic puree. Remove from heat. Beat egg. Beat some of the hot sauce into the egg. Beat egg mixture back into garlic sauce. Taste and correct seasoning.

8. Place half the eggplant slices on the bottom of a 2 quart lasagna pan or gratin dish. Spread with tomato mixture. Place the rest of the eggplant slices over the tomatoes. Pour the garlic cream sauce over the whole thing. Sprinkle with grated Parmesan cheese.

9. Bake in 350 degree oven until golden brown and bubbling, 45 minutes to 1 hour.

Grandma Grosso's Eggplant Parmigiana
Serves 8

2 medium eggplants, sliced ⅛
   inch thick
salt
4 beaten eggs
½ cup flour

2½ cups bread crumbs
½ cup olive oil, approximately
tomato sauce (see below)
2 cups grated Provolone cheese
1 cup grated Romano cheese

1. Toss the eggplant slices with a liberal amount of salt, place in a large colander and cover with wax paper. Weight with a heavy object. Let stand to drain for at least an hour, until no more liquid exudes from the slices.

2. Preheat oven to 350 degrees.

3. Beat eggs lightly in a large, shallow bowl. Set on your work surface.

4. Mix flour and breadcrumbs. Spread on a platter. Set next to eggs.

5. Dip drained eggplant slices in egg, then in bread crumb mix. Leave on a rack until all are dipped and breaded.

6. Heat oil in a wide, heavy skillet. Fry breaded eggplant until well browned on both sides. Add oil as necessary. Drain on paper towels.

7. Spread some sauce on the bottom of a lasagna pan. Arrange some eggplant slices on sauce. Sprinkle with cheeses. Continue layering until all ingredients are used, ending with sauce and cheese.

8. Bake in the preheated oven for 20 to 30 minutes until piping hot, browned and bubbly.

   This dish can be made several days ahead of time. It also freezes beautifully.

Tomato Sauce

1 tablespoon olive oil
4 cloves garlic, minced
2 large cans (1 pound 12 ounces
   each) Italian plum tomatoes,
   drained and mashed with the
   hands
1 6 ounce can tomato paste

½ cup red wine
1 tablespoon fresh basil (if
   available)
salt and pepper to taste (go easy
   on the salt, the eggplant will be
   salty)

1. Heat oil in a sauce pan. Saute garlic lightly in oil, but don't let it brown. Add tomatoes and all remaining ingredients.

2. Simmer for ½ hour, partially covered.

Chef Louis' Zucchini Fish
Serves 4

When I went to Chicago to meet King Tut several years ago, I also met Chef Louis Szathmary; two legendary characters in one day. King Tut I met through 55 dazzling artifacts at the Field Museum; Chef Louis in his offices above the Bakery, his famous restaurant in Chicago. The King Tut exhibit was wonderful—his gold and jewels were dazzling—but Chef Louis was definitely the more interesting of the two. Although he came here from Europe some years ago with a Ph.D. in psychology from the University of Budapest and experience as a journalist, he is now thoroughly ensconced in the food business as a restaurateur, a consultant, a cookbook author and a columnist.

Chef Louis gave me the zucchini fish recipe, and the cauliflower paprikash that follows. Cooking is creative and satisfying in many ways, but it is fun above all; zucchini fish stresses the fun. The fish are a sort of culinary witticism; zucchini trimmed and cut into the shape of fish, breaded and then fried. As a "fish" dinner, they are amusing and very delicious. When you cook zucchini fish, invite the rest of your family or some friends to prepare it with you. They should get into the spirit of things by carving up a good catch; sharks, whales, dolphins, whatever comes to mind. It's marvelous kitchen therapy and the whole zany operation fosters a great sense of cooking camaraderie. And of course, when the fish are to be served, be sure to tell the dinner guests about the ones that got away.

4 young zucchini approximately 6 to 7 inches long, 1½ inches in diameter
salt and pepper to taste
approximately ½ cup all-purpose flour
1 whole egg beaten with 1 tablespoon cold water
1 cup fine dry bread crumbs
¾ to 1 cup oil for frying

1. Split zucchini lengthwise. Discard two thin slices from the middle where it is soft and pulpy. Trim the halves lengthwise to approximately ⅜ inch thickness so you have two flat pieces. With a sharp paring knife cut each into the shape of a fish.

2. Sprinkle the fish shaped zucchini pieces with salt and pepper, coat with the flour, shake it, then dip into the egg wash, finally in the bread crumbs.

3. When they are all breaded, fry them in hot oil for about a minute to a side or until golden brown.

Place on absorbent paper to drain. Serve at once with lemon.

Chef Louis' Cauliflower Paprikash
Serves 4

1 head firm white cauliflower, 1½
  to 2 pounds
1 tablespoon corn oil
1 tablespoon butter
4 tablespoons finely minced onion
2 tablespoons Hungarian paprika
1 tomato peeled, seeded and
  chopped
⅓ cup finely chopped green
  pepper

3 tablespoons flour
1 cup tomato puree mixed with 1
  cup warm water
salt to taste
1 quart water with 1 tablespoon
  salt
2 cups sour cream at room
  temperature

1. Wash and drain cauliflower, breaking it into flowerets about as large as a lime.

2. In a heavy pot or saucepan, melt fat, add onions and cook, stirring for about a minute over high heat. Lower heat to medium, cover and cook for 2 or 3 minutes, stirring occasionally. Remove cover, increase heat to high again, add half the paprika, quickly stir it in and add chopped tomato and green pepper. Lower heat to medium, cover pot and cook for another 3 minutes.

3. Meanwhile, with a small whisk stir flour into tomato puree. Mixture should not be lumpy. (The best way is to add the liquid to the flour and whisk constantly.) Add salt and stir mixture into pot with whisk.

4. Drop cauliflower pieces into rapidly boiling salted water, bring to a boil again and boil vigorously, uncovered, for about 1 minute. Drain and gently stir cauliflower into paprika sauce. Cover and simmer over low heat for 20 minutes, stirring occasionally and being careful it doesn't scorch. If you prefer, bake in a preheated 350-degree oven for 30 minutes, stirring only once very gently.

5. Before serving, ladle some of the paprika sauce into sour cream, stir and add remaining paprika. Add this to cauliflower mixture and fold it in. Transfer to a serving platter. Surround it with elbow macaroni or wide noodles. Sprinkle with freshly chopped parsley or snipped dill weed and serve at once.

Chapter 5

Vegetables, Salads, Dressings

Vegetables

Stuffed Artichoke
Serves 6

One's first sight of an artichoke at the dinner table can be intimidating, but even though at first the whole process may seem a bit bizarre, eating an artichoke is one of life's pleasures.

An artichoke contains, over its heart, a fuzzy choke of prickly, unpleasant texture. It is not edible and should be removed during the cooking process. After removal of the choke, the artichoke can be stuffed with any one of a number of stuffings, and baked until tender but not falling apart. My favorite artichoke stuffing is a combination of bread, mint, garlic, and parsley.

When faced at the table with this steamy, fragrant, stuffed thing, stay calm. Begin picking off the leaves one by one with your fingers. Place each leaf in your mouth with the tender meaty part against your upper teeth. Pull against your teeth to scrape off and eat that tender meat. Discard the scraped leaf. (A bowl or plate should be provided on the table for the litter of discarded leaves).

When each leaf has been scraped of its tender portion, you will find yourself at the heart. In a restaurant, it is often necessary to dechoke it yourself at this point. The heart is the prize, your reward for bravely eating your way through a thistle in the first place. (Yes, the artichoke is a member of the thistle family). The heart can be eaten easily with a knife and fork and is, indeed, delicious.

I think it was Kingsley Amis, the English novelist, who suggested that an artichoke uses up more calories in the eating than it contributes. Unfortunately, this has no basis in fact but it must be admitted that eating an artichoke is a lot of work for the diner. It's worth it, however, as you will see.

6 artichokes
acidulated water: large bowl of
   water, mixed with lemon juice
   or vinegar
6 quarts boiling water in a
   non-reactive pot
¾ cup chopped fresh parsley
1 tablespoon crumbled mint or
   3 tablespoons fresh, chopped

2 slices good white bread,
   trimmed of crusts and crumbled
2 to 3 large cloves garlic, minced
⅓ cup olive oil
Salt and pepper to taste
stock
2 tablespoons olive oil
lemon wedges

1. Cut off artichoke stem and trim its base so that it can stand upright. Dip cut edges in acidulated water to prevent discoloration. Snap off tough outer leaves. Slice an inch off the top of each artichoke and dip in acidulated water again. With scissors, trim the pointy tips from all the leaves. Dip again.

2. Immerse the artichokes in the boiling water. Drape a piece of doubled cheesecloth over the pot so that it covers the artichokes and keeps them wet. (They tend to bob and float). Boil, uncovered, except for the cloth, for 10 minutes. Drain and cool slightly.

3. Preheat oven to 350 degrees.

4. Spread open the leaves of each artichoke. Pull out the cluster of pale yellowish, purply leaves covering the heart. With a teaspoon, scrape out and discard all the prickly, hairy choke covering the heart.

5. Mix thoroughly the parsley, mint, bread, garlic, oil, salt, and pepper. Put some stuffing into the center of each artichoke. Stuff any remaining stuffing between the big outer leaves. Arrange the artichokes in a baking dish that will hold them snugly in one layer. Pour in stock to the depth of two inches. Sprinkle with 2 tablespoons olive oil. Cover baking dish with foil. Bake for 40 minutes to 1 hour, or until the base of each artichoke is very tender when pierced with the tip of a sharp knife. Serve hot with the pan juices, or cold with lemon wedges.

Asparagus

Long stemmed roses and clever bouquets of springtime flowers are charming, but not nearly as welcome as fat bunches of perfect asparagus. Green vegetable haters look at asparagus and mutter— like the little boy in the New Yorker cartoon—"I say it's spinach and I say the hell with it"; they are missing one of life's great pleasures. I must admit, though, that when asparagus is out of a can or frozen or improperly cooked, I say the hell with it, too.

Fresh springtime asparagus is much too good to serve with other things; it deserves to be presented in solitary magnificence as a separate course. Plan to serve overflowing platters of perfectly cooked stalks with bowls of bearnaise or hollandaise sauce for dipping purposes. Eat the stalks with your fingers, dipping each one into the sauce between bites. This method of serving and eating asparagus is so wonderful that I often do it as a springtime meal-in-itself with no following course—it's a pity to clutter up an exquisite asparagus happening with roasts or cutlets.

To cook the stalks perfectly, they must be peeled first. This sort of dogmatic culinary declaration inevitably produces groans of complaint and outraged assertations—"Why, I've been cooking asparagus for 40 years and I've never peeled it yet!"—but I assure you that peeling first makes all the difference in the world. Peeled asparagus can be cooked very quickly; it retains a heavenly crunch and lack of fibrousness that is impossible in an unpeeled stalk. Cut off the tough woody portion of each stalk, and then peel the trimmed stalk with a swivel-blade vegetable peeler, from the bottom up to the buds. If the bunch of peeled, trimmed asparagus must wait an hour or so before cooking, stand it in a glass of water, as if it were a bunch of flowers. To cook it properly, use one of the following methods:

1. Take a glass ceramic coffee pot (not metal, please) and partially fill it with water. Bring it to a boil.

Meanwhile, tie your trimmed, peeled asparagus in a bundle, using kitchen string. Leave one stalk out of the bundle as a test piece. When the water boils, stand the bundle and the test piece in the water so that the tips are not submerged. If the coffee pot is too full, empty out some water.

Partially cover the pot and reduce the heat to a brisk simmer. Simmer for 3 to 7 minutes (depending on size), no more. Let the test piece be your guide. The vegetable should still have some crunch (crisp-tender is the convenient expression usually applied). Then drain well, blot on paper towels, and serve at once with lemon juice, melted butter, and freshly ground pepper, or bearnaise sauce or hollandaise sauce.

2. If you don't have a glass ceramic coffee pot, you might want to try a shallow skillet. Fill it with some water, less than halfway. Bring to a boil. Spread the trimmed, peeled asparagus on the bottom of the skillet, reduce the heat to a brisk simmer, and partially cover the skillet. Again, simmer for 3 to 7 minutes only. Drain and serve as described above.

3. If you have a steamer, this method is the best way of all to cook asparagus: place the peeled, trimmed stalks in the steamer basket. Steam over boiling water for 3 to 7 minutes, until crisp-tender. Drain and serve, as above.

4. To serve asparagus as a vegetable accompaniment, for the times when you tire of total asparagus feasts, try stir-frying.

Peel and trim the asparagus and cut each stalk into 1-inch lengths. Heat some unsalted butter and peanut oil in a wide, heavy nonreactive skillet or wok. When hot, throw in the asparagus and toss it in the hot fat for one minute. Squeeze in the juice of ½ a lime, a pinch each of thyme and tarragon, and salt and freshly ground pepper to taste. Stir-fry for a minute or so more and serve at once. This should be very crisp.

Asparagus Milanese
Serves 4

2 pounds fresh asparagus
¾ cup freshly grated Parmesan cheese

salt and pepper to taste
½ cup butter
4 eggs

1. Preheat oven to 200 degrees.

2. Trim and peel asparagus and cook it according to method 1, 2, or 3.

3. Butter a shallow baking dish. Spread half of the cooked, hot asparagus in the dish and scatter half the Parmesan over it. Spread the remaining asparagus over the cheese and sprinkle with the remaining cheese. Season to taste. Place in the oven to keep warm.

4. Melt butter in a wide, heavy skillet. Fry the eggs in the butter very gently. They should just poach in the butter—you do not want tough, burnt, and frazzled whites. When the whites are set but the yolks are still soft, slide the eggs, butter and all, onto the asparagus in the baking dish, and serve at once.

Each diner gets a pile of asparagus, a puddle of butter and an egg. It does not hurt to eat this asparagus with the fingers—dabble each stalk delicately in the butter and egg yolk, and then eat blissfully.

Asparagus with Proscuitto
Serves 4-8

48 stalks fresh asparagus
8 slices proscuitto
⅔ cup melted butter

1 cup freshly grated Parmesan
cheese

1. Preheat oven to 350 degrees.

2. Trim and peel the asparagus, and cook according to method 1, 2, or 3.

3. Butter a shallow baking dish. Wrap 6 of the cooked stalks in each slice of proscuitto. Place, seam side down, in the buttered dish. Pour the melted butter over the rolls and sprinkle with Parmesan. Place in the oven and cook until thoroughly hot, about 15 minutes. Serve at once.

Note: for a very festive springtime brunch, combine this dish with the preceding Asparagus Milanese. Each diner gets a proscuitto-wrapped bundle and a fried egg-topped bundle. It makes a feast that satisfies the most fanatic asparagus lovers.

Chinese Dry Fried Green Beans
Serves 6

1 cup peanut oil
1½ pounds green beans, trimmed
½ pound ground lean pork
1 scallion, sliced thinly
1 clove garlic, minced
1 thin slice ginger root, minced
2 teaspoons sugar

1 teaspoon cider vinegar
2 tablespoons soy sauce
salt to taste
1 teaspoon hot pepper paste
    or shredded hot peppers
    (more or less to taste)
few drops sesame oil

1. Heat oil in a wok. When very hot, throw in the green beans. Stir them in the hot oil for 5 to 8 minutes, or until they are slightly shriveled. Drain very well and pour away oil. (Oil may be reused at a later time). Set beans aside in a colander to drain.

2. Throw the ground pork, scallion, garlic, and ginger root into the wok and cook, stirring over high heat, for 2 to 3 minutes, until the pork is cooked. Drain and discard the fat that has been rendered from the pork.

3. Add the beans and pork back to the wok. Add sugar, vinegar, soy sauce, salt and hot pepper paste and cook, stirring, for one minute more. Add a few drops of sesame oil and serve at once.

Green Beans in Tomato Cream
Serves 6

2 pounds green beans, trimmed
4 tablespoons butter
1 large onion, cut in half and
  sliced thinly into half moons
1 green pepper, cut in half, and
  sliced thinly
5 tomatoes, peeled, seeded, juiced,
  and diced (use canned if good
  fresh ones are out of season)

½ cup chopped parsley
2 tablespoons chopped fresh basil
salt and pepper to taste
1 tablespoon flour
1 cup sour cream, at room
  temperature

1. Steam the beans over boiling water until crisp-tender, about 5 to 7 minutes. Rinse under cold water and drain well.

2. Melt butter in a heavy skillet. In it, saute the onion and green pepper until tender.

3. Add tomatoes and toss and cook until they begin to render their juices. Add beans, parsley, basil, salt, and pepper. Cook briefly, until it is all piping hot.

4. Whisk flour into sour cream. Stir some hot liquid from the skillet into the sour cream, then stir cream mixture into the vegetables in the skillet. Simmer for 5 minutes. Taste and adjust seasonings.
  Serve at once.

Cabbage in Wine
Serves 6

4 tablespoons butter
1 green cabbage, cored, halved,
  and sliced into thin strips

salt and pepper to taste
1 cup dry white wine
pinch sugar (optional)

1. Heat butter in heavy skillet.

2. Add cabbage and toss to coat with butter.

3. Add salt, pepper and wine. Cook over high heat until wine has reduced considerably and cabbage is tender but not mushy. Taste and correct seasonings. Add sugar if taste is too acid.
  Serve at once.

Cabbage Flan
Serves 6-8

1/4 pound butter
1 large green cabbage, cored,
   halved and sliced into strips
   (about 6 cups)

2 cups whipping cream
1/2 teaspoon nutmeg
salt and pepper to taste
5 eggs, lightly beaten

1. Preheat oven to 350 degrees.

2. Heat butter in a deep, heavy pot. Toss the cabbage in the hot butter until it is crisp-tender. It will greatly reduce in volume. Place cabbage in a quiche dish.

3. Beat cream, nutmeg, salt, and pepper into eggs. Pour the mixture over the cabbage. Bake in preheated oven for about 45 minutes or until golden brown and set. (A knife inserted near the center will emerge clean). Serve at once.

Carrots in Wine
Serves 6

1/4 cup butter or oil
1 medium onion, cut in half, and
   sliced into thin half moons
2 pounds carrots, scraped and
   sliced thinly

salt and pepper to taste
1/2 cup cream sherry
1 tablespoon chopped fresh parsley

1. Heat butter in a deep heavy skillet. Saute onion until it begins to get limp.

2. Stir in the carrots and cook, stirring, for 2 or 3 minutes.

3. Season with salt and pepper and pour in the wine. Bring to a boil, reduce heat, and simmer covered, for about 15 minutes, until the carrots are tender but not mushy. Stir in parsley and serve hot.

Heinz's Honeyed Carrot Shreds
Serves 4

2 tablespoons butter
1 teaspoon honey

2 cups julienned carrots
salt to taste

1. Melt butter in a heavy skillet. Stir in honey, and let the butter and honey cook together gently for one minute.

2. Stir carrots into honey-butter mixture. Toss and stir the carrots for one minute. Add salt to taste. Serve at once.

Cauliflower with Fontina
Serves 4-6

*1 head cauliflower, trimmed and
   separated into flowerets
boiling water
1 tablespoon butter*

*⅓ cup whipping cream
salt and pepper to taste
1 cup grated Italian Fontina
   cheese (about ¼ pound)*

1. Steam cauliflower over boiling water for 2 or 3 minutes, until partially cooked but still quite crunchy. Refresh under cold, running water and set aside.

2. Heat butter in a heavy skillet that can be covered. Toss cauliflower in the butter, over medium heat, until heated through and beginning to brown. (Do not let the butter burn). Pour in cream and boil rapidly, stirring all the while, until the cream is reduced by about half and thickened. Add salt and pepper to taste.

3. Reduce heat, sprinkle on cheese and cover skillet. Let sit over lowest heat for 3 or 4 minutes, until the cheese has melted and melded with the cream into a delicious sauce. Serve at once.

Cauliflower Mornay
Serves 8

*2 heads cauliflower, trimmed and
   cut into flowerets
2 cups mornay sauce (see index)*

*1 cup grated Swiss cheese
½ cup bread crumbs
pinch cayenne pepper*

1. Preheat oven to 375 degrees.

2. Steam cauliflower over boiling salted water until crisp-tender.

3. When cooked, but not overcooked, drain cauliflower in colander, and run cold water over it to stop the cooking. Dry on paper towels.

4. Fold cauliflower and mornay sauce together. Scrape cauliflower and sauce into a shallow baking dish. Cover with grated cheese and bread crumbs. Sprinkle with just a bit of cayenne pepper.

5. Place in preheated oven, uncovered, for about 30 minutes, or until browned and bubbly.

Sauteed Cucumbers
Serves 6

5 medium cucumbers
salt
3 tablespoons butter
½ teaspoon dried tarragon
  (1½ teaspoons fresh)

1 tablespoon fresh chopped
  parsley
salt and pepper to taste

1. Peel the cucumbers, cut them in half lengthwise and scrape out the seeds with a teaspoon. Slice the cucumbers about ½ inch thick. Place them in a nonmetallic bowl and salt them liberally. Let them stand to sweat for ½ hour. Rinse and dry the cucumbers.

2. Heat the butter in a wide, heavy skillet. Toss the cucumbers in the butter over medium heat, for about 3 minutes, then add the remaining ingredients. Continue tossing and cooking for an additional 2 or 3 minutes, or until the cucumbers are cooked but still slightly crisp. Serve at once.

Braised Leeks
Serves 6

12 large leeks, all the same size
1 cup well seasoned chicken stock
¼ cup dry white wine

4 tablespoons butter
salt and pepper to taste

1. Preheat oven to 350 degrees.

2. Trim leeks—cut off tip and beard; cut off and put aside most of the green portion (save it for stocks), leaving just 1 inch of green on the leeks. Peel off the outer layer of fiber.

3. With a sharp knife, slash through part of the white bulb and up through the remaining green portion. Wash leeks well under cold running water, holding them apart at the slash to wash away sand. Dry each leek.

4. Place leeks in 1 layer in a shallow, buttered baking dish. Pour the stock and wine over the leeks and dot with butter. Season with salt and pepper. Cover the baking dish tightly.

5. Bake leeks in the preheated oven for ½ hour.

6. Uncover the baking dish. Raise oven temperature to 450 degrees and cook leeks for an additional 15 minutes. Turn the leeks with tongs and cook for 5 to 10 minutes more. They should be browned and tender but not falling apart. Pour cooking juices into a saucepan. Keep leeks warm. Boil liquid rapidly until reduced by ⅔. Pour over leeks and serve.

Mushrooms

Mushrooms are fungi, sprouting mysteriously in meadows and woods, offering a sort of culinary Russian roulette to those who dare to pick and eat them. Of the thousands of mushroom species that grow, some are delicious and wholesome, some bitterly unpleasant but harmless, some mildly toxic, and a few (the infamous *amanita phalloides*, for instance), deadly. Because of the difficulties involved in differentiating safe fungi from fatal, most mushroom fanciers feast on morels, chanterelles, ceps and field mushrooms only in their dreams. When the time comes for an actual mushroom feast a trip to the supermarket yields lovely blue-lined baskets of *agaricus bisporus;* although they lack the glamour and romance of mushrooms gathered at dawn, they are familiar, delicious, and quite safe.

Despite their lack of glamour, it would be unwise to dismiss the common, cultivated *agaricus* as mundane; it has a compelling earthy taste and a bitey tenderness of texture that make it very special. When purchasing the mushrooms, look for unblemished firm caps that are as tightly closed as possible underneath so that the grayish-brown gills are not exposed. Store the mushrooms in the refrigerator unwashed, in a loosely covered basket or in a plastic bag that has had a few holes punched in it. Mushrooms that remain closely covered soon become slimy. When you are about to use your mushrooms, do not wash them in an abundance of water, as they will soak it up like a sponge, only to later deposit it in your sauce. Wipe them with a damp towel, or if they need more vigorous cleaning, rinse them quickly under cold, running water and then dry at once. Trim the tough tips of the stems, and the mushrooms are ready for use. Never peel them. Canned mushrooms are a culinary abomination and are certainly no substitute for the real thing; don't even think of using them.

Carbo's Burgundy Mushrooms
Serves 2

A lovely mushroom dish from Carbo's Restaurant in Atlanta. Serve it as a separate course with crusty bread to soak up the juices, or as an accompaniment to grilled beef.

1½ tablespoons butter	½ teaspoon flour
1½ tablespoons oil	pinch thyme
2 tablespoons diced onions	salt and pepper to taste
15 medium whole mushrooms, stemmed (save stems for soups, stews, or duxelles)	½ cup Burgundy wine chopped parsley

1. Heat butter and oil in a heavy skillet. Add onions and saute until tender and browned.

2. Add mushrooms, flour, thyme, salt, and pepper. Continue to saute for 2 minutes more.

3. Add wine and let reduce by about half. Pour into serving dish. Sprinkle with parsley.

Russian Mushrooms
Serves 4

These mushrooms serve as a sauce for hamburgers, veal, chicken, or steaks, or—if the amount of sour cream is reduced—they can be ladeled over crisp toast as a delicious first course, light lunch or light supper.

½ ounce European-style dried mushrooms
½ cup hot water
3 tablespoons butter
1 pound fresh mushrooms, trimmed and sliced
1 onion, cut in half and thinly sliced into half-moons

½ to 1 tablespoon flour
1 to 2 cups sour cream, at room temperature (Use the greater amount if you plan to use the mixture as a sauce.)
salt and pepper to taste

1. Rinse dried mushrooms and soak in hot water for at least two hours. Drain and reserve the water. Strain the water if it is gritty. Trim off any tough stems and chop the dried mushrooms.

2. Melt butter in a heavy skillet. Saute fresh mushrooms and onions until the mushrooms begin to render their juices. Add chopped dried mushrooms. Simmer until quite a lot of liquid is in the pan. Add mushroom soaking liquid to the skillet and bring to a boil.

3. Whisk flour into sour cream. Stir some hot liquid from the skillet into the sour cream. Then pour the cream into mushrooms, stirring constantly. Simmer, stirring, until the mixture is thick and hot. Season to taste.

Curried Mushrooms
Serves 4-6

4 tablespoons clarified butter
2 pounds fresh mushrooms,
   trimmed and sliced
2 onions, thinly sliced
2 cloves garlic, minced
5 canned Italian plum tomatoes,
   drained and chopped

¼ teaspoon each: ground cumin,
   cinnamon, coriander
cayenne pepper to taste
pinch ground cloves
½ teaspoon turmeric
salt to taste

1. Saute mushrooms in hot butter with onion and garlic, until soft (about 5 minutes).

2. Add tomatoes and stir.

3. Add spices. Stir to coat thoroughly.

4. Cook for about 5 minutes at high heat until almost all liquid has cooked down. Serve as an accompaniment to curries.

Mr. Ma's Mushrooms
Serves 6-8

One evening, I complained to Frank Ma, owner of the Hunan Restaurant in Sandy Springs, that most Chinese restaurants, whatever their quality, use canned mushrooms. On my next visit he surprised me with a heaping platter of these mushrooms—a sort of Chinese version of mushrooms a la Grecque.

3 pounds small mushrooms,
   cleaned and trimmed of any
   woody stems
2 cups chicken stock
½ cup dry sherry
½ cup soy sauce

2½ tablespoons sugar
2 peeled cloves garlic
1 thin slice ginger root, peeled
sesame oil

1. Place mushrooms in a deep, heavy pot. They will greatly reduce as they cook, so don't worry if they overfill the pot. Add all remaining ingredients.

2. Bring to a boil. Reduce to a brisk simmer and cook, uncovered, stirring occasionally, until the mushrooms are deep mahogany brown and the liquid is greatly reduced.

3. Remove mushrooms to a bowl. Boil down remaining liquid until almost a glaze in the pan. Pour over mushrooms. Sprinkle with a few drops of sesame oil. Serve hot or at room temperature.

Duxelles
About 3 cups

Not all hashes are made out of cooked meats. Duxelles, one of the most famous and useful hashes in culinary literature is made from mushrooms; it is a rich, flavorful mixture that freezes well, and lends itself to all sorts of interesting uses. The classic recipe for duxelles directs the cook to squeeze the hashed raw mushrooms in the corner of a kitchen towel in order to extract all moisture. This practice has always horrified me, not only does the moisture get squeezed away, but a good deal of the flavor as well. My version eliminates this step and calls for rapid boiling of the mushrooms and their juices instead. The result is a highly flavored mushroom hash, suitable for omelets, crepes, quiches, stuffed mushrooms, sauces, or whatever else your imagination indicates. You do not need the freshest, whitest mushrooms with tightly closed caps for duxelles; older mushrooms that have begun to open and darken will give the hash a better, more intense flavor. Once they have turned slimy, however, they are unfit for consumption, so check them before you buy.

4 tablespoons butter
3 tablespoons corn oil
2 pounds mushrooms, (or 2
  pounds mushroom stems),
  cleaned, trimmed, and minced

3 tablespoons Madeira
¼ cup whipping cream
salt and pepper to taste

1. Heat butter and oil in a deep heavy skillet. Add mushrooms and toss them in the hot fat until they are limp, and begin to exude their liquid. As they cook, they will greatly reduce in volume.

2. Add Madeira and cream. Cook over high heat, stirring occasionally until almost all liquid is gone.

3. Add salt and pepper to taste. Lower heat, and cook until all liquid is absorbed and the mushrooms are dry. Be careful not to scorch them.

Browned Onions

These will keep in the refrigerator for a week or more. They are good as a base for stews and soups, and wonderful on hamburgers or in crepes and omelets.

1 cup clarified butter or
1 cup rendered chicken fat or
1 cup corn oil

3 pounds onions, cut in half and
thinly sliced into half moons

1. Preheat oven to 350 degrees.

2. Combine melted fat and onions in a shallow, wide baking dish.

3. Bake, uncovered, for about 1½ hours or until deeply browned but not burnt or crisp. Stir occasionally during this time. Store in the refrigerator.

Savory Onion-Noodle Kugel
Serves 8

½ pound wide egg noodles
½ cup butter
4 cloves garlic, chopped coarsely
4 large onions, chopped coarsely
4 eggs, separated, at room
temperature

½ pound creamed cottage cheese,
at room temperature
1 cup sour cream, at room
temperature
salt and pepper to taste
pinch of cream of tartar

1. Preheat oven to 350 degrees.

2. Cook noodles to the al dente stage.

3. Meanwhile, melt butter, cook the garlic and onions slowly in the hot butter until deeply golden brown, but not burnt.

4. Drain noodles, rinse, and drain again. Toss in a large bowl with butter-onion mixture.

5. Beat egg yolks. Beat in cheese, sour cream, and a liberal amount of salt and pepper. Stir mixture into noodles.

6. In a clean bowl, with a clean beater, beat egg whites, with cream of tartar until they form stiff peaks. Fold beaten whites into noodle mixture.

7. Pour into a buttered 1½-quart shallow baking dish. Bake in preheated oven for 40 to 45 minutes, or until puffed and golden.
    Serve at once.

Baked Vidalia Onions

Vidalias take well to being baked, like potatoes. This is the simplest of dishes, but very satisfying. It's the kind of thing you find yourself suddenly longing for, in the middle of the winter, when Vidalia season seems far away.

1. Preheat oven to 375 degrees.

2. Wash 1 Vidalia onion for each person you plan to serve.

3. Place unpeeled onions in a shallow baking dish. Bake for 1 to 1½ hours, until onions are tender, but still retain a hint of crispness.

4. When tender, cut a small slice from each of the onions, and slip the skins off.

Serve hot, with plenty of sweet butter, salt and pepper, or cold with lemon juice and olive oil.

Potatoes

Sometime in the sixteenth century, a gastronomically-minded Spanish sailor brought a batch of potatoes home to Europe from the Highlands of the Andes. As often happened with foodstuffs from the New World, the earthy, delicious tubers were met with reactions of revulsion and distrust. People throughout Europe refused to have anything to do with the potatoes; they were believed to be evil, decadent and as poisonous as deadly nightshade. Over the years, three important influences helped to establish potatoes as a delicious and wholesome food; Frederick the Great sent the armed military into a small Prussian town to forcibly teach the starving peasants to eat potatoes; August Parmentier served elegant French potato feasts to the elite of several continents and presented Marie Antoinette with potato blossoms to wear in her hair; and the Irish—the first to accept the mysterious tuber—flourished on their potatoes, until the entire crop was decimated by the tragic blight of 1846.

Today we eat potatoes as a matter of course with no thought at all of their turbulent history. They appear as an integral part of many meals, whether it's a fast food hamburger with fries, something gravyish with mashed, or a steak with baked.

Baked Potatoes

Baked potatoes are a true delicacy; I have always felt they were far too good to be relegated to the status of an accompaniment. When properly made, a steamy, floury, butter drenched potato can stand on its own. To do it correctly, wash the potato well; rub it with oil or butter if you want a soft skin, or leave it dry if you prefer it crisp; pierce it in a few places with a fork or a thin skewer, and bake it directly on the oven shelf at 400 degrees for 45 minutes to an hour. Never wrap it in foil or it will steam rather than bake. The potato is done when it yields softly to a gentle squeeze. When done, split it open by perforating it lengthwise and breadthwise with a fork and then pinching open. Insert a lump of sweet butter, a dollop of sour cream, a shower of grated Gruyere, a knob of Boursin cheese, a spoonful or so of caviar, a scattering of crumbled bacon, some mustard, whipped cream cheese mashed with chopped smoked salmon, or whatever else takes your fancy. A lovely, informal dinner for friends might consist of a big, napkin-lined basket of crisp baked potatoes and an array of bowls containing all those things that go so well in the potatoes. The guests split their own potatoes and insert their own filling. Make sure that you use the big, oblong, Idaho bakers; they are the best for baking and mashing. The smaller waxy potatoes are for boiling and re-frying as hash browns.

Perfect Fries

These are easy to make and invariably delicious; the "frying" is done in a very hot oven.

Large baking potatoes, peeled and cut into ¾-inch cubes (As you peel and cube each potato, drop the cubes into a bowl of cold water to avoid discoloration.)

mixture of olive oil and peanut oil
salt

1. Preheat oven to 450 degrees.

2. Pour oil into a shallow roasting pan to a depth of about ¼ of an inch. Heat to smoking in the preheated oven. Drain and dry the potatoes.

3. Carefully spread the well dried potatoes in the hot oil (if they are all wet, they will splatter.) Let bake for 35 to 45 minutes, stirring occasionally, until golden brown and crisp on the outside.

4. Scoop potatoes out of pan with a slotted spoon. Drain well on paper towels, sprinkle with salt and serve at once.

Roesti *(Swiss Fried Potato Cake)*
Serves 6

4 large baking potatoes   *salt and pepper to taste*
water to cover   *3 tablespoons hot water*
¼ pound butter

1. Boil potatoes in water to cover, until tender but not falling apart, about 30 minutes.

2. Drain and cool in the refrigerator, preferably overnight.

3. Peel potatoes and shred them into long strips, as long as possible, using the large holes on a grater.

4. Melt butter in a large well seasoned cast iron or enameled skillet that can be covered. Add potatoes and seasoning and stir gently with a spatula until butter is absorbed.

5. Lightly press potatoes down in the pan with the spatula. Sprinkle the hot water over the potatoes and cover the skillet.

6. Cook over a moderately low light for 30 to 45 minutes. The potatoes should form a beautifully crusty brown bottom.   Check heat frequently so potatoes do not burn.

7. When done, loosen the potato cake all around with a spatula and turn out onto a plate, crusty side up. Serve at once.

Potato Pancakes
Serves 6

6 medium baking potatoes   *½ cup flour*
2 eggs   *oil or clarified butter*
1 onion   *sour cream or applesauce*
1½ teaspoons salt

1. Peel potatoes. Grate them in *long* strips (use the large holes on the grater), into a bowl of cold water.

2. Beat eggs in a bowl. Grate onion into beaten eggs. Stir in salt and flour.

3. Drain potatoes very well, squeezing out all excess moisture. Stir together potatoes and egg-flour mixture.

4. Pour oil to about ½-inch depth in wide, heavy skillet, and heat until hot but not smoking. Drop potato mixture into the hot oil by the heaping tablespoon. Flatten each dollop of batter into a flat pancake. Fry on each side until golden brown and crisp. Drain on paper towels. Serve at once with sour cream or applesauce if desired.

Mashed Potatoes with Mushrooms and Leeks
Serves 8-10

6 large baking potatoes
boiling water to cover
3 tablespoons butter
1 bunch leeks, trimmed, washed
  and thinly sliced
2 tablespoons butter
1 tablespoon oil
2 pounds mushrooms, thinly
  sliced

salt and pepper to taste
¼ pound soft butter, cut into
  pieces
¾ cup sour cream, at room
  temperature
salt and pepper to taste
1 cup sour cream, at room
  temperature

1. Cook potatoes in boiling, salted water until tender.

2. Meanwhile, heat butter; cook leeks until tender and golden. Set aside.

3. Heat butter and oil in a large skillet. Cook mushrooms, stirring frequently, until they begin to render their juices. Turn up heat, and continue cooking until they are almost dry. Season with salt and pepper and set aside. Preheat oven to 350 degrees.

4. When potatoes are tender, drain and peel. Put them through a ricer into mixer bowl. Beat in soft butter, ¾ cup sour cream, salt and pepper.

5. Spread half the potatoes on the bottom of a shallow baking dish. Spread the mushrooms over the potatoes and the leeks over the mushrooms. Spread with 1 cup sour cream and cover with remaining potatoes. The dish can be made in advance and refrigerated at this point. Bring to room temperature before continuing.

6. Bake, uncovered, at 350 degrees for 45 minutes to 1 hour, or until browned and bubbling.

Potato Gnocchi *(Italian Potato Dumplings)*
Serves 4-6

3 large baking potatoes
1½ cups unbleached white flour
2 teaspoons salt
2 tablespoons olive oil

2 eggs, lightly beaten
additional white flour
boiling salted water
¼ pound melted butter

1. Boil the potatoes in their skins until thoroughly cooked. Cool slightly and peel.

2. Put potatoes through a ricer. Measure 4 cups of riced potatoes into a large bowl. Add flour and salt. Add oil and toss with a fork. Add eggs and stir until a sticky dough is formed.

3. Lightly flour your work surface. Turn out dough and knead it 15 to 20 turns until it is smooth and pliable. Pull off a chunk of dough and roll it between your palms and on the floured surface into a rope a little thicker than your finger. Cut the rope into 1-inch pieces. If desired, dent each piece lightly with your finger, or with the tines of a fork. Place the gnocchi on a floured baking sheet or platter. Repeat until all dough is used.

4. Boil a large quantity of salted water in a deep pot. Drop the gnocchi, a few at a time, into the boiling water and cook until they rise to the top. Have a baking dish waiting, with ¼ pound melted butter in it. As the gnocchi rise to the top, remove them with a skimmer or slotted spoon, and mix them with the butter in the baking dish. When all the gnocchi are cooked and mixed in butter, serve at once, or cover tightly and keep warm in a *very* low oven for one to two hours. Serve sprinkled with grated cheese if desired.

Gratin of Potatoes and Cheese
Serves 8

This dish is a star; serve it with simple accompaniments so that it can be appreciated in its full glory. It's very good with beefsteak with tarragon, beefsteak with pepper, garlic-stuffed pork roast, (see index), or as a vegetarian main dish. The gratin is incredibly calorific, but it's more than worth it.

2 large cloves garlic, peeled and flattened
4 large Idaho potatoes, sliced paper thin (Slice at the last minute so that they do not darken. Do not soak in cold water.)

salt and pepper to taste
2 cups grated Gruyere cheese
1 quart whipping cream

1. Preheat oven to 325 degrees.

2. Rub the bottom and sides of a gratin dish with garlic. Leave garlic in the dish.

3. Cover with a layer of the potatoes. Sprinkle on some salt, pepper and cheese. Pour some cream over the whole thing. Repeat until all the potatoes, cream and cheese are used.

4. Place the pan, uncovered, in the oven. (Put a baking sheet underneath to catch spills). Bake for 1 hour or more, until the top is browned and the cream has cooked down to a thick sauce.

Note: This dish is as good at room temperature as it is hot; it makes a sensational picnic dish.

Potato-Mushroom Gratin
Serves 8

Mushrooms and potatoes are culinary soul mates. This classic gratin is a variation of the previous one.

1 large clove garlic, peeled and
   flattened with a kitchen mallet
4 large Idaho potatoes, sliced
   paper thin
1 pound mushrooms, cleaned,
   trimmed and sliced

1 cup thinly sliced scallions,
   green and white parts
salt and pepper to taste
1½ cups grated Swiss cheese
2 cups whipping cream

1. Preheat oven to 325 degrees.

2. Rub the bottom and sides of an oval gratin dish thoroughly with garlic. Discard garlic.

3. Build the gratin in the dish as follows: Layer potatoes, mushrooms, scallions, a sprinkling of salt and pepper, cheese and cream, repeating until you have used it all.

4. Bake in the oven for 1 hour or more, until the potatoes are done, the cream and mushroom liquid have cooked down to a thick, mocha-colored sauce, and the top is golden brown. Let stand for 10 minutes or so before serving.

Potato-Leek Custard
Serves 6

2½ pounds boiling potatoes
boiling salted water
3 tablespoons butter
6 leeks, trimmed, cleaned, and
   thinly sliced
2 cups grated Swiss cheese—
   Gruyere or Emmenthaler

1½ cups milk
salt and pepper to taste
nutmeg to taste
3 eggs
½ cup grated Swiss cheese

1. Cook potatoes in boiling salted water until tender but not mushy. Cool and peel. Slice thinly.

2. Meanwhile, melt butter in a wide, heavy skillet, saute leeks in hot butter until tender. Preheat oven to 375 degrees.

3. Butter a 2-quart baking dish. Layer potatoes, then leeks, then cheese. Continue layering ending with a top layer of potatoes.

4. Beat milk, salt, pepper, and nutmeg into eggs. Pour over potatoes. Cover with remaining ½ cup grated cheese.

5. Bake, uncovered, for 30 to 40 minutes or until custard is set and the top is nicely browned.

Squash Boats

small yellow squash   *salt and pepper to taste*

1. Cut squash in half. With a small spoon, carefully scrape out the seeds, leaving boat-shaped, hollowed squash halves.

2. Steam over boiling water for a very few minutes. The squash must not get mushy.

3. Season lightly with salt and pepper.

Fill the squash boats with steamed asparagus stalks or stir-fried snow pea pods and serve as a decorative vegetable accompaniment.

Squash with Bacon
Serves 8

Squash cooked in this manner is good for brunch, topped with poached eggs or as an accompaniment to corned beef hash. Two versions follow, a summer version and a winter one.

Winter Version

½ pound bacon, very coarsely diced

3 large onions, cut in half and sliced into thin half moons

2 green peppers, cut in half and sliced thinly

½ cup chopped parsley

1 large can plum tomatoes, drained and roughly chopped with the hands

10 to 12 zucchini, trimmed and sliced ¼ inch thick

salt and pepper to taste

¼ cup additional chopped parsley for garnish

1. Place bacon in a large, deep heavy pot. Heat. When half cooked or a little less, stir in onion and green pepper. Let them sizzle together for 3 minutes or so, then add remaining ingredients except garnish.

2. Cover. Cook, stirring frequently, until the zucchini are cooked and tender but not mushy.

3. Garnish with additional parsley and serve.

Squash with Bacon, Summer Version
Serves 8

½ pound bacon, coarsely diced
3 large onions, cut in half and
    sliced into thin half moons
2 green peppers, cut in half and
    coarsely diced
½ cup chopped parsley
3 tablespoons chopped fresh basil,
    if available

7 ripe, summer tomatoes, peeled,
    seeded and coarsely chopped
10 to 12 yellow squash, trimmed
    and very coarsely diced
salt and pepper to taste
¼ cup additional chopped parsley
    for garnish

1. Place bacon in a large wok or skillet. Heat. When half cooked or a little less, stir in onion and green pepper. Let them sizzle together for 3 minutes or so, then add remaining ingredients except garnish.

2. Cook, uncovered, stirring and tossing, until the squash is cooked and tender but not mushy.

3. Garnish with additional parsley and serve.

Squash with Walnuts
Serves 6

3 tablespoons olive oil
3 tablespoons butter
1 pound zucchini, summer
    squash, or mixture of both
    trimmed and cut into ¼-inch
    slices

½ cup walnuts, coarsely chopped
juice of 1 lemon
salt and pepper

1. Heat the oil and butter in a wide heavy skillet. Saute the squash, tossing them in the oil, for 3 to 4 minutes until they begin to get tender.

2. Add the nuts, lemon juice, salt and pepper, and cook, stirring and tossing, a minute or two more to blend flavors. Do not let the zucchini get mushy. Serve at once.

Zucchini Agrodolce
Serves 6

6 to 8 medium zucchini, trimmed
¼ cup olive oil
3 cloves garlic, minced
¼ cup wine vinegar
¼ cup chicken stock

¼ cup pine nuts
¼ cup white raisins
2 tablespoons capers
salt and pepper to taste

1. Cut zucchini in half crosswise and lengthwise, then cut into finger length pieces about 2 inches long and ½-inch wide.

2. Heat oil in a deep pot that can be covered. Add zucchini and garlic and stir and cook them for a few minutes. Add vinegar and stock, stir and and bring to a boil. Reduce heat and simmer covered for 10 minutes.

3. Uncover and add remaining ingredients. Stir and cook for 3-5 minutes more. The zucchini must remain somewhat crisp. Cool uncovered.

Serve at room temperature.

Spinach with Croutons
Serves 6

4 tablespoons butter
2 tablespoons olive oil
1 large onion, minced
1 large clove garlic, minced
3 pounds fresh spinach, washed well, trimmed of tough stems, and chopped. (You may substitute 3 packages of frozen, chopped spinach, defrosted, drained and squeezed as dry as possible)

¾ cup whipping cream
½ cup bread crumbs
½ cup grated Parmesan
salt and pepper to taste
⅛ teaspoon nutmeg
4 tablespoons butter
2 slices good white bread, trimmed of crusts and cut into small cubes

1. Heat butter and oil, saute onion and garlic until tender. Stir in spinach. Cook, stirring over low heat until butter is absorbed and spinach is tender.

2. Stir in cream, breadcrumbs, cheese, salt, pepper and nutmeg. Heat through gently.

3. Heat 4 tablespoons of butter in a skillet. Saute bread cubes until golden. Sprinkle over spinach. Serve at once.

Stir-fried Snow Peas
Serves 4-6

2 pounds snow pea pods
2 tablespoons butter
2 tablespoons corn oil

juice of ½ lime
salt and pepper to taste
pinch of thyme

1. String the snow pea pods. Heat the butter and oil in a wide, heavy skillet or wok. Toss the snow peas in the hot fat. Squeeze in the lime juice. Toss and cook until they are shiny and partially cooked. They must remain *very* crisp and bright green.

2. Season with salt, pepper and thyme. Serve at once.

Note: I like to serve these in the spring time with stir-fried fresh asparagus, (see index). Arrange a heap of the snow peas on a platter next to a heap of the asparagus.

Pisto Manchego
Serves 8-10

¼ cup olive oil
3 large onions, cut in half and
  sliced into half moons
3 cloves garlic, minced
2 large green peppers, sliced
2 large cans tomatoes (1 pound,
  12 ounces each), drained and
  chopped
½ teaspoon dried basil

salt and pepper to taste
1 eggplant, unpeeled, cut into ½-
  inch cubes, salted and allowed
  to sweat for ½ hour in glass or
  ceramic bowl
1 package frozen lima beans,
  thawed
1 package frozen artichoke hearts,
  thawed

1. Heat oil in a wide, heavy skillet. Saute onions and garlic for a few minutes. Add green pepper and cook until vegetables are tender.

2. Add tomatoes, basil, salt and pepper. Cook until mixture is thick and savory.

3. Rinse and dry eggplant cubes. Stir them into the tomato mixture. Cover and cook for 15 minutes.

4. Stir in limas and artichoke hearts. Taste and adjust seasonings. Simmer, covered, until everything is tender, about 15 minutes. This is delicious reheated, so it can be made in advance. It is also good cold, with lemon wedges.

Ratatouille
Serves 8

Eggplant when sauteed, soaks up an unbelievable amount of oil, even if the oil is very hot and the eggplant slices dry. In my version of the French vegetable stew known as ratatouille, the eggplant slices are brushed with a small amount of oil and baked. The result is a lighter, less oily dish.

1 medium eggplant, sliced ¼-inch thick (cut slices in half if eggplant is very wide)
6 medium-sized zucchini, sliced ½-inch thick (do not peel the vegetables)
salt
6 tablespoons olive oil
3 onions, sliced
2 large cloves garlic, minced

2 green peppers, sliced
additional olive oil, if necessary
1 large can (1 pound, 12 ounces) tomatoes, drained and chopped
salt and pepper to taste
½ cup fresh chopped parsley
1 teaspoon basil (1 tablespoon fresh)
½ cup grated Parmesan cheese (optional)

1. Preheat oven to 450 degrees.

2. Place eggplant in a glass or ceramic bowl and zucchini in another. Salt both and let stand to sweat for about ½ hour. Rinse, then dry on paper towels.

3. Heat the oil in a heavy skillet. Toss zucchini in the hot oil, until crisp-tender and lightly browned. With a slotted spoon, transfer the zucchini to a colander placed over a bowl to drain. Set skillet aside without wiping out.

4. Lightly oil a baking sheet. Place eggplant slices on the sheet in one layer. Lightly brush them with oil. Place in the oven for 15 minutes or so, or until lightly browned. Drain on paper towels. Reduce oven temperature to 350 degrees.

5. In the oil remaining in the skillet, saute the onions, garlic, and peppers until tender. Add more oil if necessary. Stir in the tomatoes, salt, pepper, parsley, and basil. Turn up heat and cook for 4 to 5 minutes to blend flavors and evaporate the tomato liquid.

6. Place the tomato mixture and the drained vegetables in a baking dish and stir well to combine. Sprinkle with the Parmesan cheese, if you choose to use it.

7. Cover the baking dish and place in the preheated oven for ½ hour, or until the vegetables are very tender and the whole mixture is bubbling. (The ratatouille can be made the day before. The flavor will improve.)

Salads

Heinz Sowinski's Avocado Salad on A Bed of Sprouts
Serves 4

1 cup alfalfa sprouts
2 avocados
Walnut-Lemon Dressing (see
    index)

4 tablespoons chopped crisp bacon

Divide the sprouts among four chilled salad plates. Halve the avocados, remove pits, and peel. Slice each avocado half and place each half on a bed of sprouts. Spoon a scant tablespoon of dressing over each avocado half, sprinkle with bacon, and serve.

Liz Terry's Italian Green Bean Salad
Serves 4

1 pound crisp-cooked, cooled
    green beans
1 small onion, minced
½ cup grated Parmesan cheese
6 tablespoons olive oil
2 tablespoons wine vinegar

1 teaspoon Dijon mustard
salt and pepper to taste
watercress
handful of black olives
2 ripe, summer tomatoes, cut into
    wedges

1. Combine green beans with onion and Parmesan cheese.

2. In another bowl, combine olive oil, wine vinegar, mustard and salt and pepper. Pour over bean mixture.

3. Arrange on watercress. Garnish with black olives and tomatoes.

Corn Salad
Serves 6

Frozen kernel corn is a very decent product. In some parts of Europe corn is considered pig fodder, but Americans know that it is a jewel among vegetables. To properly enjoy corn, however, it must be plucked from the stalk directly into a pot of boiling water. Even an hour after harvest is too long, the sweet and succulent vegetable begins to change and most of the magical flavor is gone. At the freezing plant, the kernels are cut off the cob, parboiled and frozen into neat packages in record time. Loss of flavor is minimal.

¼ cup olive oil
1 cup scallions, sliced, green and
white parts
½ cup green pepper, minced
1 large clove garlic, minced
4 cups kernel corn, very fresh or
frozen

juice of 1 lemon
salt and pepper to taste
½ cup dry white wine
1 tablespoon chopped fresh thyme
2 tablespoons chopped parsley

1. Heat olive oil. Cook the scallions, peppers and garlic until soft, but not browned. Stir in the corn, lemon juice, salt and pepper. Stir and cook for one minute.

2. Stir in wine. Raise heat and bring to a brisk simmer. Simmer for 3 to 5 minutes until the corn is cooked, but not mushy. Stir in the herbs. Drain corn and reserve liquid. Boil liquid briskly until reduced by one-half. Pour over corn. Serve chilled or at room temperature.

Cucumber Salad, Hungarian Style
Serves 4

2 cucumbers, peeled and sliced
paper thin
salt
3 tablespoons white wine vinegar
3 tablespoons cold water
¼ teaspoon hot Hungarian
paprika, (or ¼ teaspoon sweet
Hungarian paprika and a pinch
of ground red pepper)

½ teaspoon sugar
1 cup sour cream
additional paprika for garnish

1. Place cucumbers in a non-metallic bowl and salt well. Let stand to sweat for 1 hour.

2. Drain in a colander. Squeeze the cucumbers in your hands to extract as much moisture as possible. Put them in a bowl with the vinegar, water, paprika, red pepper if needed and sugar. Toss until sugar is dissolved.

3. Stir in sour cream. Taste and add salt if necessary. Sprinkle with additional paprika. Serve well chilled.

Yogurt Cucumbers
Serves 6

5 medium cucumbers
salt
8 ounces plain unflavored yogurt
¼ teaspoon ground cumin
2 tablespoons chopped scallions,
  green and white parts

2 tablespoons chopped parsley
pinch cayenne pepper
salt and pepper to taste

1. Peel the cucumbers, cut them in half lengthwise and scrape out the seeds with a teaspoon. Slice the cucumbers about ¼ inch thick. Place them in a non-metallic bowl and salt them liberally; let them stand to sweat for about ½ hour. Rinse and dry them.

2. Put the dried cucumbers in a bowl. Stir in the yogurt and all the remaining ingredients. Refrigerate until serving time. Serve as a curry accompaniment.

Cucumber Cottage Cheese Salad
Serves 6

5 medium cucumbers
salt
2 cups cottage cheese
4 tablespoons sour cream
1 tablespoon mayonnaise

½ cup fresh chopped parsley
2 tablespoons prepared
  horseradish (or to taste)
salt and pepper to taste
juice of ½ lemon

1. Peel the cucumbers and cut them in half lengthwise, scrape out the seeds with a teaspoon. Slice them about ¼-inch thick. Place them in a non-metallic bowl and salt them liberally. Allow them to sweat for ½ hour. Rinse and dry them.

2. Force the cottage cheese through a sieve or fine strainer into a bowl. Beat in the sour cream and mayonnaise. Gently, but thoroughly, fold in the remaining ingredients including the cucumbers. Serve at once. (This salad becomes watery if it stands).

Simple Orange-Onion Relish
Serves 4-6

5 large, juicy naval oranges
1 large Vidalia onion (or other
  sweet onion), coarsely chopped

salt and a generous amount of
  pepper to taste
3 tablespoons olive oil

1. Peel and section oranges over a bowl, to catch their juice. Be sure to remove the bitter white pith. Discard peel but reserve juice.

2. Dice orange sections. Place in a glass bowl with the remaining ingredients and reserved orange juice. Toss together well and serve.

Orange-Onion Salad
Serves 6

2 cups romaine, washed, dried,
  and torn into bite-sized pieces
1 Vidalia onion (or other sweet
  onion) coarsely chopped
2 naval oranges, peeled and
  sectioned (make sure all white
  pith is removed), halve each
  orange section

½ pound mushrooms, sliced
1 green pepper, coarsely chopped
6 strips bacon, fried crisp,
  drained, and crumbled
¼ cup coarsely chopped
  pimientos.
½ cup chopped fresh parsley
white wine vinaigrette (see index)

1. Combine salad ingredients in a large bowl.

2. Pour in dressing. Toss dressing and salad together. Serve at once.

Potatoes Vinaigrette
Serves 6

3 pounds small new potatoes
boiling water to cover
½ cup olive oil
3 tablespoons white wine vinegar

½ cup thinly sliced scallions,
  green and white parts
½ cup fresh chopped parsley
salt and pepper to taste

1. Boil the potatoes in salted water to cover until cooked but not at all mushy.

2. Peel the potatoes while still very warm. Use an oven mitt to hold them if necessary. (The skins will slip right off).

3. Slice the peeled potatoes about ¼ inch thick and place in a glass or ceramic serving bowl.

4. Add the oil and vinegar and toss very, very gently.

5. Add the parsley, scallions, salt and pepper and toss gently again. Serve warm, or at room temperature.

Greek Salad
Serves 8

Salad

2 cups romaine lettuce, torn into
  bite-sized pieces
2 cups escarole, torn into bite-
  sized pieces
3 large ripe tomatoes, cut into
  eighths
2 cucumbers, peeled and sliced
  ¼-inch thick

1 large green pepper, seeded,
  trimmed, and cut into strips
12 radishes, trimmed
¾ cup crumbled Feta cheese
3 scallions sliced, green and white
  parts
½ cup fresh chopped parsley
1 cup Greek black olives

Dressing

1 cup olive oil
6 tablespoons red wine vinegar
6 tablespoons fresh lemon juice

2 teaspoons dried crumbled mint
2 teaspoons dried oregano
salt and pepper

1. Wash and dry greens thoroughly. Place them in a large bowl with the remaining salad ingredients.

2. Combine the dressing ingredients in a screw-top jar and shake vigorously.

3. Pour the dressing over the salad. Toss and serve at once.

Tomatoes

Ripe, juicy, and almost unbearably flavorful, tomatoes are the most eagerly awaited of the summer's bounty. Originally cultivated by the Indians of South and Central America, tomatoes were brought to Europe by the Conquistadores. Over the years the delicious red fruit has established itself as an important component of almost all the cuisines of the world. For a long time, however, tomatoes were not universally accepted as a wholesome food; they triggered a response of total distrust and suspicion in certain quarters. The Puritans, for instance, with their instinctive dislike of anything that tasted or felt good, considered the tomato a poison. In England, it was thought to be a deadly aphrodisiac and as a result was shunned by all but the most decadent. As late as 1830, an American physician warned that a dose of raw tomatoes would bring on foaming and frothing at the mouth, appendicitis, high blood pressure, and death. Despite this dismal beginning, the tomato has become one of the most popular and versatile foods in the world. It is found in all sorts of classic preparations, from the tomato sauces of the Mediterranean to ketchup; from gazpacho to bacon and tomato sandwiches.

Winter tomatoes—those pallid, tennis ball-like objects found in supermarkets—are not worth the trouble, but oh! those summer beauties. During the summer, cooks who delight in seasonal foods banish their trusty Italian canned tomatoes to the nether regions of the pantry shelves, and indulge in an orgy of tomato eating. The best way to eat them is sliced, salted and gobbled, but eventually even this gloriously primeval practice palls. Fortunately, there is a wealth of simple recipes that use the tomato without destroying its taste and texture. The simplest involves slicing them and arranging them on a plate with a splash of olive oil, a hint of vinegar, and a handful of fresh chopped basil. Slices of good Mozzarella cheese can be alternated with the tomato slices for a substantial summer salad.

Should you choose to try a more complex tomato salad that requires peeled tomatoes, keep the tomato taste intact—do not cook them to death. To peel them, immerse them in boiling water for 10 seconds only. The skins will slip off easily, but the tomato itself will not begin to cook inside. To seed and juice the fruit, cut it in half and gently squeeze out the juice. Remove the seeds with your fingers. You will be discarding a basically indigestible portion of the fruit; all the nutrients and wonderful flavor will remain.

Tomatoes Stuffed With Swiss Cheese Salad
Serves 6

6 large summer tomatoes
salt
8 ounces Swiss cheese, cut into
  ½-inch cubes
½ cup fresh chopped parsley
1 tablespoon fresh chopped basil
½ cup thinly sliced scallions,
  green and white parts

½ cup chopped green pepper
6 tablespoons olive oil
2 tablespoons white wine vinegar
salt and pepper
1 small clove garlic, finely minced

1. Slice off the stem end of each tomato. Scoop out the seeds and pulp. Salt the insides lightly and invert on paper towels to drain.

2. Combine the cheese, parsley, basil, scallions, and green pepper in a bowl.

3. In a screw-top jar, combine the remaining ingredients and shake vigorously. Pour it over the cheese mixture. Toss it gently with two wooden spoons.

4. Fill each tomato with an equal amount of the cheese mixture.

Tomato-Green Pepper Salad, Morrocan Style
Serves 4

4 large summer tomatoes, peeled,
  seeded, and coarsely chopped
4 large green peppers, peeled,
  seeded, and coarsely chopped
  (see note)
1 tablespoon chopped fresh chili
  pepper

½ cup chopped fresh parsley
2 cloves garlic, minced
salt and pepper to taste
¼ teaspoon ground cumin
1 teaspoon paprika
1 tablespoon lemon juice
3 tablespoons olive oil

Combine all ingredients in a glass bowl. Chill for several hours before serving.

Note: To peel peppers, place directly on the flame of a gas stove (one on each burner). As the peppers blacken and char, turn them with tongs. When they are completely blackened, close them in a paper bag for 15 minutes. Then peel under running water—the skins will slip right off. Lacking a gas stove, place peppers on a baking sheet in a 450 degree oven. Turn with tongs, every 5 minutes or so. When the peppers are blackened, proceed as above.

Ron Cohn's Tomato-Pepper Salad, Hungarian Style
Serves 4

In his restaurant, Hal's, in Atlanta, Ron Cohn serves this salad all year long, but it reaches magnificent heights with summer tomatoes. I like to serve it in soup bowls as a first course; it will seem like a Hungarian gazpacho.

¼ cup wine vinegar
¼ cup olive oil
1½ to 2 tablespoons sugar
salt and pepper to taste
5 medium-sized summer
* tomatoes, peeled, seeded,*
* juiced, and coarsely chopped*

2 to 3 medium size green peppers,
* seeded, and coarsely chopped*

1. Combine vinegar, oil, sugar, salt, and pepper in a jar and shake well.

2. Combine green peppers and tomatoes, toss with dressing, and serve at once on lettuce-lined plates, or chill for a few hours, and serve in soup bowls.

Italian Uncooked Tomato Sauce With Pasta
Serves 4

One of the appeals of this fresh-tasting dish is the same as in a hot fudge sundae; the contrast of the temperatures. The hot pasta and the cold sauce are wonderful together.

10 to 12 beautiful summer
* tomatoes, peeled, seeded, and*
* juiced—at room temperature*
1 clove garlic, minced
salt and pepper to taste
½ cup fresh chopped parsley

⅓ cup fresh chopped basil (omit if
* not available, do not substitute*
* dry)*
good olive oil
lemon wedges

1. Chop tomatoes coarsely and place in a bowl.

2. Stir in garlic, salt, pepper, parsley, and basil. Serve at once with 1 pound of hot linguini. Serve on hot plates. Pass a cruet of olive oil and wedges of lemon. Each person takes some hot linguini, tops it with sauce, and adds lemon juice and olive oil to taste.

Avocado-Tomato-Onion Salad
Serves 6

2 firm, ripe tomatoes, cut into eighths
1 large Vidalia onion (or other sweet onion) cut in half and sliced thinly into half moons
1 ripe avocado, halved, pitted, peeled, and sliced ¼-inch thick

¾ cup Greek olives, pitted and halved
½ cup chopped fresh parsley
lemon vinaigrette (see index)

1. Combine salad ingredients in a bowl.

2. Pour lemon vinaigrette over salad, toss, and serve at once.

Consuelo's Watercress-Tomato Salad, Philippine Style
Serves 4-6

1 bunch watercress
4 to 5 summer tomatoes, cut into eighths

1 bunch thin scallions, trimmed and sliced, green and white parts
salt

1. Steam watercress over boiling water for 10 seconds. Rinse at once under cold running water. Blot dry. Trim off woody stems. Cut watercress into 1-inch pieces, remaining stems, leaves, and all.

2. Place watercress, tomatoes, and sliced scallions in an attractive bowl. Toss together lightly and allow to stand for about an hour.

3. Salt lightly, toss again and serve.

Note: When good tomatoes are out of season, substitute 1 box cherry tomatoes, each tomato halved.

Dressings

Heinz's Walnut-Lemon Dressing

Since this dressing contains no vinegar, it is excellent if wine is to be served with the salad course.

½ cup walnut oil
juice of 1 large lemon
juice of 1 large lime
2 ounces finely chopped toasted walnuts

1 teaspoon chopped capers
½ teaspoon sugar
salt to taste
pinch of white pepper

Combine all ingredients well. Store in a covered jar until needed.

White Wine Vinaigrette

¾ cup dry white wine
½ cup olive oil
¼ cup white wine tarragon vinegar

1 clove garlic, crushed
salt and pepper to taste

Combine all ingredients in a screw-top jar. Shake vigorously before using.

Lemon Vinaigrette

6 tablespoons olive oil
2 tablespoons white wine vinegar
juice of ½ lemon

1 garlic clove, minced
salt and pepper to taste

Combine dressing ingredients in a screw-top jar. Shake vigorously before using.

Mustard Vinaigrette

⅓ cup wine vinegar
2 tablespoons Dijon mustard
½ cup olive oil

½ cup corn oil
salt and pepper to taste

1. Beat the wine vinegar into the mustard with a small wire whisk.

2. Still whisking slowly, add oils in a thin stream. The mixture will be thick, creamy, and emulsified.

3. Beat in a frugal amount of salt and pepper. Herbs may be added if desired, although I think it's better without. For a wonderful first course or light summer lunch, serve new potatoes, steamed in their skins, with bowls of mustard vinaigrette for dunking.

Mayonnaise

This is very simple, yet it makes a brilliant addition to a menu; we have become much too accustomed to commercial mayonnaise in a jar. For a first course, serve the homemade stuff mounded in a clear glass bowl surrounded by a bouquet of beautiful raw vegetables. The mayonnaise may be varied with the addition of any of these: crushed garlic (crush it with a kitchen mallet, *not* a garlic press), paprika—hot or sweet, curry spices, a tablespoon or so of good caviar, or some mashed ripe avocado.

3 egg yolks, at room temperature
salt and pepper to taste
2 teaspoons white wine vinegar
2 teaspoons Dijon mustard
¾ cup olive oil

¾ cup corn oil
1 to 2 tablespoons lime or lemon juice
1 to 2 tablespoons boiling water

1. With a wire whisk, stir together the egg yolks, salt and pepper, vinegar, and mustard.

2. Add the oils by droplets, whisking very hard. As the mayonnaise begins to thicken, add oil in larger driblets, whisking it in vigorously all the while.

3. When all the oil has been absorbed, whisk in the lemon or lime juice. Then, to stabilize the sauce, whisk in the boiling water.

Remoulade Sauce

3 cups mayonnaise (preferably homemade)
2 teaspoons Dijon mustard
4 tablespoons capers
4 tablespoons chopped cornichons
4 tablespoons chopped fresh parsley

1 teaspoon paprika
½ cup chopped scallions, green and white parts
few drops of Tabasco sauce
½ tablespoon dried tarragon, crumbled

Mix all together with wire whisk. Ripen in the refrigerator 1 hour.

Sorrel Mayonnaise

½ cup mayonnaise (preferably homemade)
½ cup sour cream
½ cup freshly whipped cream
1½ tablespoons Dijon mustard

1 tablespoon sorrel puree (see index)
½ cup fresh sorrel chiffonade (see index)

Fold all ingredients together, gently but thoroughly. Serve with boiled shrimp, salmon, poached scallops, or smoked salmon.

Chapter 6

Grains, Breads

Grains

Kasha With Pine Nuts
Serves 6

This buckwheat groat pilaf and the following cracked wheat pilaf make delightful alternatives to rice or potatoes.

2 eggs, lightly beaten
2 cups coarse kasha (buckwheat groats)
4 cups chicken stock, combined with ½ cup dry sherry and brought to a rolling boil

salt and pepper
2 ounces pine nuts

1. Stir the eggs into the kasha. Mix until the kasha grains are well coated with egg.

2. Heat a large, heavy skillet. Stir the kasha in the skillet over moderate heat until it is dry and each grain is separate, and it gives off a delicious, toasty odor—5 minutes or more. Place kasha in a large pot that can be covered.

3. Add boiling stock and sherry, salt and pepper to pot. Stir a few times.

4. Cover pot, simmer over lowest heat for about 30 minutes. All liquid should be absorbed, and the kasha tender. Toss in the pine nuts, fluff with a fork and serve. This is also delicious with an addition of sauteed mushrooms and onions.

Wheat Pilaf
Serves 4

3 tablespoons butter
1 small onion, finely chopped
1 cup coarse cracked wheat
  (bulghur)

½ teaspoon ground coriander
¼ teaspoon ground cumin
salt and pepper to taste
1¾ cups boiling stock

1. Heat the butter in a heavy pot that can be covered. Saute the onion until tender. Add the wheat and stir it in the hot butter until lightly browned.

2. Add the seasonings and stir until the wheat is coated. Stir in the stock. Immediately cover and simmer on lowest heat about 20 minutes, or until the wheat is tender but not mushy, and all the stock is absorbed. Fluff with a fork and serve.

Tabooley (Cracked Wheat Salad)
Serves 8

From the women of the St. Elias Church, in Atlanta.

1 cup cracked wheat (bulghur)
water
½ cup fresh lemon juice
¼ cup olive oil
4 bunches parsley, stemmed and
  finely chopped
4 bunches scallions, trimmed and
  finely chopped

1 cup fresh mint, finely chopped
4 pounds summer tomatoes,
  peeled, seeded, and juiced,
  finely chopped
salt and pepper to taste

1. Soak the wheat in water to cover. It will expand greatly. After 30 minutes, squeeze with your hands to drain it, and place it in a bowl.

2. Toss in the lemon juice and olive oil. Toss in the remaining ingredients. Mix it all together thoroughly. Serve as an hors d'oeuvre with romaine leaves, or serve as a salad.

Perfect Rice, Method I

Use in Oriental menus; the grains will be cohesive.

1. Rinse white, long grain rice under cold water.

2. Pour rice into a saucepan. Place hand flat on surface of rice. Pour in cold water until it just barely covers the middle knuckle of your middle finger. Add a bit of salt, if desired. Cover pan and place over high heat.

3. When the cover begins to jiggle and steam with the pressure of boiling water, *do not uncover,* but reduce heat to its lowest point for 30 minutes.

4. Uncover, place kitchen towel over pan, recover over towel and leave until ready to use.

Perfect Rice, Method II
3 cups cooked rice

Use in Occidental menus; each grain will be separate.

4 quarts boiling salted water   1 cup rice

1. Sprinkle the rice slowly into the boiling water. If the water stops boiling, keep stirring the rice until it begins to boil again. Boil the rice for 10 minutes.

2. Drain the rice in a colander, rinse well under hot water tap.

3. Scrape the rice onto a long length of double thick, damp, cheese-cloth. Bring the ends of the cheesecloth up to completely enclose the rice. Place the cheesecloth wrapped rice in the colander.

4. Place the colander in a deep pot containing an inch or two of boiling water. (The water should not touch the rice bundle). Cover the pot tightly, with foil if necessary, and steam over medium heat for 30 minutes or until the rice is tender and fluffy.

Rice Salad with Apricots
Serves 6

3 cups cooked rice
6 tablespoons olive oil
2 tablespoons white wine vinegar
½ teaspoon ground cumin
salt and pepper to taste
1 cup dried apricots, coarsely
* chopped*

¾ cup unsalted almonds
1 cup fresh chopped parsley
¾ cup thinly sliced scallions,
* green and white parts*
juice of 1 lemon (more or less,
* to taste)*

1. While the rice is still warm, place it in a bowl and toss it gently with the oil, vinegar, cumin, and salt and pepper. When the rice is thoroughly coated with the dressing, set it aside to cool.

2. Soak the dried apricots in boiling water to cover for 15 minutes. Drain.

3. Toss the apricots, almonds, parsley, scallions, and lemon juice into the cooked rice.

4. At serving time, garnish, if desired, with additional parsley, chopped apricots, and slivered almonds.

Rice Pulao, East Indian Style
Serves 6

2 tablespoons clarified butter
2 tablespoons corn oil
2 thin slices peeled ginger root,
   minced
1 small green pepper, chopped
2 small onions, chopped
2 carrots, peeled and chopped
¼ teaspoon cinnamon
¼ teaspoon turmeric

pinch ground cloves
2 canned tomatoes, well drained
   and chopped
5 cups water
2 cups rice
salt and pepper to taste
¼ cup each: cashews, shelled
   pistachios, and raisins
5 cups boiling chicken stock

1. Preheat oven to 450 degrees.

2. Heat butter and oil. Saute ginger root, green pepper, onions, and carrots in butter and oil until onion is limp. Add the spices. Stir the vegetables and spices in the hot oil until they are well blended.

3. Add tomatoes, increase heat, and cook for 2 or 3 minutes. Set vegetables aside until needed.

4. Bring water to a boil. Add rice and boil 2 minutes.

5. Drain, place rice in a heavy pot that can be covered. Add salt, pepper, nuts, and raisins to rice.

6. Stir in vegetables and add boiling stock.

7. Stir once or twice. Cover pot. Bake in preheated oven 30 to 35 minutes, or until rice is cooked, and the liquid absorbed. Uncover, place kitchen towel over pan, recover over towel, and leave until ready to serve.

Wild Rice
Serves 8

Although wild, it is not a rice—wild rice is actually an aquatic grass. Methods of cleaning and packaging wild rice have changed in the last few years; the washing, soaking, and preboiling specified in many recipes are no longer necessary. The length of cooking time and the amount of liquid used will vary with different brands of wild rice; it is best to experiment. Don't be afraid to add more liquid, or to cook a little longer, but wild rice must remain somewhat crunchy to be at its best; be sure not to overcook. In spite of its high price, this spectacular grain (the only native American grain) is worth finding and cooking; wild rice is one of the most delicious of American foods.

4 tablespoons butter
2 carrots, peeled and chopped fine
1 stalk celery chopped fine
½ cup green onions, thinly
  sliced, green and white parts
1½ cups wild rice

3 cups chicken stock
¼ teaspoon thyme
1 Turkish bay leaf or ½ California
  bay leaf
salt and pepper to taste

1. Preheat oven to 350 degrees.

2. Heat butter in a 2½-quart pot that can be covered. Saute vegetables until tender. Add wild rice and stir so that vegetables and rice are well combined. Add stock, herbs, and seasonings. Bring to a boil. Cover and bake for 45 minutes, or until all liquid is absorbed, and the wild rice is cooked. (It should remain somewhat crunchy).

Note: This reheats well—sprinkle with some dry vermouth, dot with a bit of butter, and place in a covered pot in a 350 degree oven for about ½ hour.

Wild Rice Pancakes

If you are lucky enough to have leftover wild rice, you will be able to have wild rice pancakes for breakfast.

Use one large egg for every cup of leftover wild rice. Beat egg. Stir into rice. Heat ¼ inch of combined butter and oil in a heavy skillet. Drop the mixture by spoonfuls into the hot fat. Flatten into pancakes and fry until crisp on both sides. Serve hot with real maple syrup.

Bread

There is nothing quite as satisfying as wrestling a recalcitrant hunk of yeast dough into submission. The whole process of bread-making is totally gratifying in a very primitive way. When I'm up to my elbows in dough, with flour in my hair, on my nose, and lightly coating every doorknob in the house, I feel like nothing less than the Great Earth Mother herself, the Goddess of Grain. The whole bread baking ritual, from the initial testing of the water temperature to the final hysterical feeling of self congratulation when the fragrant perfect loaves emerge from the oven, is pure glory.

Although a mystique has grown around yeast doughs, home bread baking is extremely easy; probably the easiest of all kitchen activities. Making bread is very different from making cakes and pastries; there is a tremendous amount of leeway involved. Once a few simple rules are understood and once the yeast is working, it is almost impossible to ruin a loaf of bread. For those who want to plunge headfirst into the visceral, dramatic and elementally satisfying world of home bread baking, here is a brief guide that should help demystify the process.

Equipment

All you really need for the production of a perfect loaf is a bowl, a baking sheet, and an oven. Dough hooks and food processors fill me with dismay—they do shorten the kneading time, but they also deprive the baker of the therapeutic fun of hand kneading. Earth mothers and fathers, and grain gods and goddesses, have no need for such effete contraptions.

Check your oven with an oven thermometer to make sure the thermostat is working properly, and get yourself a large crockery bowl for mixing the ingredients and starting the dough. Measuring cups and spoons, a whisk and a long handled wooden spoon are convenient to have as well.

Flour

All-purpose flour, bleached or unbleached, is the most convenient for the home baker. Flour contains a protein called gluten. It forms the web that allows the yeast to rise the dough. Hard wheat flour contains more gluten than soft wheat, therefore, hard wheat flour is usually used for bread and soft wheat flour for cakes and pastries. All-purpose flour is a blend of both; it is easy to work with and produces excellent home breads.

Whole wheat flour is the white flour before processing, sifting, bleaching, and reenrichment. It contains the germ, endosperm, and bran (outer covering) of the wheat kernel. This brown flour can produce as much gluten as white flour, if not more, but the bran and germ are sharp and tend to cut the developing strands of gluten, producing a loaf of less volume than a comparable white loaf. An all whole wheat recipe can produce a lovely loaf, but it will be more compact than a white bread. Many recipes combine whole wheat flour with white flour to produce a finished product with the color and texture of the former and the height and lightness of the latter.

Rye flour is milled from kernels of rye grain. Rye does not have the same kind of gluten as wheat flour. A yeast bread made from rye flour alone will resemble a brick, but the brick might be easier to slice. As a result, rye flour is usually combined with wheat flour, either whole wheat or, for more volume, whole wheat and white. Pumpernickel is dark rye meal. If it is unobtainable, it may be replaced with rye flour, although a baker will often sell you a few pounds of pumpernickel meal for a nominal price.

Miller's bran and wheat germ may be added back to any white bread recipe for flavor, texture, and nutrition. If miller's bran is elusive, use whole bran cereal in its place. A tablespoon of bran or wheat germ can replace a tablespoon of flour in every cup of flour used. A dough that contains a significant amount of whole grain flour will be harder to knead than a comparable white dough, and the rising time will be longer. The finished bread, however, will be gutsy, hearty, and loaded with character.

Yeast

Yeast is a living organism. As it grows, it releases carbon dioxide gas. As a yeast dough is kneaded, its gluten is developed into a web-like structure. The carbon dioxide gas gets trapped in the gluten framework and causes it to expand. This, in turn, causes the dough to rise. For first time bakers, this impressive rising of the dough usually results in joyous hysteria. There is no moment to compare with that first magical rising of your first bread dough. To insure the reality of that moment, the temperature of the water used to dissolve the yeast must be correct; too hot and the organisms will die; too cold, and they will continue to sleep peacefully. The temperature of the water should be 100 to 115 degrees, but it is not necessary to fool with thermometers. Simply let the water tap run, and hold your wrist under the flow. When it feels *comfortably warm*, it is just right to mix with the yeast. Not hot, not cold or neutral, but comfortably warm. If you are prone to fever, abandon this method and invest in a thermometer.

The most convenient yeast for a home baker is the granular kind, found in packets in the supermarket. Always check the expiration date on the back, and buy it well before that date has occurred. Only buy the yeast if the grocer has kept it refrigerated, then bring it home and store it in your refrigerator for use. A package of yeast yields about one tablespoon.

Steps to a Perfect Loaf

1. Do not sift the flour. Measure by spooning the flour out of its bag into a one cup measuring cup until the cup is overflowing. Level off with a knife, and dump the cupful into your bowl. Do this operation over a sheet of wax paper so that the overflow will not be wasted.

2. Always remember that the amount of flour called for in a recipe is approximate. The amount of liquid that flour will absorb varies with the weather, the brand of flour, the humidity, the moistness of the baker's hands, and other variables. As you bake bread over and over again, you will learn to tell when enough flour has been added by the feel of the dough. After a while, you will not need measuring cups at all.

3. Dissolve the yeast first, in water of the proper temperature, then add any other liquids called for in the recipe, and salt, seeds, sugar, and so on, if needed. If eggs are to be used, add a bit of flour to the dissolved yeast and liquids, and then add the eggs.

4. Begin adding flour to this wet, yeasty, possibly eggy mess. Use a wooden spoon or your hand to mix the flour until a shaggy dough is formed, then turn it out onto a floured surface and begin kneading. Kneading is simply working the dough until the gluten network is formed and the yeast has begun to work. It is extremely pleasurable, and excellent exercise for the arms, shoulders, and back. Knead in the remaining flour until the dough feels smooth, alive, nonsticky, and elastic, and then *stop adding flour*. You may find that you have added less flour than the recipe calls for, or a bit more. Remember that it depends on a number of variables, and may change from one time to the next. The kneading itself consists of folding, pushing, and turning the dough rhythmically on your floured surface. It will be unmanageable and messy at first; then, as you work at it with vigor, it will become smooth and lively, and seem to push back against your hands. It will take about 15 minutes for the dough to progress from shaggy and unmanageable to smooth and satiny—a bit longer for whole grain

doughs. If, during the kneading process you feel the need to rest your complaining muscles, cover the dough with a clean cloth and let it and your aching arms relax for a few minutes. Then continue until the dough feels ready. To test if the dough has been kneaded sufficiently, poke two fingers gently into the dough. If the resulting indentations spring back, the dough is ready for the next step; if not, knead a few minutes more and try again.

5. Now the dough is ready to rise in a large, clean, well-buttered bowl. The bowl in which you have done all your combining and mixing is fine—just wash and dry it well, and butter it thoroughly on the bottom and sides. Form the dough into a nice fat ball (it feels marvelous at this stage) and put it into the bowl. Turn it to coat it with butter, so that it does not form a crust while it rises. Cover the bowl with a clean towel or with plastic wrap and place it in a *warm draft-free* place to rise (the carbon dioxide gas pushing against the gluten strands) until it has doubled in bulk. This will take from one to two hours depending on the nature of the dough and the amount of yeast used. One of the best places for worry-free dough rising is in the turned off oven, with a pan of boiling water on the oven floor. During this time you can nap, call your mother-in-law, or read a modest amount of *War and Peace*.

There is a simple way of determining whether or not the dough has risen sufficiently—when it looks about doubled, gently poke a finger hole in the dough (if you are too enthusiastic in your poking, the whole airy edifice will collapse, so be careful), recover the dough, and wait a few minutes. If the hole remains, the dough has risen sufficiently—if it has filled up, leave the dough to rise a little more.

6. At this point, the dough is ready for punching down (this deflates the gas-filled gluten frame), shaping into loaves, and a second rising before baking. If time is a problem, and you are not ready for this final stage, the dough may be punched down, kneaded a few times and left to rise again in the bowl. This can be done several times with no harm to the bread. Each rising will be a little shorter than the previous one, and will give the bread a finer texture. If, for some reason, you cannot finish baking although the dough is ready, simply punch it down, cover the bowl and refrigerate. The action of the yeast will continue, but very slowly. Anytime you are in the vicinity of the refrigerator, give the dough a swift punch. On the next day, bring it to room temperature, let it rise and continue with the recipe.

7. The dough is now ready to be shaped into loaves. I find the best and most convenient way to bake them is free form, on a

baking sheet. After punching down, the dough should be kneaded a few turns and allowed to rest for a few moments. Then pat and nudge the lively dough into the proper shape. (At this point the dough is so alive that it is practically talking back to you). Place the loaves on a baking sheet that has been greased or sprinkled with a generous amount of coarse cornmeal. The cornmeal method imparts a delicious crunchy bottom to your loaf; it is a marvelous texture foil to the tenderness of the crumb (the inside of the loaf). If the dough is not a particularly stiff one, it may be shaped and placed in a buttered loaf pan. Either way, it must then have its final rising. This last rising will take about one half the time of the previous one, and will have to be in some alternate warm, draft-free place because at this time the oven should be preheating for the final baking. You will need to gauge this rising by eye; a finger poke will mar the finished loaf. When the loaves have doubled, ease them into the oven, and let them bake the specified amount of time.

8. During the first part of the baking, an impressive phenomenon, "oven spring", occurs; the yeast gives its final push to the gluten web before it is killed by the heat of the oven. The loaf will rise still more during this time, then it will begin to set. Finally, it will begin to turn a deep golden brown. If it is made with no shortening and no sweetening (some of the best breads in the world are made with only flour, water, yeast, and salt), it will need some help to get brown. During the baking of such bread, place a pan of boiling water on the oven floor. Several times during the baking period, spray the loaves with water. If you have a toy water pistol around the house, use it for spraying purposes. If anyone sees you shooting the bread, explain that you are killing the evil spirits that threaten the success of your loaf, and leave it at that.

Many other kinds of breads brown nicely by themselves, but a nice shiny glaze can be achieved by brushing the loaves before baking with egg yolk and water, egg whites and water, whole egg and water, cornstarch and water, or just plain old water. Use a pastry brush to apply the glaze. If you like a bread with a tender crust, brush the loaves with melted butter as they emerge from the oven, but when you rob a loaf of its crustiness, you are also depriving it of a good deal of character.

9. The trickiest part of the whole process is checking the loaves to determine doneness. There are several ways to check: first, the loaves should be a deep golden brown and should smell like bread; second, when you knock each loaf on the bottom with your knuckles, it should emit a hollow sound. (If a voice says, "Come in", go lie down); and third, a skewer or cake tester in-

serted all the way in will emerge clean. If there is any doubt, put the loaves back in the oven for a few minutes. The baking time is always approximate; it depends on your oven, your pan, and so on. Sometimes it is ready before the time specified in the recipe, so always check it during baking. If, when the loaf emerges from the oven, you cut into it and it is not done (it will show little doughy unbaked lumps), simply shove it back into the oven for a few minutes. The cut edges may dry out a bit, but otherwise it will be fine. Cool the finished bread on racks. Never wrap it until it is completely cool—if it lasts that long.

10. The best part comes last. Cut into the finished loaf with a good, serrated bread knife. Taste a slice, and then try to restrain yourself from rushing headlong into the street to press pieces of your masterpiece on helpless passersby. Also restrain yourself from immediately eating the whole thing. The moment that you taste the first slice of your own fresly baked loaf is a heady one. It's a good bet that you will never buy a packaged bread again.

The following four loaves represent my idea of perfect bread. Crusty, dense, chewy, and intensely flavorful, they put squishy-soft store-bought loaves to shame. The corn rye is the closest I have been able to get to the old fashioned Jewish corn rye I remember so vividly from my childhood. I was always the one to run to the corner baker at the last minute for a hot loaf, right out of the oven. I would wander home with my nose buried in the bag, inhaling the remarkably yeasty fragrance of the freshly baked, freshly sliced loaf. By the time I arrived home, both heels and a slice from the middle were gone—it was impossible to carry such a loaf home and leave it untouched. The combination of hard, crunchy crust and tender, yeasty flavorful crumb is unforgettable—I spent years trying to duplicate it in my kitchen. This version comes close. It makes excellent sandwiches, and is marvelous with ragouts and other saucy dishes. Dabble thick slices in the sauce on your plate and eat it uninhibitedly. There are few gastronomic pleasures to equal it.

Old Fashioned Corn Rye
1 large loaf

1 package yeast
½ cup warm water
  (100 to 115 degrees)
2 cups warm water
2 tablespoons kosher salt
1 tablespoon caraway seeds
3 cups rye flour

1 cup mashed potatoes (instant
  mashed potatoes work well,
  believe it or not)
5 to 6 cups unbleached white
  flour
corn meal

1. Combine yeast with ½ cup warm water in a large bowl. Stir with a fork or small whisk. Add remaining water. Add salt and caraway seeds. Stir in rye flour 1 cup at a time, the potatoes, and the white flour 1 cup at a time, until a soft dough is formed.

2. Turn dough out onto floured surface. Knead vigorously for 20 to 25 minutes until smooth and elastic. Knead in up to 1 more cup of white flour if needed. Let dough rest while you wash, dry and butter the bowl. Knead the dough another few times, form into a ball and place it in the bowl. Turn it to coat with the butter. Cover with a clean kitchen towel and put in a warm draft-free place to rise until doubled in bulk, 1 to 1½ hours. It has risen sufficiently when you can poke a finger into the dough and the hole remains.

3. Flour your fist and punch down the dough. Knead a few times, then shape into a round, plump loaf, and place it on a large cornmeal-sprinkled baking sheet. Cover with a clean kitchen towel and place it in a warm, draft-free place to double in bulk. Meanwhile, preheat the oven to 375 degrees.

4. When loaf has doubled, slash it lightly in 2 places with a sharp knife. Brush it with cold water. Bake it for 1 to 1½ hours, until a knuckle rap produces a hollow sound. Brush with water twice during the baking process. Cool thoroughly on a rack.

Whole Wheat Continental Bread
3 loaves

2 packages yeast
½ cup warm water
   (100 to 115 degrees)
2½ cups warm water
2 tablespoons kosher salt

3¼ cups whole wheat flour
3¼ cups unbleached white flour
corn meal

1. Combine yeast with ½ cup warm water in a large bowl. Stir with a fork or small whisk. Add remaining water. Add salt.

2. Stir in flour 1 cup at a time, beginning with whole wheat. Use a whisk until dough becomes stiff, then switch to a wooden spoon.

3. Turn dough out onto a well floured work surface. Knead rhythmically for 10 to 15 minutes until the dough is smooth, springy, nonsticky, and elastic. Add more flour as you knead if necessary. The dough is ready if you can poke 2 fingers into it and the resulting indentations spring back.

4. Cover the dough with a cloth to rest while you wash, dry, and generously butter the bowl. Knead the dough a few more turns, then form into a ball and place it in the bowl. Cover the bowl and put it in a warm, draft-free place until the dough has doubled in bulk, 1½ hours. It has risen sufficiently when you can poke a finger into the dough and the hole remains.

5. When doubled, flour your fist and punch the dough down. Knead it a few times and then let it rest.

6. Sprinkle 1 large or 2 small baking sheets with a liberal amount of corn meal. Divide the dough into 3 equal parts. While you work with 1 piece, keep the other 2 covered. Flour your work surface. Pat, push, and cajole each piece of dough into a loaf shape, fatter in the middle than at the ends. Place loaves on baking sheet. With a sharp knife, slash the loaves lightly at 2-inch intervals. Cover with a cloth and place in a warm, draft-free place, to rise until doubled, about ½ hour. Meanwhile, preheat oven to 400 degrees.

7. Bake for 35 to 50 minutes in the oven with a pan of boiling water on the oven floor. Spray the loaves with water several times during the baking process. To test for doneness, rap the bottom of the loaf with your knuckles. The loaf should sound hollow. Also, a skewer inserted through the bottom should come out clean. Cool on wire racks, but these are delicious right out of the oven.

Pumpernickel
3 large loaves

1½ cups unbleached white flour
1½ cups whole wheat flour
2 cups rye flour
½ cup bran buds
½ cup yellow corn meal
½ cup wheat germ
1 tablespoon unsweetened cocoa
1 tablespoon instant coffee
2 tablespoons kosher salt
1 tablespoon caraway or fennel
  seeds
1 cup mashed potatoes

4 tablespoons butter
2 packages yeast
½ cup warm water (100 to 115
  degrees)
3 cups warm water
½ cup molasses
up to 7 cups additional
  unbleached white flour
corn meal
1 egg beaten with 1 tablespoon
  water

1. Combine first 12 ingredients in a large bowl.

2. Combine yeast and ½ cup warm water in another bowl. Stir with a fork or small whisk. Add 3 more cups of warm water and ½ cup molasses. Stir the flour mixture into the liquid, 1 cup at a time.

3. Beat the mixture well with a wooden spoon. Beat in enough additional white flour to form a soft, shaggy dough (2 to 3 cups more).

4. Flour work surface. Turn out dough and begin kneading. Knead in more white flour as needed to produce a smooth, nonsticky dough (3 to 4 cups more). Knead vigorously for about 20 minutes until the dough is smooth and lively. It is kneaded sufficiently when a lightly poked finger hole in the dough springs back. Let the dough rest, covered, while you wash, dry, and butter the large bowl.

5. Knead the dough a few more turns. Form it into a ball and place it in the buttered bowl; turn it so that it is covered with butter. Cover bowl with plastic wrap or a clean kitchen towel and place in a warm, draft-free place until the dough has doubled in bulk. This will take about 1½ hours. When you think it is ready, gently poke two holes in the risen dough and cover it again for about 5 minutes. If the holes remain, the dough has risen sufficiently.

6. Flour your fist and punch down the dough. Turn it out and knead a few times and then let it rest covered, for 5 minutes.

7. Cut the dough into 3 equal pieces. Shape each piece into a plump round loaf. Sprinkle a large baking sheet or two smaller ones with cornmeal. Place balls of dough on sheets. Leave plenty

of room around them for they will expand considerably. Cover with a towel or plastic wrap and place in a warm draft-free place until they have doubled in bulk (40 to 45 minutes).

8. Preheat oven to 375 degrees. Beat egg with 1 tablespoon water in a small bowl.

9. When loaves have risen, brush them with egg-water glaze. Place in preheated oven and bake for 1 hour or more, until done. They are done when· they emit a hollow sound when thumped on the bottom with the knuckles. Also, a thin skewer inserted all the way into the loaf will come out clean. Cool the loaves on wire racks.

Challah (Jewish Sabbath Bread)
1 monumental loaf

3 packages yeast
2½ cups warm water
  (100 to 115 degrees)
2 tablespoons honey
1 tablespoon kosher salt
¼ cup vegetable oil
2 cups unbleached white flour

3 eggs
3 to 4 cups unbleached white
  flour
1 egg yolk mixed with 1 teaspoon
  water
poppy seeds

1. Combine yeast and water in a large bowl.

2. Stir in honey, salt, oil, 2 cups of flour and eggs. Stir with a whisk.

3. Beat in remaining flour, 1 cup at a time. Switch from the whisk to a wooden spoon as the dough gets stiffer.

4. Turn dough out onto floured surface and knead for about 15 minutes until smooth, satiny, and very lively. This is a very responsive dough. It is very easy to work with and feels about as smooth and soft as a baby's bottom. The dough has been kneaded sufficiently when 2 lightly poked finger holes spring back. Let the dough rest, covered, while you wash, dry, and oil the large bowl.

5. Form the dough into a ball and place it in the bowl. Turn it so that it is coated with oil. Cover with a clean kitchen towel or plastic wrap and place it in a warm, draft-free place until the dough has doubled in bulk, about 1½ hours. To check for proper rising, gently poke 2 holes in risen dough, and leave for 5 minutes. If holes remain, the dough is ready.

6. Flour your fist and punch down dough. Turn out and knead a few times. Then let it rest, covered, for a few minutes. Grease a large baking sheet.

7. Divide the dough into 2 equal parts. Set 1 part aside covered. Divide the remaining piece into 3 equal parts. Gently pull, roll and stretch each piece into a thick rope. Starting in the middle, braid the ropes, first down one end, then the other. Pinch the ends together and center the braid on the buttered sheet. Divide the remaining piece of dough into 4 equal parts. Set 1 piece aside, covered. Form the 3 pieces into ropes and braid as before, but this braid should be smaller than the first. Set second braid securely on top of first braid. Pinch the braids together. Pull and stretch the last piece of dough into a short fat rope. Twist it several times. Place it on top of the second braid. Pinch the dough together so that it doesn't fall off. Cover the entire loaf with a clean dry cloth or plastic wrap. Place in a warm, draft-free place to double in bulk, about ½ hour.

8. Preheat the oven to 400 degrees. Mix egg yolk and water in a small bowl.

9. When the loaf has risen, brush it with the egg yolk glaze and sprinkle liberally with poppy seeds. Bake for 45 minutes to 1 hour. It is done when it is golden, and a knuckle thump on the bottom produces a hollow sound. Also, a skewer inserted into the loaf will emerge clean. This bread is delicious right out of the oven. Be careful or it will vanish before it even cools.

Note: For an alternate shape, do not braid the risen punched down dough. Instead, gently pull, stretch, and roll all of the dough into a long thick rope. Coil the rope into a large snail-like spiral. Put the spiral on the oiled pan, and continue with the recipe as written.

Betty's Rolls
About 2½ dozen. Use what you need, freeze the rest.

Betty Harris made these every day when we both worked in a small Atlanta restaurant. As she walked in each morning, her movements were always the same; she would take off her hat with one hand, reach for the yeast with the other, and get down to work. She worked completely by ear and by eye. I asked her for the recipe, but she could never explain what she did with such ease every day. Finally, one day I followed her around the kitchen armed with measuring and writing utensils, determined to obtain the formula for her feather light rolls. This recipe is the result. The rolls make excellent hamburger buns, simply use a glass of the appropriate size when cutting the dough.

4 packages yeast
hot tap water
¼ pound butter cut into small
   pieces
1 quart milk
6 tablespoons sugar

1 tablespoon salt
9 cups unbleached, all-purpose
   white flour
2 eggs, lightly beaten
melted butter

1. Dissolve the yeast well in just enough hot water to cover. (The water should feel comfortably warm to your wrist).

2. Combine butter, milk, sugar, and salt in a saucepan. Heat to lukewarm. (Again comfortably warm).

3. Place 8 cups of flour in a very large mixing bowl. Stir in the milk mixture and 2 eggs. Stir in the dissolved yeast. Beat in up to 1 cup more flour until a sticky dough is achieved.

4. Beat the whole mixture vigorously with a wooden spoon but do not overbeat. Stop beating when the mixture follows the spoon in a slightly rubbery way.

5. When the dough reaches this elastic stage, scrape it out onto a pan to rest. (It will be very sticky). Wash the big bowl, dry it, and butter it. Dump the dough back into the bowl, spread the top surface with a film of softened butter, cover with plastic wrap, and put it in a warm place to rise until doubled in bulk. This will take about 1 hour. The best place for rising is in the turned off oven with a pan of boiling water on the oven floor.

6. When doubled, remove dough from oven and preheat oven to 500 degrees. Flour your fist and punch the dough down. Flour your work surface and rolling pin. Turn dough out onto work surface and roll to about ½-inch thick. The dough will still be somewhat sticky so keep the rolling pin and the surface of the dough well floured.

7. Grease several baking sheets. Cut the dough into circles of desired size with a glass and place the circles on the greased sheets. Gather up any scraps into a ball, roll out and cut into additional circles.

8. Brush all circles of dough with melted butter and let rise until doubled (about 20 minutes).

9. Place baking sheets in 500 degree oven. Do them in batches if necessary. Bake only until browned, about 7 or 8 minutes. Check them carefully.

These are delicious right out of the oven, but they can be cooled and used later in the day. They also freeze very well.

Stollen-Patisserie Bothe
two stollen

Edgar Bothe's stollen, a typical Austrian Christmas sweet yeast bread, is easy to make and freezes beautifully; several can be made before Christmas and stashed away in the freezer. They make excellent, edible gifts.

1 pound, 2 ounces raisins—dark, light, or combination
hot water
¾ cup milk (approximately)
2 packages dry yeast
4 cups unbleached, all-purpose white flour
½ teaspoon salt

2 tablespoons sugar
¼ pound butter, softened
1 egg
1 ounce grated lemon peel
4 ounces chopped candied citron (optional)
melted butter
powdered sugar

1. Soak raisins in hot water to cover.

2. Heat milk to lukewarm (100 to 115 degrees). Dissolve yeast in the milk.

3. Combine flour, salt, sugar, butter, egg, and yeast-milk mixture in a large bowl. Stir, adding more flour if necessary, until a stiff dough that clears the sides of the bowl is achieved. If dough is too dry, add a bit more milk, but don't let it get sticky.

4. Place the dough on a floured surface, and knead vigorously until smooth, shiny, and elastic (about 10 minutes). Wash and dry the large bowl.

5. Drain raisins in a colander and shake dry. Shape the dough into a ball and return it to the bowl. Spread the raisins, lemon peel, and citron over the dough and cover the bowl lightly with plastic wrap or a clean cloth. Let rise in a warm place for approximately 15 minutes.

6. Knead again in the bowl, distributing raisins, lemon peel, and citron uniformly throughout the dough. Use additional flour if the dough is sticking, but guard against crushing the raisins. Let rise again for 10 minutes, then divide the dough into two parts of equal weight. Shape these into balls and let rest for 10 minutes.

7. Flatten the balls with a rolling pin, dusting with flour whenever necessary. Roll the dough into ovals. The longest diameter on each oval should be 7 inches. Using the longer diameter as a folding line, fold the ovals almost, but not quite in half. The bottom edge of the folded oval should extend a bit beyond the top.

8. Line 2 baking sheets with baking parchment, or butter and flour the sheets. Place stollen on the sheets and let them rise in a warm, humid environment until tender and at least 1½ times their original size. (This may take as long as 2 hours. A turned off oven with a pan of boiling water on the oven floor is the best place for the rising).

9. When the stollen have risen sufficiently, remove them and the pan of water from the oven. Preheat the oven to 350 degrees. Bake the stollen for about 35 minutes, until they are a deep brown color, and a knuckle thump on their undersides produces a hollow sound. Cool them on racks, then brush generously with unsalted melted butter and sprinkle with powdered sugar.

Frank Ma's Onion Pancakes
18 pancakes

These flaky, flat Chinese breads are not easy to make, but if you love Oriental food, they are worth the effort. Forming the pancakes properly takes practice—you will probably need to make a few batches before you get them exactly right.

3 cups boiling water
7 cups unbleached, all-purpose
   flour
1½ bunches scallions

½ cup peanut or corn oil
salt
peanut or corn oil

1. In a bowl, stir water gradually into flour with 2 chopsticks or a wooden spoon. Stir it vigorously until it forms a rough dough. Knead it in the bowl, turning the bowl as you knead until the dough is smooth. If it seems too dry and crumbly, add up to ½ cup hot water.

2. Form the dough (it will still be somewhat rough, not like a yeast dough) into a ball, cover directly over its surface with a damp towel, and let it rest for 20 minutes. It can be kept well covered with plastic wrap for up to 2 days in the refrigerator.

3. Pound the scallions with your hand or the side of a cleaver or knife to soften up a bit. Slice thinly, green and white parts. Place in a small bowl.

4. Flour board or work surface liberally. Knead dough until soft, smooth, and pliable.

5. Work with half the dough at a time. (Keep the other half well-covered). Flour top of dough and grease a large rolling pin. Roll out dough until it is a large, roughly rectangular sheet, about ⅛-inch thick.

6. Evenly spread approximately ¼ cup vegetable oil over the sheet of dough. Sprinkle salt evenly over dough. Sprinkle on half the sliced scallions evenly.

7. Start with long end, roll up dough into a long, sausage shape, as if you were rolling up a rug. It will be about 2½ feet long. With a sharp knife, cut it into 3-inch lengths.

8. Flour your hands, flour open ends of each section of rolled dough. Holding the open ends in your floured palms, twist each section of rolled dough gently between the hands, twisting in opposite directions with each hand, to seal ends, flouring hands as needed as oil leaks out. They must be sealed very well. Compress each gently between the palms into round cakes about 1-inch thick and 2-inches wide.

9. With a smaller rolling pin, roll each cake into flat circles about ¼-inch thick, 6½ inches wide.

10. Heat large skillet. Pour in oil to a depth of ⅛ inch. Fry pancakes, 2 at a time, on moderately high heat. When lightly browned on one side turn and cook until nicely browned and crispy on the second side, less than 5 minutes. Drain on paper towels. As the oil gets dirty and burned looking, pour it out, wipe out skillet, and start again.

11. When all the pancakes are done, serve at once in a Chinese menu with soup, hors d'oeuvre, or cold dishes.

Chapter 7

Desserts

Chocolate

Chocolate desserts are magical in their remedial properties. According to some, they have the restorative powers of penicillin, chicken soup, and a Fred Astaire movie, all rolled up into one seductive foodstuff. When culinary therapy is in order, try a chocolate bread pudding (see egg chapter) or one of the following.

Chocolate Mousse
Serves 8

*9 ounces semi-sweet chocolate
  chips*
¼ cup sugar
3 tablespoons hot strong coffee
2 eggs

2 egg yolks
1 cup whipping cream, scalded
*4 tablespoons orange brandy
  or rum*
whipped cream (optional)

1. Place chocolate chips, sugar, coffee, eggs, and yolks in container of electric blender in the order given. Turn blender on high, immediately uncover and pour in hot cream in a steady stream.

2. Add brandy. Blend for 1 minute on high.

3. Pour into dessert glasses or goblets. Chill until set.
   Garnish each serving with whipped cream, if desired.

Chocolate Loaf
Serves 8

8 ounces semi-sweet chocolate
1/4 cup orange liqueur
1/2 pound softened butter
2 tablespoons super fine sugar
2 egg yolks
1 cup, tightly packed, ground
  blanched almonds (about 6
  ounces, ground in the blender)

2 egg whites
pinch cream of tartar
12 Petite Beurre biscuits,
  broken into raggedy pieces,
  approximately 1 x 1½ inches
  each
whipped cream

1. In a heavy saucepan, melt the chocolate with the liqueur over a low light, stirring it occasionally. When melted, set it aside to cool.

2. Cream the butter against the side of a mixing bowl until it is very smooth. Beat in the sugar, then the yolks, one at a time. Incorporate them well. Beat in the ground almonds and the cooled chocolate. Scrape the mixture into a large bowl and wash and dry the mixer bowl.

3. Beat the egg whites with the cream of tartar until they hold firm peaks. Quickly fold them into the chocolate mixture with a rubber spatula. Gently fold in the broken biscuits.

4. Lightly oil an 8½ x 4½ x 2½ loaf pan. Pour in the mixture and spread it evenly with a spatula. Cover well and refrigerate for several hours.

5. To serve, run a knife around the loaf, cutting down to the bottom. Dip the bottom of the pan in hot water, invert on a chilled platter and rap the platter on the table. Repeat if necessary. The loaf should unmold nicely. Serve in thin slices with whipped cream.

Chocolate-Potato Torte

5 ounces unsweetened chocolate
1 teaspoon instant coffee
1/4 pound butter, softened
1½ cups sugar
5 egg yolks

1 teaspoon orange extract
2 cups hot mashed potatoes
  (instant mashed potatoes
  work fine)
whipped cream

1. Line a 4-cup shallow baking dish with parchment paper.

2. Melt the chocolate with the coffee in the top of a double boiler, over simmering water.

3. Cream the butter with an electric beater. Beat in the sugar. Beat in the yolks, one by one. Beat very well.

4. Beat in the chocolate-coffee mixture and the orange extract. Beat in the potatoes.

5. Spread the mixture in the prepared dish. Smooth the top and cover with wax paper. Refrigerate for several hours or overnight.

This torte may be made several days in advance. Serve in thin slices, with whipped cream, if desired.

Ruth Jenkins's Fudge Brownies

These rich and sybaritic brownies are from an excellent cookbook on traditional southern foods; "Four Great Southern Cooks" from DuBose Publishers.

1 cup sugar	*2 eggs*
¼ pound butter, melted	*1 cup pecans or walnuts, chopped*
2 squares bitter chocolate, melted	*pinch salt*
½ cup flour	*1 teaspoon vanilla*

1. Grease and flour a 1½-quart shallow baking pan.

2. Place all ingredients into a mixing bowl and stir until mixed well.

3. Spread the batter in the prepared baking pan and place in a cold oven.

4. Set oven to 450 degrees for 5 minutes, then set back to 300 degrees. Bake for 20 minutes. They will be a bit soft, but dry on top. Cut into squares when cool.

Maureen's Mississippi Mud Brownies

½ pound butter, softened	*¼ teaspoon salt*
2 cups sugar	*⅓ cup unsweetened cocoa*
4 eggs	*1 to 1½ cups chopped pecans*
2 teaspoons vanilla	*or walnuts*
1½ cups all-purpose flour	

1. Preheat oven to 350 degrees.

2. Grease and flour a 9 x 13-inch shallow baking pan.

3. Cream butter and sugar. Add eggs and blend well. Add vanilla.

4. Sift flour, salt, and cocoa together and mix well into blended mixture. Add nuts.

5. Bake in prepared pan 30 to 40 minutes. Let cool thoroughly before cutting into squares.

Butterscotch Brownies

¼ pound butter
2 cups brown sugar
1 cup flour
2 teaspoons baking powder

¼ teaspoon salt
2 eggs
1 teaspoon vanilla
1 cup pecans

1. Grease and flour a 9 x 13 inch shallow baking pan.

2. Preheat oven to 350 degrees.

3. Melt butter. Stir in sugar. Cool.

4. Sift together flour, baking powder and salt.

5. Beat eggs into cooled butter-sugar mixture and stir in all other ingredients.

6. Spread in prepared pan.

7. Bake in preheated oven for 25-30 minutes. They will appear somewhat soft when removed from the oven. Cut and serve while still warm.

Cream Cheese Mousse
Serves 6

8 ounces cream cheese, at room
  temperature
1½ tablespoons whipping cream
1 cup confectioners sugar

1½ tablespoons lemon juice
½ teaspoon vanilla
1 cup whipping cream, whipped
fresh raspberries or strawberries

1. Cream the cheese until light and fluffy. Beat in the cream and sugar and continue beating until very smooth.

2. Beat in lemon juice and vanilla. The mixture must be very smooth.

3. Gently fold in the whipped cream. Spoon the mixture into individual dessert goblets or into a glass serving bowl. Chill overnight. Garnish with fresh berries.

Yogurt-Cream Mousse
Serves 6

2 cups whipping cream
2 cardamom pods, lightly crushed
1½ envelopes plain gelatin
  (1½ tablespoons)
½ cup cold water

pinch salt
½ cup sugar
2 cups plain yogurt
raspberries, fresh or frozen

1. Scald the cream with the cardamom pods in a heavy-bottomed saucepan. Meanwhile, soften the gelatin in the cold water.

2. When the cream is scalded, add the salt and sugar, stir until dissolved. Stir in the softened gelatin. Cool to room temperature. Discard cardamom.

3. Strain the mixture into a bowl. Whisk the yogurt to smooth it out. Stir the yogurt and the cream mixture together. Pour the mixture into a 5 cup, lightly oiled mold. Chill several hours.

4. Unmold onto an attractive serving dish and garnish with the berries.

   Note: This tastes best on the day it is made.

Farina Mousse
Serves 6

¼ cup farina (Cream of Wheat)
½ cup granulated sugar
2 cups milk
1 cinnamon stick

1 envelope plain gelatin
  (1 tablespoon)
¼ cup cold water
1 cup whipping cream, whipped

1. Combine the first 4 ingredients and very slowly bring them to a boil, stirring constantly. Do not let them scorch.

2. Turn heat to lowest point and simmer about 5 minutes still stirring, until thick and cooked.

3. While the farina mixture is simmering, soften the gelatin in the cold water.

4. Stir the gelatin thoroughly into the farina. Discard the cinnamon stick.

5. Cool to room temperature.

6. Gently fold in the whipped cream.

7. Pour into a glass bowl. Chill several hours or overnight.

Souffleed Farina Pudding
Serves 4-6

This pudding was inspired by a traditional Greek dessert. Serve it after a Greek or Middle Eastern meal.

softened butter
1 to 2 tablespoons sugar
¼ pound butter
1 cup farina (regular Cream of Wheat)
1 cup sugar
¾ cup cinnamon
pinch of salt
2 cups half and half

6 egg yolks, at room temperature
8 egg whites, at room temperature
pinch of salt
pinch of cream of tartar
¼ cup raisins, soaked in warm water and drained
¼ cup coarsely chopped walnuts
whipped cream (optional)

1. Preheat oven to 350 degrees.

2. Rub the sides and bottom of a 1½-quart souffle dish with softened butter. Sprinkle in sugar and turn the dish to coat the bottom and sides with it. Shake out excess. Set dish aside.

3. Melt butter in a wide saucepan. Stir in farina and sugar. Stir the mixture constantly over low heat, for about 15 minutes, until it begins to brown delicately. Stir in cinnamon and salt.

4. Whisk in half and half. Bring to a boil, reduce heat and cook, stirring constantly until the mixture is smooth and thickened. Set aside to cool slightly.

5. Whisk in the egg yolks, one by one, whisking well after each addition.

6. Place the egg whites in a very clean bowl. Add salt. Begin beating them with a clean whisk. As the whites begin to get foamy, add the pinch of cream of tartar. Continue beating them at high speed until they hold firm peaks, but do not let them get dry and clumpy.

7. Immediately scoop up ¼ to ⅓ of the beaten whites with a rubber spatula and stir them into the farina base, using the spatula to stir them well.

8. Then immediately dump the remaining beaten whites onto the lightened farina mixture. With the spatula, fold the whites and the base together, using an over-under motion and turning the bowl as you fold. Do not overfold. A few white streaks won't hurt.

9. With a large kitchen spoon, spoon half the souffle mixture into the prepared dish. Sprinkle with the raisins and nuts. Spoon in the remaining mixture. Bake for 35 to 40 minutes, until puffed and firm. Serve at once, with whipped cream if desired.

Heinz Sowinski's Baked Apples
Serves 4

4 medium baking apples
  (winesap or rome beauty)
lemon juice
1 cup Chablis
2 cloves
½ cinnamon stick
½ cup raisins

½ cup chopped almonds
4 teaspoons brandy
4 teaspoons honey
4 tablespoons Advocaat liqueur
whipped cream
sliced almonds

1. Preheat oven to 350 degrees.

2. With a swivel bladed vegetable peeler, peel a band of skin from around the circumference of the apple. Core the apple. Rub the peeled surface and the inside of the apple with lemon juice to prevent discoloring.

3. Place apples in a 1½ to 2-inch deep glass baking dish. Pour the Chablis around apples, and add the cloves and cinnamon stick.

4. Fill each apple with an equal amount of raisins, almonds, and brandy. Drizzle one teaspoon honey over each apple. Bake the apples for about ½ hour. They should be tender enough to eat with a spoon, but not falling apart.

5. Pour one tablespoon Advocaat Liqueur over each apple. Top with whipped cream and sliced almonds, and serve at once.

Susan Steel's German Apple Cake

This cake has a thin, buttercake base, a thick layer of apples, and a crumbly topping. It's the sort of cake that disappears while still warm.

Crumble

⅔ cup all-purpose flour
⅓ cup granulated sugar
½ teaspoon cinnamon (optional; it can be added if the apples lack flavor)

2½ ounces butter, softened

Cake

2½ ounces butter, softened
½ cup granulated sugar
2 eggs
¼ teaspoon vanilla extract
1 teaspoon lemon extract

¾ cup self-rising flour
⅓ cup cornstarch
4 tablespoons milk (approximately)

Topping

2 large apples, peeled, cored, and thinly sliced (toss apples with lemon juice to prevent darkening)

1. To make crumble: sift flour, sugar and cinnamon together; work in butter with your fingers until the mixture is crumbly—it will resemble corn meal. Set aside.

2. Butter and flour a 9 x 13-inch oblong glass ceramic baking dish. Preheat oven to 350 degrees.

3. Cream butter and sugar together. Beat in eggs and flavorings.

4. Sift flour and cornstarch together and beat into the butter-sugar mixture with enough of the milk to make a smooth batter with a heavy dropping consistency.

5. Pour the batter into the prepared pan. Spread and smooth it with a rubber spatula. Arrange apples over the batter, leaving about ½ inch clear around the rim. Sprinkle crumble over the whole thing.

6. Bake for 30 to 40 minutes in the 350 degree oven, until the cake browns and pulls away from the sides of the pan, and a toothpick tests clean. Serve the cake out of the dish.

This cake is marvelous hot, right out of the oven.

Cheese Cake

Crust

1½ cups graham cracker crumbs   6 tablespoons melted butter
¼ cup sugar

Filling

5 8-ounce packages cream cheese,   3 tablespoons fresh lemon juice
. at room temperature   5 whole eggs
3 tablespoons flour   2 egg yolks
1¾ cups sugar   ¼ cup whipping cream
3 tablespoons vanilla

1. Combine crumbs and sugar. Add melted butter and mix to moisten. Press this mixture on the bottom and part way up the sides of a 10-inch springform pan. Place in the refrigerator to chill while making filling.

2. Preheat oven to 500 degrees.

3. Cream the cream cheese in an electric mixer until soft and fluffy.

4. Beat in the flour. Beat in the sugar, a little bit at a time. Beat in the vanilla, the lemon juice, the eggs and egg yolks 1 at a time, and the cream, beating very very well between additions.

5. Pour cheese mixture into the prepared springform pan. Bake at 500 degrees for 12 minutes.

6. Turn oven down to 200 degrees and bake for 45 minutes.

7. Turn oven off and leave cake in the oven for 15 minutes.

8. Remove pan from oven and cool on rack for 1 hour.

9. Refrigerate the cake in the pan for 5 hours before removing side of pan. This is very important; the cake may collapse if the 5 hour period is cut short.

Rugelach *(Nut-Filled Crescents)*
32 Crescents

8 ounces cream cheese	½ cup granulated sugar
8 ounces butter	½ cup raisins
2 cups flour	½ teaspoon cinnamon
confectioners sugar	1 cup chopped walnuts

1. Remove cream cheese and butter from refrigerator and let soften for 15 minutes.

2. Place cream cheese, butter, and flour in a bowl and work it all together with the hands until smoothly amalgamated. Form into a ball, wrap well with plastic wrap and refrigerate for at least an hour. (It can remain in the refrigerator for a week if necessary).

3. Preheat oven to 350 degrees. When the dough is chilled, dust your work surface with confectioners sugar, and roll out half the dough at a time. Leave remainder in the refrigerator. Roll into a circle, about ¹⁄₁₆ of an inch thick, giving the dough quarter-inch turns as you roll, and sprinkling with a bit of confectioners sugar to prevent sticking. Work quickly; when the dough loses its chill, it is difficult to work with.

4. Cut the circle of dough like a pie, into 16 wedges. Combine granulated sugar, raisins, cinnamon and walnuts in a bowl. Sprinkle each wedge with mixture and roll, from the wide edge to the point, into a crescent. Place crescents on an ungreased cookie sheet. Refrigerate. Repeat with second half of dough.

4. Bake for 15 to 20 minutes or until lightly browned. Do not overbake; they will still be a bit soft when done. Cool on a rack.

Darlene Gereb's Lepan *(Hungarian Custard Pie)*

Crust

½ batch cream cheese dough (see preceding recipe)	confectioners sugar

Filling

½ pint sour cream	3 eggs
2 teaspoons minute tapioca	¼ teaspoon vanilla
¾ cup sugar	

1. Preheat oven to 350 degrees.

2. Dust your work surface with confectioners sugar, and roll out the dough to fit a 9-inch pie pan. The dough should be about ¼ of an inch thick. Press the dough into the pan.

3. Beat together the sour cream, tapioca, and sugar. Beat the eggs, then beat them thoroughly into the sour cream mixture with the vanilla. Pour into the dough-lined pie pan. (It should fill it about ¾ full).

4. Place in the oven for 25 to 35 minutes, until the crust is browned and the custard is puffy and set. It should remain a bit runny in the center. Let cool for a few minutes, but this is wonderful when still warm; don't let it get too cool before tasting.

Meringues
1 dozen Large Meringues, or 2 dozen Small

These are fun and easy because you put them in the oven, turn off the oven, and forget all about them until the next morning.

2 egg whites *pinch cream of tartar*
1 teaspoon vanilla *⅔ cup sugar*
pinch salt

1. Line a cookie sheet with cooking parchment. Grease. Preheat oven to 350 degrees.

2. Beat egg whites with vanilla and salt. When they begin to get foamy, add cream of tartar. When they hold soft peaks, begin adding sugar gradually. Beat until very stiff and shiny; the mixture will look like marshmallow cream.

3. Drop onto prepared sheet by the teaspoon or the tablespoon, depending on desired size. Place sheet in oven and immediately *turn oven off*. Leave the meringues in the turned-off oven overnight. Do not open door until the next morning.

To serve, place two meringues in a bowl, separated by a scoop of ice cream, and topped with whipped cream. These meringues keep well. Store them at room temperature, covered with plastic wrap.

Variation: Michael's Cookies
1½ dozen large cookies, 3 dozen small cookies

Fold into the stiffly beaten egg white mixture 1 cup coarsely chopped walnuts and/or 1 cup chocolate chips. Spoon onto prepared pan and bake according to preceding recipe.

Helen Lee's Mocha Hazelnut Torte

On a visit to New York, Helen Lee ate a slice of dacquoise at the Windows on the World Restaurant in the World Trade Center. "Why, I'll bet I can make something like this," she said to herself as she lingered over every delicious bite. At home in Atlanta she told her friend Claudette, chef-proprietor of Claudette's French Restaurant in Decatur, that the problem of excess egg whites— separated from yolks destined for hollandaise sauce—was solved. Helen toted home a batch of egg whites and worked up this version of dacquoise. Her torte is now a staple on Claudette's dessert menu.

Torte

1 cup egg whites, at room temperature
pinch of salt
pinch cream or tartar
¾ cup granulated sugar

1½ cups ground, unsalted hazelnuts (can be ground in a blender or processor, but do not grind to a powder)

Icing

1 pound unsalted butter, softened
1 pound confectioners sugar
3 egg yolks

4 teaspoons instant coffee dissolved in ½ cup rum
3 ounces unsweetened chocolate (optional)

1. Preheat oven to 250 degrees.

2. Line a 12 x 16 inch baking sheet with baking parchment. Grease.

3. Beat egg whites with salt. When they begin to get foamy, add cream of tartar. When they hold soft peaks when the beater is withdrawn, begin beating in sugar gradually. Beat until egg whites are stiff and shiny. (They will look something like marshmallow cream.) With a rubber spatula, fold in ground nuts.

4. Spread the meringue on the lined cookie sheet. Spread and smooth it evenly to the edges of the pan.

5. Bake the meringue in the 250 degree oven for 1½ to 2 hours, until set and dry. Remove from oven and let cool. Carefully split it into 3 equal pieces with a knife or spatula. (Don't worry if it cracks a bit—the icing will hide it later). Peel off the parchment.

6. Cream the softened butter with the sugar; beat in the egg yolks one by one. Add the rum-coffee mixture slowly, beating all the while. If you prefer chocolate to mocha, add 3 ounces unsweetened chocolate which has been melted in a double boiler and cooled.

7. Spread the icing between the 3 meringue layers, and over the top and sides.

Keep this cake refrigerated. Remove from refrigerator an hour before serving.

Sweet Noodle Pudding
Serves 6

½ pound wide egg noodles
4 eggs
⅔ cup sugar
1 cup sour cream

grated rind of 1 lemon
¾ cup yellow raisins
4 tablespoons butter

1. Preheat oven to 375 degrees.

2. Cook noodles.

3. Meanwhile, beat eggs with sugar. Beat in sour cream. Stir in lemon rind and raisins.

4. Drain noodles. Rinse under hot running water. Place in large bowl and toss with butter. Stir in egg-sour cream mixture. The noodles should be well coated with the mixture.

5. Pour the noodles into a buttered, shallow, 1½-quart baking dish. Spread them evenly in the dish. Bake for 30 to 40 minutes, until the top is lightly browned and crispy and the pudding is set. (A knife inserted near the center will emerge clean). Cut in squares and serve warm.

Ron Cohn's Palacsinta *(Hungarian Crepe Dessert)*
12 to 14 crepes

3 eggs
1¼ cups flour
1 cup milk
1 teaspoon sugar

pinch of salt
1 cup carbonated water
clarified butter for cooking

Note: read advice on crepes in the egg chapter first.

1. Mix eggs, flour, milk, sugar, and salt to make a smooth pancake-like batter. Let rest for 1 or 2 hours.

2. Stir in carbonated water at the last minute, just before cooking.

3. Heat 8-inch crepe pan. When hot brush with butter. Pour small ladleful of dough into pan, twist to cover entire pan. When top of the batter bubbles, turn over and cook 4 or 5 seconds longer. Brush pan with butter for each Palacsinta. Keep warm covered with wax paper.

233

Filling I for Palacsinta

Ron Cohn's Apricot Jelly

12 ounces dried apricots   *brandy or cherry liqueur to taste*
½ cup sugar (approximately)

1. Put dried apricots in saucepan with water to cover, cook over low heat until apricots disintegrate into a jelly. Add liqueur and sugar to taste. Place some jelly across one end of pancake and roll. Top with powdered sugar which has been standing with a vanilla bean.

Filling II for Palacsinta

Darlene Gereb's Cheese Filling

This can be varied with grated lemon peel, a dash of vanilla, or brandy, if desired.

8 ounces cream cheese   *milk*
½ cup (approximately) sugar

1. Beat cream cheese with sugar to taste and enough milk to make a spreadable mixture.

2. Spread some cold filling on each warm palacsinta, roll up, and serve.

Macaroons-Maison Robert
About 2½ dozen

Robert Reeb has been delighting Atlantans with his traditional French confections and pastries for several years now. His shop—tea room, Maison Robert, is filled with glorious examples of pastry art. The macaroons—chewy almond-paste cookies with or without chocolate filling—are delicious, and easier to make at home than you might think. Keep them well wrapped to preserve freshness.

2 pounds almond paste   *1 cup egg whites*
2 cups plus 4 tablespoons   *additional granulated sugar*
  granulated sugar

1. Preheat oven to 375 degrees.

2. In an electric mixer, with a paddle-shaped beater if possible, blend almond paste and sugar very well until the mixture is crumbly. (Make a shield of wax paper if necessary to keep bits of the mixture from flying out).

3. Add the egg whites and beat at medium speed, with the same paddle-shaped beater (if such a beater is not available, beat on low speed) until the mixture is smooth and fluffy, about the consistency of mashed potatoes.

4. Line 2 or 3 cookie sheets with baking parchment. Grease. Fill a pastry bag fitted with a number 8 round tip with the almond mixture. Pipe onto the parchment covered sheets. Each macaroon should be about 1½ inches in diameter. Leave 1½ inches between each one. Sprinkle each with a bit of sugar.

5. Place the pans in the oven. After 5 minutes, rotate position of pans so that the macaroons cook evenly. Bake for 10 to 15 minutes longer, until the macaroons are lightly browned. Do not overbake—they will be somewhat soft when done. Cool on pan.

Note: To make tiny, chocolate-filled macaroons, use a number 4 tip on your pastry bag, and pipe out macaroons that are about ½ inch in diameter. Bake for 5 to 10 minutes. Make chocolate filling as follows:

1 cup whipping cream

1 pound semi-sweet chocolate, chopped; or 1 pound semi-sweet chocolate chips

1. Bring whipping cream to a boil in a deep heavy pot. Immediately turn off heat.

2. Stir in chocolate. Stir gently until melted and perfectly smooth. Cool.

3. Spread this mixture on half of the tiny macaroons. Top with the remaining macaroons to form chocolate-filled sandwiches. You may also dip the larger macaroons into the chocolate mixture. Cool, chocolate side up.

Strawberries and Cream

I can imagine no other dessert when fresh strawberries are in season.

strawberries
dry white jug wine

sour cream
brown sugar

1. Rinse strawberries in an inexpensive dry white wine. Do not use water. Leave them unhulled. Drain and pile on a platter.

2. Place a small bowl of sour cream and a small bowl of brown sugar in front of each diner. The strawberries are held by the stems, dipped first into the sour cream, then into the sugar, and popped into the mouth.

Orange Pears
Serves 8

2 cups water
1 cup sugar
julienned zest of 2 oranges
juice of 2 oranges

8 firm ripe pears, peeled
1 cup Kirsch or orange brandy
whipping cream

1. Combine water, sugar, orange zest, and juice in a large pot that can be covered. Add pears.

2. Bring to a boil, reduce heat and simmer, covered, until pears are tender, but not mushy (20 to 30 minutes). Stir pears in liquid several times during cooking period.

3. Cool in the syrup. When cool, add liqueur. Pass the cream at the table.

Almond Curd
Serves 6

This is a very refreshing Chinese dessert that goes well after any heavy meal, but is particularly appropriate after a Chinese one.

2 envelopes (2 tablespoons)
  unflavored gelatin
½ cup cold water
1¼ cups boiling water
½ cup sugar

1½ cups milk
1 tablespoon almond extract
food coloring (optional)
1 can mandarin oranges or 1 can
  litchis

1. Soften the gelatin in the cold water for 5 minutes.

2. Add to the boiling water with the sugar. Stir until the gelatin dissolves.

3. Add the milk and almond extract and stir. If desired, a few drops of food coloring can be added.

4. Pour the mixture into a shallow, 1½-quart baking dish and chill several hours until set.

5. When set, cut the gelatin into 1-inch cubes and place cubes in a deep bowl. Add the oranges or litchis and their juice. Stir gently to combine the gelatin cubes and fruit.

Chapter 8

Sauces, Miscellaneous

Sauces

Bearnaise Sauce

The sauce of my dreams is bearnaise, that creamy emulsion of tarragon-enriched egg yolks and butter. When fresh tarragon is at its best and most abundant, I inevitably go into a frenzy of bearnaise production. Bearnaise has a sister sauce, lemon-flavored hollandaise—it is traditionally served with vegetables and poached eggs, while bearnaise is saved for chicken, beef, and fish. My advice is to throw tradition to the winds when fresh tarragon is in season and serve bearnaise with everything. Of course, it would be improper to serve it with everything all at one meal; that would be too much of a good thing. My favorite way with bearnaise is as a first course with a single, lightly steamed vegetable. Young, tender green beans, broccoli, asparagus and new potatoes are all sublime with bearnaise; any one of them arranged on a pretty plate with an accompanying pool of the golden, green-flecked sauce makes an elegant and delicious first course. The best way to eat this course is with the fingers, dipping each vegetable into the sauce first. Serve an arrangement of all the vegetables around the pool of sauce for a wonderful, late summer main dish.

There are many ways to make bearnaise; the easiest is with a blender or food processor, but the resulting sauce will have a raw, homogenized quality that is very unsatisfying. A double boiler method appears in most cookbooks, but it's tricky—if the water accidentally boils, the egg yolks scramble and what should be a lovely, thick creamy sauce turns into an unattractive mass of scrambled eggs. The most efficient method is to use a wire whisk and a large, heavy pot directly on the stove. (Do not use an aluminum or cast iron pot, the sauce will turn an ugly gray.)

If you are not used to making egg yolk emulsion sauces, you may develop bearnaise elbow—in the midst of all the beating, it will feel as if your arm is about to fall off onto the kitchen floor. To avoid this dread affliction, have another person standing by to take over the whisk for a few seconds while you rest. Anyone can do it—my nine year old son spells me when bearnaise elbow seems imminent.

Excessive heat is the enemy of bearnaise; if you don't watch it carefully, your sauce will be sabotaged. Should the sauce reach temperatures above 140 degrees, it will separate; two distinct layers will form, eggs on the bottom, pools of liquid butter on the top. At this point, it is redeemable; simply put a fresh, room temperature egg yolk in a clean pot, whisk it briskly, then whisk in the separated sauce.

If the sauce reaches temperatures above 175 degrees, it will curdle—the yolks will scramble and the whole mess will be completely ruined. The only thing to do in such a case is to stamp off to bed and cry yourself to sleep.

Bearnaise Sauce

½ cup white wine
⅓ cup tarragon wine vinegar
2 tablespoons minced shallots
2½ tablespoons chopped fresh
    tarragon

1 tablespoon chopped fresh parsley
salt and pepper
3 egg yolks, at room temperature
1 cup clarified unsalted butter,
    melted but warm, **not** hot

1. Combine first 6 ingredients in a saucepan. Bring to a boil, reduce heat and simmer briskly until almost all liquid has evaporated. Cool thoroughly.

2. Place cooled tarragon mixture and the egg yolks in a large, heavy saucepan over low heat. Use an asbestos pad or flame tamer under the pot. Whisk the yolks quickly and vigorously. As they begin to poach, they will turn frothy, custardy, and thick. Watch your heat. If too high, the yolks will scramble. After 3 or 4 minutes, remove from the heat.

3. As soon as you remove the pot from the heat, begin whisking in the warm (not hot) butter—driblet by driblet. Keep whisking hard and fast. If the butter is not too hot and you whisk constantly, the egg yolks will expand as they absorb the butter, and the sauce will be lovely, creamy, and thick. Do not make more than an hour or so ahead of time. Do not reheat.

Serve with peeled, lightly steamed asparagus; peeled, lightly steamed broccoli, barely cooked tender young green beans or new potatoes, in their skins. Of course, the sauce is excellent on chicken, fish, beef, and poached eggs as well. Add a tablespoon of tomato paste and a tablespoon of whipping cream to make sauce choron—good on beef and fish. Fresh mint substituted for the tarragon makes sauce paloise—very good with lamb.

Hollandaise Sauce

⅓ cup water
1 tablespoon fresh lemon juice
salt and pepper to taste

3 egg yolks, at room temperature
1 cup unsalted, clarified butter,
* melted but warm, not hot*

1. Combine water, lemon juice, salt, and pepper. Boil vigorously until reduced to about two tablespoons. Cool thoroughly. Make sauce according to the bearnaise recipe, substituting the lemon mixture for the tarragon mixture.

Pesto Sauce
1½ cups

Once you make and taste this earthy, pungent sauce, you will probably feel compelled to have a thriving basil plant near the kitchen at all times.

4 to 5 cups fresh basil leaves
5 tablespoons parsley leaves
2 cloves garlic
2 ounces pine nuts

salt and pepper to taste
½ cup grated Parmesan cheese
¾ cup olive oil
¼ cup grated Parmesan cheese

1. Place basil, parsley, garlic, pine nuts, salt and pepper, ½ cup cheese and olive oil in blender jar. Blend to a rough, coarse paste.
2. Scrape into a bowl. Stir in ¼ cup additional grated cheese.

To serve, toss with hot linguine or fettucini, stir into summer vegetable soups, fold into omelets, or spoon onto cooked fish. To store the sauce, refrigerate with a film of olive oil on its surface.

Mornay Sauce

Mornay sauce is a simple white sauce (bechamel) to which cheese has been added. Both bechamel and mornay sauces are out of fashion in some cooking circles; indeed for a long while I myself refused to make them because I grew up thinking them pasty, sometimes lumpy, always flavorless concoctions. They always seemed to be blanketing something even more unsavory than themselves; elderly leftovers, for instance, that should have remained left, or overcooked chicken with canned peas.

The basic sauce consists of a roux—melted butter to which flour is added—and warm milk or cream. If the roux is cooked gently until golden, the sauce will not taste pasty from insufficiently cooked flour. If a wire whisk is used to stir the warm liquid into the roux, and the stirring continues as the sauce simmers, then it will not be lumpy. And finally, if flavorful ingredients are added to this basic formula, the sauce will certainly not be flavorless.

I always add cooked down sherry to the roux before adding the warm cream. This imparts a subtle, aromatic change to the basic sauce. At the end, when the grated cheese is folded in, it should be done gently so that it incorporates into the sauce as it melts. If stirred in too vigorously, the cheese will form strings, causing the mixture to resemble the top of a pizza, rather than the lovely velvety mornay sauce it should be.

This sauce can cover a multitude of good things. If you do like chewy melted cheese (and who doesn't) a layer of grated cheese can cover the sauce which in turn covers something delicious like poached eggs on English muffins or crisp-tender cauliflower.

The whole thing then goes under the broiler or in a hot oven until bubbling and lightly browned. This is splendid fare indeed, quite a change from questionable leftovers in paste sauce.

Mornay Sauce
About 2 cups

1 cup cream sherry
4 tablespoons butter
3 tablespoons finely chopped
  shallots, or scallions
4 tablespoons flour
1½ to 2 cups half and half,
  scalded

salt and pepper to taste
pinch of nutmeg and cayenne
  pepper
3 tablespoons Gruyere cheese,
  grated

1. Place the sherry in a saucepan. Bring to a boil, stand back, and let the sherry flame. Reduce heat a bit and simmer briskly until reduced to half. Set aside.

2. In a heavy saucepan, melt butter, saute the shallots. Whisk in the flour, and cook, stirring over medium heat, for about 3 minutes until the roux is a light golden color.

3. Whisk the sherry into the roux. The mixture will be quite thick. Whisk in the scalded half and half. Add salt, pepper, nutmeg and cayenne. Bring to a simmer and simmer slowly for 10 minutes or so, until smooth and thickened. Stir frequently with your wire whisk.

4. Turn off heat and gently fold in grated cheese, with a rubber spatula. Taste for seasoning and adjust if necessary.

Set sauce aside until needed. Cover with a piece of plastic wrap right over the surface to prevent a skin from forming.

Cumberland Sauce
2 cups

1 orange	1 tablespoon chopped shallots or
1 lemon	scallions
water	⅔ cup red currant jelly
1½ tablespoons cornstarch	1 teaspoon sugar
⅔ cup port	pinch cayenne pepper

1. Remove the zest from the orange and lemon with a zester or swivel-bladed vegetable peeler and sliver the zest. Parboil in water to cover for 2 minutes. Drain and set aside.

2. Squeeze the juice from the orange and half the lemon. Stir the cornstarch into the juices until it dissolves.

3. Bring the port to a boil. Simmer the shallots in the port for one minute. Add the jelly and the sugar and stir until they are thoroughly dissolved. Add the slivered citrus zests.

4. Stir in the cornstarch mixture and bring to a boil, stirring constantly. When the mixture thickens nicely, remove from heat and season with cayenne. Cool and then refrigerate. Serve cold with pate, turkey, game, or roast pork.

Cranberry-Apple Sauce
4 cups

1 pound fresh cranberries
2 cups sugar
2 tart apples, peeled, cored, and
  diced
⅛ teaspoon ground cloves
⅛ teaspoon allspice

¼ teaspoon cinnamon
zest of 1 lemon, cut into julienne
  strips and parboiled
zest of 1 orange, cut into julienne
  strips and parboiled
½ cup coarsely chopped walnuts

1. Toss together the cranberries, sugar and apples. Place the mixture in a 2-quart pan that can be covered.

2. Cover pan. Cook over medium heat until mixture comes to a boil. (Add no liquid. The apples will render plenty of juice.)

3. Uncover and stir in the spices. Cover and simmer for 12 to 15 minutes more, or until thickened and most of the berries have popped.

4. Stir in orange and lemon zest.

5. Cool and refrigerate. When cold, stir in walnuts. This will keep for weeks, well covered, in the refrigerator.

Chunky Apple Sauce

8 ounces dried apples
water
1 to 2 teaspoons lemon juice

1 teaspoon cinnamon
½ teaspoon nutmeg
½ cup sugar or to taste

1. Soak apples in water to cover overnight. (12 hours).

2. Boil in water until very tender and beginning to fall apart. Drain.

3. Mash apples with potato masher.

4. Beat in remaining ingredients. Cool, and store in the refrigerator.

Miscellaneous

Rendered Chicken Fat
2 cups fat

1 pound chicken fat and fatty skin   1 onion, minced

1. Cut fat and skin into pieces. Put them into a heavy skillet and heat.

2. When the fat starts to melt, add the onion. Let cook over moderate heat until the fat has completely melted and the skin pieces and onion are deeply browned.

3. Strain the liquid fat into a clean jar. Cover and refrigerate.

4. Scrape the browned onion and cracklings into a jar. These are the "grebenes" and considered a great delicacy. Use in chopped liver, mashed potatoes, or kasha.

Sorrel Chiffonade

Wash sorrel leaves well. Strip the leaves from the ribs and stems. Gather the leaves into a heap, and shred them with a sharp chef's knife.

Sorrel Puree
½ cup puree

2 tablespoons butter   4 cups sorrel chiffonade

Heat butter in a non-reactive saucepan. Cook sorrel gently in butter, stirring until it forms a soft, dark green, dry mass. Scrape into a glass or ceramic container and refrigerate. This freezes well. Make several batches when sorrel is in season, and freeze for the winter.

Chapter 9

The Emergency Shelf

Even the most secure people occasionally fall prey to insecurity dreams. An actor dreams of unlearned lines and total confusion on stage; a student dreams of lost classrooms and missed exams, a writer, of forgotten deadlines and blank sheets of paper. One of my personal nightmares involves hordes of unexpected company at my door, clamoring for some of the food they remember from their last visit. In my dream, the glorious piles of fresh produce, interesting meats and assorted cheeses that usually stock my refrigerator have dwindled to nothing, and all the supermarkets in the world are closed. This frightening dream does not occur very often, but when it does, I spend the next day restocking my emergency shelf. It's the comforting presence of all those neatly arranged cans and packages on the shelf that keeps the nightmares at bay. Recipes using such staples are certainly not for everyday, but they work wonders when the fresh stuff has run out, and the hungry multitudes are waiting to be fed.

Artichokes a la Grecque

½ cup raisins
½ cup dry vermouth
1 can artichoke hearts, packed in water, (8½ ounces) drained and quartered

6 tablespoons olive oil
2 tablespoons white wine vinegar
salt and pepper to taste

1. Combine raisins and vermouth in a saucepan. Bring to a boil, reduce heat and simmer for 5 to 10 minutes, until almost all liquid is absorbed.

2. Toss remaining ingredients in a bowl. Add raisins. Chill.

Braised Chinese Mushrooms
Serves 4-6

2 cups dried Chinese or Japanese
  mushrooms
hot water
1½ tablespoons peanut oil
1 thin slice ginger root, peeled
  and minced

2 tablespoons soy sauce
1½ teaspoons sugar
¼ cup chicken stock
sesame oil

1. Rinse mushrooms. Place them in a bowl and cover with hot water. Let soak for ½ hour. Drain and squeeze dry. Trim off tough stems. Cut each mushroom in half.

2. Heat oil in a wok or heavy skillet. Throw in ginger and mushrooms. Stir fry over medium heat for one minute.

3. Combine soy sauce, sugar and stock. Pour over mushrooms. Simmer until almost all liquid is absorbed. Sprinkle with a few drops of sesame oil, and serve at once as an hors d'ouevre.

Corn Chowder
Serves 4

3 slices bacon, diced
3 scallions, trimmed and sliced,
  green and white parts or 1
  small onion finely chopped
1 potato, cooked, peeled and diced
  (optional)
1 16 ounce can cream style corn

1 corn-can half and half or milk
  (use reconstituted powdered
  milk if you're out of everything
  else)
pinch thyme
salt and pepper to taste

1. Cook bacon and scallions or onion together in the bottom of a heavy pot until scallions are limp and bacon is almost crisp. Add potato, and stir in the hot bacon fat.

2. Pour in corn, half and half, thyme, salt and pepper. Bring to a simmer and let simmer for 10 minutes or so. Pour into a comfortable, capacious mug or pottery bowl and sip soothingly.

Mexican Corn Bread

1 16 ounce can creamed corn
1 cup corn meal
3 eggs
1 teaspoon salt
½ teaspoon baking soda

¾ cup milk (reconstituted
  powdered milk is fine)
⅓ cup melted butter
1 cup grated sharp Cheddar cheese
2 tablespoons butter

1. Preheat oven to 400 degrees.

2. Combine the first 7 ingredients in a large bowl. Add half the cheese. Stir together.

3. Place butter in a 1½ quart round oven proof casserole. Put the casserole in the oven until the butter is hot and melted. Immediately pour in the batter. Sprinkle with remaining cheese.

4. Bake for 40 minutes. Serve warm, in wedges.

Bean Salad With Tuna—Italian Style
Serves 8

1 15½ ounce can red kidney
  beans
1 15½ ounce can white kidney
  beans (cannelini beans)
1 15½ ounce can chick peas
1 7 ounce can tuna
1 cup sliced scallions, if available
½ cup chopped fresh parsley, if
  available (do not substitute
  dried parsley)

salt and pepper to taste
½ teaspoon oregano
½ teaspoon basil
2 cloves garlic, minced
4 tablespoons wine vinegar
¾ cup olive oil

1. Drain beans and chick peas in a colander and wash well under running water. Drain again and dry with paper towels. They must be very dry.

2. Drain tuna and mash in the bottom of a large bowl. Add beans and chick peas.

3. Add remaining ingredients, except oil, vinegar, garlic and herbs, and toss gently to combine. Be careful not to pulverize the beans.

4. Combine dried herbs, garlic, oil and vinegar in a small jar and shake well. Pour over tuna and beans and mix it all up gently with your hands. Allow to marinate at least an hour, preferably more, before serving.

Desperation Cassoulet
Serves 8

This is not a real cassoulet—far from it—but someone at my table once dubbed it desperation cassoulet, and the name stuck. It is a very satisfying and delicious bean casserole made out of bits and pieces of things that are likely to be in your pantry and freezer. If you have no pork or lamb stashed away in the freezer, leave it out and increase the amount of sausage. Red kidney beans or chick peas or a combination of both may be used in place of the cannelini beans.

2 pounds well trimmed pork butt, lamb shoulder, or combination of both cut into 1 inch cubes
1 cup dry red wine
3 tablespoons olive oil
3 medium onions coarsely chopped
½ teaspoon dried thyme
salt and pepper to taste
2 cloves garlic, chopped
1 bay leaf
2 cans (1 pound 12 ounces each) tomatoes, mashed with the hands and drained

2 cans white kidney beans (cannelini beans) drained and rinsed in a colander under cold water
1½ cups chicken stock
1 pound (2 pounds if you are not using lamb and pork) smoked sausage—kielbasi, chorizo, pepperoni, etc.—sliced into ½ inch pieces (this kind of sausage keeps for a long time in the refrigerator)
1 cup plain bread crumbs
melted butter

1. Preheat the oven to 450 degrees. Place lamb and pork in a casserole or baking dish. Brown in the oven. This should take 15 to 20 minutes. When brown, add wine, cover casserole, and reduce oven to 350 degrees. Continue cooking for 1 hour.

2. Meanwhile, heat olive oil in a deep heavy saucepan or skillet. Saute onions until golden. Stir in thyme, salt, pepper, garlic, bay leaf and tomatoes. Bring to a boil, reduce heat and simmer for 15 minutes.

3. When meat has cooked for 1 hour, add tomato mixture to the casserole. Stir in the beans, stock and sausages. Cook uncovered for 45 minutes.

4. Sprinkle casserole contents with bread crumbs, and drizzle on some melted butter. Bake an additional ½ hour. Serve at once to hungry friends although the cassoulet may be cooled, refrigerated and reheated at a later time. This is the sort of dish that improves with age.

Smoked Sausage in Wine Sauce
Serves 6

1½ pounds smoked sausages, sliced into ½ inch pieces (use keilbasi, chorizo, pepperoni, whatever you have)
½ cup red wine
¼ cup Dijon mustard

¼ teaspoon thyme
salt and pepper to taste (go easy on the salt)
1 tablespoon finely chopped scallions or shallots

1. Heat oven to 300 degrees. Place sausages in a baking dish in the oven so that they render some of their fat. After 15 minutes drain on absorbent paper.

2. Meanwhile, pour wine into a saucepan. Whisk in mustard. Stir in remaining ingredients. Bring to a boil, reduce heat and simmer gently for 5 minutes, stirring almost constantly.

3. Add sausage to sauce. Serve hot.

Spaghetti with Clam Sauce
Serves 4

4 tablespoons olive oil
3 cloves garlic, minced
1 can (7½ ounces) baby whole clams

1 can (7½ ounces) minced clams
½ cup dry white wine
¼ cup fresh chopped parsley, if available

1. Heat oil in a skillet. Saute garlic in hot oil, but do not let it brown, or it will turn bitter.

2. Add the juice from the two cans of clams and the white wine to the skillet. Simmer briskly for 3 or 4 minutes to reduce the liquid slightly. Reduce heat.

3. Toss the clams in the liquid and heat through. Add salt and pepper and sprinkle with parsley, if you have it. Serve with one pound hot, freshly cooked spaghetti or linguini.

Stuffed Tomatoes
Serves 6

Save bits and pieces of leftover cheese, well wrapped, in the freezer for dishes like this. If the tomatoes are too tart, sprinkle them with a tiny bit of sugar before stuffing.

½ cup plain bread crumbs
½ cup cheese (Swiss, Parmesan, Cheddar—whatever you have) in small cubes
½ cup broken walnut meats
1 to 2 cloves garlic
½ cup fresh parsley if available
¼ cup olive oil
salt and pepper to taste
1 large can Italian pear shaped tomatoes, drained
additional olive oil

1. Preheat oven to 350 degrees.

2. Place all ingredients except tomatoes and additional olive oil in a blender jar or processor. Blend or process to a coarse paste. Use a rubber spatula to push the mixture down onto the blades if you are using a blender. If necessary, add a bit more olive oil. Season to taste.

3. Gently slit each tomato and remove seeds. Stuff with crumb mixture. Place stuffed tomatoes in a shallow baking dish. Drizzle with additional olive oil. Sprinkle with salt and pepper. Bake uncovered for 15 to 20 minutes, until hot and bubbling. Baste with the pan juices once or twice during the baking time. Serve hot.

Chocolate Fondue
Serves 6

3 Toblerone chocolate bars (3 ounces each)
½ cup evaporated milk
2 tablespoons Kirsch, orange liqueur or brandy
1 good quality frozen pound cake, defrosted and cut into cubes

1. Break up Toblerone bars. Put them in a chafing dish with the milk and liqueur. Stir over low heat until melted and smooth. Keep it warm. (This makes a lovely sauce for vanilla ice cream.)

2. Spear cake chunks on a long fork. Dip chunks into chocolate mixture and eat.

Triple Chocolate Cake

Children love this cake. Use the smaller amounts of rum and coffee if it is to be used for a children's party.

1 package good quality devils food cake mix
1 package (4 serving size) instant chocolate pudding mix
1 cup sour cream
½ cup cooking oil
¼ to ½ cup coffee
¼ to ½ cup dark rum
4 large eggs
2 cups semi-sweet chocolate chips

1. Preheat oven to 350 degrees.

2. Combine all ingredients, except chocolate chips in the bowl of electric mixer, mix on low speed briefly, just to blend ingredients together.

3. Beat at medium speed for 1 minute. Stop and scrape down sides of bowl, then beat for 1 minute more.

4. Fold in chocolate chips.

5. Pour batter into well greased and floured Bundt pan. Bake at 350 degrees for 40 minutes to 1 hour, until cake springs back when pressed lightly with the finger, near the center.

6. Cool in pan on rack for about ½ hour. Turn out gently onto serving plate. Let stand over night to allow chocolate chips to firm up.

Chapter 10

Menus

There are countless menu possibilities using the recipes in this book. The following suggestions are meant as a guide, particularly for those of you who belong to the kind of cooking group that prepares a different ethnic dinner once a month. I have included a few holiday and seasonal menus as well as ethnic ones; with a bit of imagination you will be able to put together many more.

ETHNIC MENUS

Chinese:

Everyone remembers that first seductive, compelling and utterly ravishing Chinese culinary adventure. It probably involved something Cantonese toted home from the local Chinese take-out. Those leaky cardboard cartons filled with chow mein, fried rice, and egg foo yung were once daring touches of exoticism on kitchen tables all over America, but for many of us they remain only as vague memories, fading under the assault of Mandarin delicacies and Szechuan pungencies. Gastronomically minded Americans have clasped Szechuan and Hunan cuisine in a blistering embrace; Mandarin and Peking food have been thoroughly explored and Hakka cookery and Mongolian barbecue are lurking in the wings, ready to burst into prominence. Chow mein and fried rice now appear on the menus of Hunanese and Mandarin establishments much as steaks and chops used to appear on the menus of the old Cantonese places—they serve as a sop to the timid in the party who are unwilling to go the whole way. We will undoubtedly continue working our compulsive American way through all the provinces of China until the day a food conscious astronaut returns from deep space exploration brandishing a recipe for Callistian smerp au gratin. Then Interplanetary Cuisine will become the preoccupation of restaurant goers, teachers of cookery and food writers and Chinese food will fade into stodgy oblivion. Until that extraterrestial moment, there is no harm in our Chinese culinary indulgences; indeed Chinese food is usually low in fat, high in nutrients and fairly economical.

Some of the recipes in the following menus are for homestyle Chinese food, dishes not likely to be found on restaurant menus. For the stir-fried dishes, have all ingredients prepared and on hand, and cook at the last minute. Try not to have more than one or two stir-fried dishes in any one menu.

Chinese Dinner I

Braised Chinese Mushrooms
Chinese Roast Chicken
Lion's Head
Dry Fried Green Beans
White Rice
Cold Litchis on Shaved Ice

Chinese Dinner II

Hot and Sour Soup
Steamed Whole Red Snapper
Beef With Broccoli
Five Fragrance Pork
White Rice
Seasonal Fruits

Chinese Picnic

Pon Pon Chicken
Crab, Hunan Style
Barbecued Ribs, Grilled on a Portable Hibachi
Mr. Ma's Mushrooms
Onion Pancakes
Almond Curd

Middle Eastern

Middle Eastern food is vivid, earthy and compelling. The sensual smoothness of cream salads, the lemony fibrousness of stuffed vine leaves, the crunchy bite of walnut studded chili paste, and the herb scented graininess of marinated cracked wheat are all a part of the cuisine's complexities. The recipes in the following menu are culinary heirlooms—some of them from members of Atlanta's St. Elias Church—passed down from generation to generation in Syria and Lebanon, and finally brought to America. Food processors and blenders have replaced the traditionl wooden mortars, and modern stoves have supplanted more primitive sources of heat, but despite these changes in technique of preparation, the resulting dishes have remained remarkably constant over the generations. Serve these dishes buffet style, and place a few bowls of sunflower seeds and pistachio nuts on the table as well. This is not a meal to be gulped and forgotten, but to be slowly savored, with special attention to contrast of texture and depth of flavor.

A Middle Eastern Buffet

Mahammara
Baba Ganooj
Hummus
Pita Bread
Tabooley
Stuffed Grape Leaves
Stuffed Squash
Lamb-Green Bean Stew
Souffled Farina Pudding

Greek

The Greek Orthodox Cathedral in Atlanta holds a three day festival every fall. During those days, thousands of Atlantans experience the glories of Greek gastronomy. The extravaganza of Greek culture and food always seems to be over far too soon; an unbridled urge to consume more Greek food inevitably coincides with the closing of the festival. To satisfy that urge, plan small Greek culinary festivals of your own during the year. Greek cookery is fun and the results are always hearty, sustaining, and extremely delicious. Many Greek recipes make excellent party food; they are perfect for feeding a crowd of exuberant and hungry friends.

A Greek Party

Taramasalata
Spinach-Cheese Pie
Stefado
Greek Salad
Farina Mousse

A Greek Dinner

Cheese Saganaki
Egg-Lemon Soup
Shrimp With Feta Cheese
Stuffed Eggplant or Moussaka
Souffled Farina Pudding

Philippine

The cuisine of the Philippines is a mirror of the history of those remote islands; it is a blend of Malaysian, Indian, Japanese, and Spanish. The Filippinos are a rice eating people, and their use of soy sauce, bean sprouts, bitter melon, and so on point to a strong Asian culinary base. Magellan and other Spanish explorers found the Philippines while searching for spice routes more than one hundred years before the first Pilgrims landed at Jamestown. Inevitably, Spanish missionaries followed, and Spanish overlords to govern the island villages. This very strong Spanish influence of hundreds of years of duration, laid over a basically Oriental food philosophy has produced a unique style of cookery. Philippine cookery is not particularly well known in this country, which is a pity. Philippine dishes are very easy to like.

A Philippine Country Style Dinner

Penakbit
Chicken Adobo
Tomato-Watercress Salad
White Rice
Ripe Mangoes

Jewish

Jewish cookery encompasses an enormous range of geographic influences and ethnic legacies, therefore one Jew's soul food may well be another Jew's *chozzerai*. The culinary heritage of the Sephardic Jews, who trace their roots from Spain and Portugal to Greece, Turkey, and the Levant, is quite different from that of the Eastern and Central European Ashkenazic Jews. Even within these groups, culinary styles differ. Some Sephardim dream of stuffed grape leaves and baked meat pies wrapped in paper thin pastry; Germanic Jews long for fluffy dumplings swimming in rich chicken soup, and Ashkenazim of Russian ancestry find bliss in a thick red brew of beets, greens, and fat meat. These wildly differing styles of cookery, modified and unified by the powerful mystical thread of Jewish dietary law, have become the vast culinary hodge-podge known as modern Jewish cookery.

The laws that govern the gastronomic life of an Orthodox family are stated very clearly in the Bible and result in a complicated system of forbidden foods, separation of meat and dairy products, ritual slaughter of food animals, and special feast day observances. The keeping of a kosher household is a full time, demanding job; it keeps Orthodox Jews in constant, practical touch with their beliefs. The stringent laws apply to Orthodox Jewry in all parts of the world; in times of poverty, persecution and severe emotional hardship they serve as a graphic and tangible reminder of self worth and faith.

In periods of freedom and plenty, many Jews relax their orthodoxy and ignore the ancient, time-consuming precepts described so vividly in the Bible; the majority of Jews in America today do not keep completely kosher households. But long after the strict rituals and taboos have been abandoned, long after shellfish, bacon, and other untouchables have crept into their culinary patterns, agnostic or liberalized American Jews retain a hankering for the old foods.

A Jewish Style Dinner

Chicken Liver Pate, Jewish Style
Chicken Soup
Sweet and Sour Stuffed Cabbage or Pot Roasted Brisket
Potato Pancakes or Kasha with Onions and Mushrooms
Carrots in Wine
Challah
Fruit and Nuts

Italian-American

Paul Masselli, second generation Italian-American, is a man who has been haunted all his adult life by the elusive taste memories of childhood. His devotion to the gastronomic echoes of his childhood resulted in a major career change from the head of a collection agency to sausage maker.

When Paul reminisces about his past and his extraordinary family, he creates a kind of verbal time machine. The listener is transported into a world of larger-than-life uncles, flowing pitchers of wine and gargantuan, unmatched meals.

"I remember that dried sausage was really good in a sauce," he once told me in a fit of nostalgia. "It costs nothing to dry it—they would simply hang it from the ceiling from sticks of wood. In the middle of the night, my father and his brothers would get up and hack a chunk off, eat it, and get back into bed. Sausages would be hanging in the bedrooms and all the rooms, even over their beds—one hundred pounds of sausages hanging over eleven brothers. The more adventurous of the brothers would try to take a glass of Pop's wine to go with the sausage—if they got caught, they had big trouble." As Paul told the story of his uncles and the midnight sausages, he roared with laughter. "My father and his eleven brothers and two sisters were foodaholics; they were maniacs. They all cooked—when they got married very few of the sisters-in-law cooked better than the husbands. For my grandfather there was one important meal . . . dinner. Sunday dinners were endless. If you came to my grandmother's house on a Sunday, you'd see 23 grandchildren, 11 or 12 brothers and sisters and in-laws, and all sorts of friends. They would come in and play mandolins and accordions and sing Italian songs. Dinner would last at least 11 hours."

Such joyous meals are reproducible today, even without mandolins, accordions, and dozens of relatives. Round up a bunch of friends, and have each prepare one dish. Covered dish suppers with friends have become, for many of us, a surrogate for the ritual Sunday family meals of long ago.

An Italian American Family Dinner

Melon With Slices of Proscuitto
Escarole Soup With Meatballs
Garlic Stuffed Pork Roast
Sausage Carbonara
Eggplant Parmagiana
Pop's Wine
Salad of Mixed Greens with Lemon Vinaigrette
Cheesecake
Fruit and Nuts

Italian

The ghosts of Marco Polo and Catherine de Medici haunt the dreams of those devoted to classic Italian cookery. Centuries ago, the Oriental travels of Polo had a great impact on Italian culture, particularly on gastronomy. Chinese cookery combines great artistry, economy, and intelligence; cultural sharing through Polo and his men infused Italian cookery with some of the same qualities. Several hundred years later, the young Italian noblewoman, Catherine de Medici, came to France with a culinary entourage, to marry the French youth who was to become King Henry II. This sixteenth century nuptial happening has had far reaching culinary reverberations; historically inclined gourmets tend to agree that Italy, not France, is the true cradle of gastronomy.

Elegant Italian Dinners

I
Carpaccio
Pasta With Pesto
Veal ala Valdostana
Asparagus With Butter and Lemon
Chocolate Loaf

II
Maritata
Stuffed Artichoke
Veal Antonio
Potato Gnocchi
Strawberries Steeped in Marsala

Hungarian

About one hundred years *before* Catherine de Medici made her famous marriage, Hungary was receiving the enriching, civilized Italian touch; Beatrice, daughter of the King of Naples, married Hungary's King Matthias in 1475. As Catherine would many years later, Beatrice brought a culinary dowry with her; chefs, fine china, cookware, cookery books, and exotic ingredients. This Italian influence built on a strong foundation of Magyar cookery techniques and later influenced during Hungary's dark period by a long Turkish occupation, has created a cuisine of great subtlety and delicacy. Hungarian food is a sublime combination of peasant and aristocratic tastes that is unmatched anywhere in the world.

A Hungarian Dinner Party

Beef Rolls (Serve on toothpicks, as an hors d'ouevre)
Blueberry Soup
Szekely Goulash or Stuffed Cabbage
Noodles Tossed With Butter and Poppy Seeds
Tomato Pepper Salad
Palacsintas

East Indian

The cuisines of India are complex and varied; it would take a lifetime to learn the ins and outs of their various components. The following menu is Westernized, but it captures the feeling of Indian food. Adjust the hot spices to make the food as spicy or as bland as you like it to be.

An Indian Style Dinner

Samosas
Split Pea Soup, Indian Style
Sweet Chicken Curry
Koftah Curry
Rice Pulao
Yogurt Cucumbers
Curried Mushrooms
Yogurt Cream Mousse

Up-to-the-Minute German

Nouvelle cuisine, when not carried to some of its sillier extremes, is wonderfully inventive, delicate, and satisfying. It is a cuisine that depends on appearance, interesting juxtaposition of ingredients, and the sure, light hand of the chef. Recently, Atlanta's Chef Heinz Sowinski, dabbled in nouvelle cuisine when he hosted Count Matuschka-Greiffenclau and the Atlanta Chapter of the German Wine Society. Heinz's restaurant, the Brass Key, was the location of a special dinner designed to complement an impressive selection of some of Germany's finest wines. Count Matuschka is the owner of Schloss Vollrads, one of Germany's outstanding vineyards; his personal chef designed the menu and recipes for the dinner, which was to be in the manner of nouvelle cuisine. On the day of the party, Heinz and his staff were madly at work in the kitchen of the Brass Key; the wines had been delivered, the menu was posted, the proper ingredients had been obtained, but the recipes from Germany had never arrived. Heinz, with superb aplomb and considerable talent, worked out the recipes himself, and produced a nouvelle cuisine dinner that pleased the Count, entranced the Wine Society, and highlighted the wines the way black velvet highlights diamonds.

A German Dinner in the Manner of Nouvelle Cuisine

Halibut on Eggplant, Beurre Blanc
Avocado Salad on a Bed of Sprouts, Walnut-Lemon Dressing
Breast of Chicken with Stilton Cheese Sauce
Squash Boats with Stir-Fried Snow Peas
Honeyed Carrot Shreds
Baked Apples

SEASONAL MENUS

Summer Picnics at the Symphony

Two glories of civilization are good food and good music; they nourish the soul, stir the emotions and immeasurably enrich the quality of life. Summer concerts in the park are the perfect time and place to indulge in both glories simultaneously. In Atlanta, the Atlanta Symphony Orchestra, long may it flourish, gives a series of free concerts in Piedmont park every summer; the music is magnificent, the musicians impeccable, and the setting perfect for inspired picnicking. Don't even think of munching fast foods or slurping peanut butter during the musical splendor. Symphonic picnics are occasions for culinary elegance and good taste—avoid mundane food at all costs.

For maximum enjoyment, take the time to carefully organize your picnic; plan to carry a capacious basket filled with pretty plates and napkins, corkscrew, wine glasses, tableware, and lots of garbage bags, and use insulated chests for the food and the wine. Get to the park early; by the time the conductor raises his baton, the grass will be thick with bodies, and latecomers must pick their way gingerly through a maze of arms, legs, sleeping babies, and panting dogs. The earlier you arrive, the better the choice of good spots for your picnic, and the more time you will have for leisurely dining and conversation. Part of the fun of summer park concerts is people watching; as you eat your pate and sip your Beaujolais, admire the array of individuals strolling by in varying states of interesting dress and undress.

Good picnic food should be well seasoned, able to withstand the heat without melting or spoiling (ice cream or chocolate mousse, for instance, would be a disaster) and attractive. Cold sparkling Vouvray, or a lightly chilled Beaujolais, are perfect picnic wines.

2 Symphonic Picnic Menus

I
Pain de Veau
Beef Provencal
Cold Gratin of Potatoes and Cheese
Zucchini Agrodolce
Orange Pears

II
Stuffed Grape Leaves
Chicken With Cold Sauce
Green Bean Salad
Potatoes Vinaigrette
Fruit and Cheese

Springtime Brunches
   Sunday brunch is the most civilized meal of the week. Sunday afternoons—especially during spring and summer—are made for good food, interesting conversation and wine; there is no better time for entertaining good friends. The focal point of a satisfying Sunday brunch should be single, colorful, highly flavored dish, or an intelligent selection of fresh, seasonal foods. A final course of fruit and/or cheese encourages lingering conversation around the table as the day lazily spins its quiet way into evening.

4 Springtime Sunday Brunches

I
Tomato-Green Pepper Salad, Moroccan Style
Onion Cheese Pie
Asparagus With Proscuitto
Strawberries and Cream

II
Schav
Piperade Omelet
Whole Wheat Continental Bread and Butter
Fruit and Cheese

III
Potato-Tarragon Soup
Stuffed Cabbage, Italian Style
Cream Cheese Mousse With Raspberries

IV
Corned Beef Hash Mornay
Squash With Bacon
Orange Slices Sprinkled With Red Wine and Cinnamon

HALLOWEEN

There is nothing as horribly delicious as a gleeful wallow in the elegant and frightening prose of the macabre. The works of M. R. James, H. P. Lovecraft, Oliver Onions, Shirley Jackson, Edgar Allen Poe, Roald Dahl, John Collier, and all the other masters of the horror genre make Halloween worth celebrating year after year. Every October 31, when the trick-or-treaters have been safely tucked in bed, their sticky hands and faces washed and their inevitable tummy-aches soothed, I settle down to my own ritual Halloween celebration, a happy rereading of some of my favorite horror stories. Since part of the fun of being frightened out of one's wits is in sharing the fright, I always hold a Halloween dinner party. The menu is chosen to match the literary selections; each dish designed to pay homage to an author in the genre. Several days before Halloween the guests are provided with a reading list, and on the evening of the dinner, each course is preceded by readings of excerpts from the appropriate works. Candlelight, sepulchral reading voices, and a sinister table setting are the necessities for this occasion. If your only memories of Halloween involve trudging happily from house to house on your block, collecting handfuls of execrable sweets from the neighbors, it's time to establish some grown-up traditions.

A Halloween Menu

A Glass of Amontillado
Oliver Onions' Soup (Onion Soup With Calvados)
Oliver Onions wrote *The Beckoning Fair One*, a short story about a haunted house. It appeared in a volume called *Widdershins* in 1911; since then it has been considered—along with Henry James' *The Turn of the Screw*—one of the most effectively horrifying, beautifully written ghost stories in the English language. Onions hated his name and eventually had it legally changed to George Oliver.

Lamb to the Slaughter (Lamb Leg Stuffed With Mushrooms)
Roald Dahl specializes in grotesque, bizarre short stories, written in a dead-pan, matter-of-fact style. Devotees of Roald Dahl tend to have most interesting nightmares. In his story, *Lamb to the Slaughter*, a young wife murders her husband by whacking him on the head with a frozen leg of lamb, which she then places in the oven to cook in the usual way. The police comb the house for clues and sympathize with the widow, who offers them the sizzling, fragrant lamb. As the police hungrily polish off the succulent roast, they assure each other that the case could be easily solved, if only the murder weapon would come to light.

Souffle Hill House (Potato Souffle)

The late Shirley Jackson was one of the best of the contemporary horror writers. In her novel, *The Haunting of Hill House,* the story of a modern haunting is slowly and terrifyingly unfolded. As the book progresses, Jackson's elegant and precise writing leads the reader inexorably into pure terror.

Mrs. Dudley, the unattractive and nasty caretaker of Hill House, is a marvelous cook; the protagonists consume a souffle and many other of her exquisite dishes, between bouts with fearful supernatural phenomena.

Aunt Clara's Cucumbers (Cucumber Salad, Hungarian Style)

In *The Visitation of Aunt Clara,* by Kate Barlay, the ghost of Aunt Clara visits the narrator's grandfather in Bachka, Hungary. The story is studded with descriptions of glorious Hungarian meals. The cucumber salad is typical of the time and place and might have been a favorite of Great Aunt Clara.

The Tell-Tale Heart (Yogurt-Cream Mousse in a Heart-Shaped Mold)

The menu began with a glass of Amontillado (homage to the master, Edgar Allen Poe and his story, *The Cask of Amontillado*). It ends with a culinary allusion to another of his stories, *The Tell-Tale Heart.* How I wish I were reading these two stories for the first time this Halloween. They are still eminently creepy and satisfying, even after countless rereadings, but there is nothing to compare with the numbing burst of delightful horror that occurs with one's first exposure to Poe.

THANKSGIVING

The best menus are restrained ones; beautiful vegetables are served as a separate course, one food does not overwhelm another, and the guests can still walk when they leave the table. There are exceptions, of course. Some of the ethnic dinners listed in this chapter present many foods served at once so that the diners may get a comprehensive taste of a country's cuisine. But the most notable exception to discretion and restraint is our yearly American dining ritual—the Thanksgiving dinner. At such dinners, the table groans under a heavy burden of substantial food; if the diners are not groaning as well by the end of the meal, then the holiday has not been properly celebrated.

Thanksgiving Dinner

Squash Soup in Squash
Roast Turkey With Chestnut Dressing
Cranberry-Apple Sauce
Potatoes With Mushrooms and Leeks
Pisto Manchego
Cabbage Flan
Orange-Onion Salad
Apples and Walnuts
Assorted Pies

FOURTH OF JULY

Hamburgers on the grill are perfect for the gastronomic celebration of this purely American Holiday. Children and adults always enjoy them immensely when they are properly made but most children, I find, like them very thin, and fairly well done.

A Fourth Of July Cookout

Hamburgers
Cheeseburgers
Browned Onions
Betty's Rolls
Ripe Summer Tomatoes, Sliced, and Lightly Salted
Perfect Fries
Watermelon
Brownies

About the Author

Sue Kreitzman, contributing food editor of *Atlanta Weekly*, lives in Atlanta with her husband, son and a beagle named Shallot. Although she went through college on an oboe scholarship and had originally planned a brilliant career in teaching and music, a passion for food overtook her, and she now spends her time cooking, eating and writing about it. She has been the chef in a well-known Atlanta restaurant, director of her own cooking school, author of a popular column, "In Good Taste" in the Atlanta Journal food section, and co-author of "The Nutrition Cookbook." Sue's work has appeared in *Atlanta* Magazine, *Self, Playgirl,* and *California Living* among others.

Please send me _____ copies of Sue Kreitzman's SUNDAY BEST

@ $10.95 per copy $_____.

Add postage and handling @ $1.50 per copy _____.

Georgia residents add 4% sales tax @ $.44 _____.

per copy $_____.

Total enclosed $_____.

Please make checks payable to: Sue Kreitzman's SUNDAY BEST
P.O. Box 15464
Atlanta, Georgia 30333-0464

Please send me _____ copies of Sue Kreitzman's SUNDAY BEST

@ $10.95 per copy $_____.

Add postage and handling @ $1.50 per copy _____.

Georgia residents add 4% sales tax @ $.44 _____.

per copy $_____.

Total enclosed $_____.

Please make checks payable to: Sue Kreitzman's SUNDAY BEST
P.O. Box 15464
Atlanta, Georgia 30333-0464

Please send me _____ copies of Sue Kreitzman's SUNDAY BEST

@ $10.95 per copy $_____.

Add postage and handling @ $1.50 per copy _____.

Georgia residents add 4% sales tax @ $.44 _____.

per copy $_____.

Total enclosed $_____.

Please make checks payable to: Sue Kreitzman's SUNDAY BEST
P.O. Box 15464
Atlanta, Georgia 30333-0464

Please send me _____ copies of Sue Kreitzman's SUNDAY BEST

@ $10.95 per copy $_____.

Add postage and handling @ $1.50 per copy _____.

Georgia residents add 4% sales tax @ $.44 _____.

per copy $_____.

Total enclosed $_____.

Please make checks payable to: Sue Kreitzman's SUNDAY BEST
P.O. Box 15464
Atlanta, Georgia 30333-0464

Please send me _____ copies of Sue Kreitzman's SUNDAY BEST

@ $10.95 per copy $_____.

Add postage and handling @ $1.50 per copy _____.

Georgia residents add 4% sales tax @ $.44 _____.

per copy $_____.

Total enclosed $_____.

Please make checks payable to: Sue Kreitzman's SUNDAY BEST
P.O. Box 15464
Atlanta, Georgia 30333-0464

Please send me _____ copies of Sue Kreitzman's SUNDAY BEST

@ $10.95 per copy $_____.

Add postage and handling @ $1.50 per copy _____.

Georgia residents add 4% sales tax @ $.44 _____.

per copy $_____.

Total enclosed $_____.

Please make checks payable to: Sue Kreitzman's SUNDAY BEST
P.O. Box 15464
Atlanta, Georgia 30333-0464

Re-Order Additional Copies